Records Management at the Heart of Business Processes

Digital Libraries and Collections Set

coordinated by
Fabrice Papy

Records Management at the Heart of Business Processes

Validate, Protect, Operate and Maintain the Information in the Digital Environment

Florence Ott

ELSEVIER

First published 2020 in Great Britain and the United States by ISTE Press Ltd and Elsevier Ltd

ISTE Press Ltd
27-37 St George's Road
London SW19 4EU
UK

www.iste.co.uk

Elsevier Ltd
The Boulevard, Langford Lane
Kidlington, Oxford, OX5 1GB
UK

www.elsevier.com

Notices
Knowledge and best practice in this field are constantly changing. As new research and experience broaden our understanding, changes in research methods, professional practices, or medical treatment may become necessary.

Practitioners and researchers must always rely on their own experience and knowledge in evaluating and using any information, methods, compounds, or experiments described herein. In using such information or methods they should be mindful of their own safety and the safety of others, including parties for whom they have a professional responsibility.

To the fullest extent of the law, neither the Publisher nor the authors, contributors, or editors, assume any liability for any injury and/or damage to persons or property as a matter of products liability, negligence or otherwise, or from any use or operation of any methods, products, instructions, or ideas contained in the material herein.

For information on all our publications visit our website at http://store.elsevier.com/

British Library Cataloguing-in-Publication Data
A CIP record for this book is available from the British Library
Library of Congress Cataloging in Publication Data
A catalog record for this book is available from the Library of Congress
ISBN 978-1-78548-043-0

Printed and bound in the UK and US

Contents

Preface

When I first began my work in archives in the mid-1980s, the desire to preserve the memory of organizations and to deal with documentary inflation was dominant. The business world was beginning to change and whole swathes of traditional professions were disappearing. In Alsace, an old industry, particularly the textile industry, was suffering from international competition and the loss of outlets. Therefore, in 1983, the first economic archive center was established in Mulhouse, bringing together the Mulhouse Chamber of Commerce, the Université de Haute-Alsace, the Mulhouse Industrial Society and the region's archivists. When I took over as director of the *Centre Rhénan d'Archives et de Recherches Economiques* (CERARE), my mandate was to make companies aware of their heritage, to preserve their memory and to train them in better records management.

Information technology was hardly a concern when all important records were on paper, but the need for better information management was already present. The primary concern of companies was how best to manage the inflation of documents, to find them easily and to be able to respond to regulatory issues. By providing technical assistance and training to their staff, it was possible to identify historical archives and, once trust was established, to propose the safeguarding of their heritage. Already, an integrated archiving system best suited the needs of companies and I had been able to carry out many consultations with the implementation of documentation procedures.

I left CERARE[1] and Alsace in 2006 as well as the Université de Haute-Alsace where I taught private archiving. When I moved to New Brunswick, Canada,

---

1 This associative organization was dissolved in 2009 and the collected industrial archives representing more than 3 linear kilometers of archives are now kept by the *Archives municipales de Mulhouse*.

I was offered a position as a professor of records management at the Université de Moncton, Shippagan campus, with a bachelor's degree in information management. This gave me the opportunity to do a lot of training and to work in organizations to help them organize their document management. Canada was ahead of the curve in terms of legislation and North America was already heavily impacted by the judicialization of cases and especially the legislative change in many countries around 2000. Indeed, by making digital records equivalent to paper records as evidence under certain conditions, these legislations were beginning to bring new problems of authenticity and integrity to archives. The effects began to be felt in the 2010s and to worry the archival world, which was the guarantor of the preservation of records. New documentation standards also appeared and a whole reflection on our methods and issues was carried out.

In June 2011, during the annual specialized symposium of information sciences (*colloque annuel spécialisé des sciences de l'information,* COSSI)[2] in which I participated as a member of the organizing committee and the scientific committee, I had the opportunity to meet Mr. Fabrice Papy, professor-researcher in information and communication sciences and university professor at Université Nancy 2. We talked about the problems that troubled specialists in libraries, documentation centers and archive services. Several collaborations have resulted from these discussions, including a special issue on "Problems of information governance in the age of digital records" in *Les Cahiers du numérique* in 2015.

Another more comprehensive project was to write a book on the state of progress in records management in view of the paradigm shifts brought about by the dematerialization of information. It took me some time to gather all the information and finally I opted to focus more on records management that are of particular interest to organizations and which are essential if we want to preserve the memory of institutions. A poorly identified document in a non-perennial format will not be able to be properly archived or remain intelligible for its restitution and understanding.

The role of records managers has become increasingly important and I would like to thank all my colleagues, especially Michel Cottin for his proofreading of the manuscript. These are colleagues who often do a job in the service of others, but who remain the guardians of time in a world of information that is so easy to manipulate and whose production context is often difficult to interpret if measures are not taken at a very early stage in the management of records. The stakes are

2 The name of the conference is now "*Communication, Organisation, Société du Savoir et Information*".

enormous with the dematerialization of information. They pose as many problems as they solve with regard to proof, traceability, protection of privacy, confidentiality and authenticity, but above all the durability of the information. I also hope to shed light on the good practices to be implemented in the field of records management.

Florence OTT
August 2020

Introduction

In an increasingly complex world, information has become sovereign. The means of dissemination and exchange have multiplied, leading to an increase in litigation and trials, but also to a need to find in the resulting mass of records the document that is useful for the activity, the evidence or the memory of the facts. In this age of digital technology and multiple computer media, losses, accidental distribution and poor data sharing increase the risks and the need for document traceability.

Information governance is important to promote access and sharing in order to improve the daily efficiency of an organization and to ensure the management, protection and sustainability of information and data related to activities. From this point of view, records management fits perfectly into this new paradigm. It takes into account all the processes in a given environment to manage a record, in a paper or electronic form, from its creation to its final preservation or its disposal.

The challenge facing archivists goes far beyond the age-old methods of a profession that has survived the ages, but which needs to rethink its priorities. From a material and fixed form, from the material and intellectual harmonization of research instruments, it is now necessary to handle a virtual document that is easy to modify and difficult to secure over time. The notion of archives, archiving and consultation is transformed by the digital revolution. It is no longer merely technological, but also cognitive and social.

The changes imposed by dematerialization are leading to a review of the management and circulation of information, which is becoming multifaceted, fragmented and dependent on metadata that is essential to understanding the production context and controlling long-term archiving.

Everyone is concerned with archiving, because everyone produces, receives, validates and uses documents that need to be kept. The questions that come up during our consultations in the departments are always about what to archive, for how long and who is responsible for archiving and disposal decisions. Indeed, the preservation of archives is a major issue. Previously, it followed the successive sequences of collection, appraisal, sorting and preservation. With the digital document, all these sequences are carried forward and grouped together at the very origin of the documents. This requires constant reflection and adaptation to the needs of both users and archivists. It is essential to have methods to make the management of engaging and strategic documents in companies reliable over time.

Also, our issue is particularly concerned with records in organizations, since control of document production must be done well in advance, especially since the heritage angle is no longer an end in itself. It is above all a question of contract management, the multiplication of legal and regulatory obligations, and authentic and honest documents. We will focus on the study of records processes, the policies and rules to be put in place, compliance and risk management, which is now well understood in companies even if archiving remains a crucial point far from being resolved. So, although we are not talking about the historical use of archives or their communication to researchers, good records management from the moment information is created will also promote the availability of a quality documentary heritage.

To try to understand the various issues generated by the digital world and the contribution of records management, we made a review of writings that we submitted to an experiment in the field with the collaboration of companies that have great difficulty in setting up coherent shared files. As Pierre Bourdieu pointed out, "any discourse or theory emanates from practice and returns to it[1]". We also rely on Francophone practices that take a more comprehensive view of the records lifecycle and on integrated archives management.

We have divided our book into four main chapters. The first one aims to study the various problems caused by the dematerialization of information. What are the changes in information management in which its medium and content are no longer inseparable? How does records management participate in information governance to reduce risks? Every organization needs to access its vital documents, meet its legal obligations and control its documentary mass while safeguarding its information heritage. We are also going to review the document lifecycle, which no longer follows the same model as traditional archives, but which remains a useful concept for defining the points that command the implementation of procedures. We will also review the concept of records and processes. To be qualified as an archive,

---

1 Pierre Bourdieu, *Le sens pratique*, Éditions de Minuit, Paris, p. 30, 1980.

the record must therefore be understood in its field as a trace of an activity, proof and testimony of an act or event that can be located and dated. A document can be identified not only by its content, but also by its origin, its recipient and the context in which it was created. We are also witnessing the explosion of data that will have to be managed within the framework of *open data* policies and the promotion of administrative transparency. How should they be handled, and what are the issues at stake? How can we resolve the paradox of access to information, which is a positive aspect in the face of security and privacy constraints?

The second chapter is devoted to records and records management standards, in particular ISO 15489 on records management and the ISO 30300 standards series on the business records management system. They present the objectives, the scope of implementation, the legislative and regulatory framework, the definitions of the terms used, the policies, the responsibilities of the players, the overall organization of records management and the implementation processes, the monitoring and evaluation of the system and the validation authorities. Then there is an essential part to ensure the authenticity, integrity, reliability and operability of records. The reliability of the records depends on the conditions of preservation which provide the basis for the presumption of authenticity. The preservation of digital data requires much greater conditions of protection to prevent fraud and falsifications or to guarantee the confidentiality of data. Similarly, the risks of non-disposition of documents and technological dependence will be analyzed. We will also discuss the management and preservation of e-mail, which has become essential in the collaborative aspects of an organization due to the profusion of messages it generates, but also the risks that these engaging documents can entail if they are not managed rigorously.

The third chapter examines the central aspect of the archival profession, and perhaps the most fundamental part of it, which is the appraisal of records. It will determine their lifespan, their administrative usefulness, their historical or non-historical interest, and finally their disposition. Mastery of records appraisal enables relevant information to be retained while controlling and scheduling the disposal of unnecessary records, thus reducing the volume of records to be processed and lowering the cost in the long term. In this field, we will look at the different schools of thought and the new questions that have arisen with digital documents. In this chapter, in addition to analyzing the sensitivity levels of documents, we will look at the three categories of metadata, which are descriptive, administrative and structural. In the digital world, metadata is essential because it facilitates identification and access to information, enhances its evidential value and documents changes, improves preservation and contributes to the interoperability of systems when it is standardized. Finally, proper naming of files and folders will facilitate the filing and creation of shared folders with logic based on user needs and service activities. We are going to see what criteria should be retained to achieve a good functional and hierarchical filing plan that will ensure good management of information retrieval and sharing in organizations.

In the final chapter, we will address the crucial issue of information sustainability. In any organization, electronic archiving is gradually becoming a reality or an obligation. It coexists with paper archiving where complete dematerialization of processes is not yet in place. In this sense, digitization is sometimes proposed as a solution to the problem of preservation and to encourage the dissemination of information, but here too rigorous procedures are necessary to guarantee quality records over time. We will try to distinguish electronic record management from electronic archiving, which is the only guarantee of long-term preservation. We will examine archiving strategies, including migration and the important choice of the right document formats. It must be borne in mind that a computer file is threatened by hardware, software and file format obsolescence and loss of meaning of the content. Therefore, we will try to understand how to choose the right measures for archiving files that must be able to be read again as long as necessary. Mass data storage also involves new systems such as cloud computing, which again provide solutions to some problems, but raise others. A great deal of thought must therefore be given to establishing an effective document policy that meets the challenges of a world that has never before produced so much information, even though its long-term preservation is far from assured.

1

Information and Data Management

While the digital world brings advantages by simplifying many processes, it also makes the context of records production more complex and difficult to understand according to traditional archival principles. The explosion in the volume of information leads to the multiplication of actors, the acceleration of exchanges, and the atomization and fragmentation of information with numerous digital files to replace what was formerly a paper document or the reproduction of several copies.

The dematerialization of information makes the document more fragile and more fragmented. The digital revolution is leading to a questioning of concepts and methods leading to a review of information circulation, which is becoming multi-faceted, fragmented and dependent on metadata essential for the management and preservation of information. The theory of the three ages and the practice of collecting need to be rethought. Both initiator of events and bearer of information, the digital document needs to be identified, linked to its context, processed, validated, stored and preserved. The fundamentals of document and file need to be revisited because of their fragmentation with the recombination of these units in an often-arbitrary manner. "Digital technology has also become another way of producing documents" [GUY 15c, p. 83].

It is often said that the digital time corresponds to that of the data. Older data add depth to recent data produced by scientific observation and human activities. All these elements concern or interest each and every one of us. The number of data produced in the world today likely exceeds the number of traditional paper archives. Mass data are increasing, but the quality and use of these data must be questioned. This applies in particular to open data, which requires administrations to be more transparent, but also involves controlling the handling of personal data. Here we find the paradox of data openness in the face of increased protection of personal data.

Consequently, there is an obligation to properly raise questions, and to define the requirements in more detail. The technological mechanisms to be managed in the background are often extremely complex, even complicated and expensive, while business processes increasingly require analysis and procedures with agents who need awareness and training in these new concepts and forms of work.

1.1. The digital environment and its issues

The digital environment is recomposing a new information landscape in which the virtual, the intangible and transparency are becoming the key words for sharing information with a single point of access to data by putting more and more native electronic documents online. The production of documents takes place in a context where multiplicity, accessibility and mobility prevail. Technologies such as the Internet and the mobile network have changed behaviors. The flow and volume of digital documents is reaching proportions far exceeding what already existed for paper. Access is easier, with benefits and risks. In just a few clicks, it is possible to consult a document, wherever it is stored, from a computer, tablet or mobile phone; immediacy becomes the rule.

Digital technology causes a collision between delayed time and real time. Immediacy is caused by the acceleration of traffic and information transmission channels, which generates a sense of proximity. One acts in the moment without putting one's action into perspective. For the first time, it is necessary to anticipate the risk of losing the document at the moment it is collected, or even at the moment the document is created, because the collection concerns information and the elements that will enable it to be represented, whatever the technical evolutions. Another effect is the abolition of distances and the automation of procedures. Distances are replaced by connection time. Documents must be available at all times. Operations on the documents have become transparent for the producer with a capture of the documents in a digital archiving system that can take place at any stage of their lifecycle. And, for additional protection, a consultation copy can be made available [MAN 15, p. 297]. However, the corollary of this immediacy is a rapid devaluation of the information that makes the information stated two years ago seem less relevant than the information of the day, even if it is not interesting. Moreover, there is a false sense of completeness induced by the number of references proposed by search engines without knowing the algorithms that produce them or the magnitude of the noise generated.

The challenges of the digital environment can be classified into three areas:

– control the long-term access to approved information. This means communicating information only to authorized persons, but with the certainty that it is authentic and always readable. The challenges are to share recent or older information, which involves making it available in a simple way, allowing controlled access over time and properly qualifying it;

– do not submit information but organize it and manage it, which involves the definition and application of an information management policy, specifying the purpose of each piece of information, its required retention period, its level of confidentiality and the associated access rights [APR 14b, p. 4];

– control direct and indirect costs related to information. The objective is the application of a policy to control the information stored, to limit its costs to essential needs. It also means measuring the risks through a complete knowledge of the business rules to be applied according to the contexts of the business lines and countries and to respond within set deadlines [APR 14b, p. 5].

The first characteristic of digital information is the explosion of data, due on the one hand to the democratization of information production coupled with more complex regulations that encourage more and more documentation of what we do, and on the other hand, to the very technologies that are so easily able to capture signals (medical, geographic), photograph and duplicate data. The number of information producers is increasing and so are the documents they create. In addition, the number of traces automatically created by tools is increasing, as are the capacities for storing and searching for information [FRE 13, p. 113]. We also note the massive use of messaging as a vector of information circulation. We can consider that the most important concern is for organizations to know how to manage, organize, reference, classify and sort the volumes of information, documents, e-mails, office files and exchanges for each employee. The pitfall is to drown in this flow of information while remaining concentrated in one's daily work [SER 16, p. 16]. Moreover, the mass and complexity of the information prevents us from being able to retrieve a digital "bulk", the characteristics of which are unknown. It is impossible to support office files spread over hundreds of directories without a file classification, naming scheme and version management [BAN 10, p. 76].

The form of the information has diversified although traditional records co-exist such as minutes of deliberations, contracts or official correspondence, but they are created in digital form. Exchanges between contacts take place by e-mail, and working documents are scattered in files, some of which are engaging, but drowned in the mass. External documentation is often online and data at risk take the form of digital traces such as connection or navigation traces which constitute personal data that are at the heart of regulatory news, particularly the new General Data Protection Regulation (GDPR) adopted in 2016 in France and entered into force in May 2018 [CHA 18, pp. 12–13]. Moreover, the issue of confidence in digital archival records lies less in the uncertainty of their actual identity and reliability than in the breakdown of the traceability of the origin of the records [DEL 15a, p. 281]. It is difficult to make employees realize that with the use of powerful tools, accessible to all, and instantaneous production, infinitely distributed, that it leads to a total, but often uncontrolled, traceability of the actions carried out. It is difficult to identify the traces that need to be preserved and destroyed. Often, no one is responsible for identifying the risk that the created record may generate. The challenge now lies not only in the proper management of the traces produced, but in the control of the production of the traces. For it is easier to take the time to avoid leaving traces than to try to erase unfortunate digital traces.

The most disruptive factor is the fragmentation of information into countless forms, media, producers and locations, due to technology that allows everyone to produce information and traces very quickly anytime and anywhere on the networks, mixing personal and professional tools. This dissemination of actors, tools and documents encourages the increase in volume by multiplying the intermediate files created and stored automatically when only the final document was manually archived yesterday [CHA 15a, pp. 63–64].

Previously, the contextualization attributes of the content, such as date and signature for example, were written on the document medium. Now, these contextualization attributes form traces that are not visible on the document because they are autonomous from it. However, it is these attributes that give confidence in the content of the documents. The receipt, publication or notification dates are contextualization attributes that are inseparable from the record itself. Maintaining the intrinsic link between the record and these different contextualization attributes is more complex in the digital environment [GUY 15c, pp. 83–84].

The digital object distinguishes its content from its medium. An archive is information and no longer a materially constituted record. It is no longer a question of preserving parchments, films, papers, but lines of code. Everything needs to be rethought, organized, financed, and operated in a technological environment that is poorly designed to support foundations and in a context of extreme industrial competition [DEL 12a, p. 12]. Thus, content and medium are no longer inseparable, whereas this characteristic was essential for the traditional work of diplomacy. What is even more disturbing is that information alone will not be enough to be preserved, but it must be able to be represented again in a new technological environment for new uses, for new communities with new presentations. Information becomes by definition elusive. The modus operandi does not change. It is a matter of being able to take charge of the information content in its production context, but also by integrating all the elements that make it possible to enter and qualify this information throughout its lifecycle [BAN 12b, p. 49].

Digital technology multiplies the possibilities of manipulation since each part of the record can become a unit of manipulation or the cohesion and coherence of the record becomes unintelligible. They can be modified, copied, exchanged and distributed without any checks. It is also difficult to identify the validated version of a document and to have access to the relevant information needed for decision-making [DIS 12, p. 4]. The authoritative copy must then be fixed, constituting a common and shareable reference. The information thus constituted, transmitted, documented and maintained with integrity must make it possible to prove through the time chain that it is indeed what it claims to be. It is a question of evaluating a document with respect to its production context. Because of the technological obsolescence gap, great importance must be attached to encoding formats that are preferably open and, if possible, standardized. In addition to traditional back-up devices, replication of information to remote sites and good traceability of information are also important [BAN 12a, p. 223].

After production, the memory problem was a second challenge to be solved. As early as the First World War, attempts were made to reduce the growing mass of documents by destruction or substitution using increasingly sophisticated sorting procedures according to the criteria of non-utility of the time. Substitution by microfilm raised high hopes as early as the 1930s. Computerization became the norm in the mid-1970s when the problem of electronic memory was solved and new media, such as tapes, floppy disks, videodisks and hard disks, appeared [DEL 12b, p. 187].

The challenge of electronic archiving has become a major one for organizations. This progression is linked to the daily life of organizations that encourage their teams to organize and preserve office content, photos, and videos, and to index files to make them accessible, then to archive them according to the management cycle. But, faced with the enormous mass of files, how do you identify in the office mass between shared servers, external hard drives, and relevant files to be preserved, files that need to be kept beyond a period of active utility [SER 16, p. 34]? The constraints and needs that weigh on electronic archiving are far from insignificant. The electronic business process must plan and prepare for the archiving of records and data from the moment they are created, particularly if the information contained in the records is to be preserved for the long term. Indeed, the dematerialization process must be able to restore the information intact. In order to do this, it will be necessary to set up a management system that will follow the lifecycle of the information and guarantee that each record and piece of data will be systematically captured or recorded in the various systems, ensuring this guarantee of integrity. Analyses are unavoidable when we consider that dematerialization and electronic archiving must guarantee that all records and data will be gathered, identified, selected and classified. They will also have to be kept on a medium and in a format suitable for the purpose of exploiting and consulting them both as evidence and as information [RIE 10, p. 57]. Producers are not bound by any legal constraint for preservation. The democratization of production, open data policies that facilitate access and the possibility of free re-use, opens up the best and worst possibilities. The break is there between uses that almost instantaneously escape the objectives of digital document creation [DEL 15a, p. 282].

In addition, when organizations rely on trusted third-party archivers to store their digital records in the cloud, it can result in serious problems. Even if these third-party archivers provide their clients with full guarantees of security and confidentiality, the risks of technological and legal dependency are great. Retention may take place in countries whose legislation does not meet the requirements of the organization [DEL 15a, p. 283].

However, the great fundamentals stand up well in the digital age when it comes to evaluating and criticizing sources in accordance with the principle of provenance and respect of fonds. The issues of integrity and reliability call into question the know-how derived from the science of diplomacy. These principles can serve as a basis for finding a methodology in the face of increasingly fragmented and changing information [BAN 12b, p. 48].

In the digital environment, as in the case of conventional information media, the process of selecting, recording, and preserving an organization's records can be summarized in three points:

– the organization, management and preservation of records that have evidential, cultural or historical value. For the selection of electronic records, it is necessary to ensure immediate accessibility to information, the possibility of technical conversion, the long-term durability of the medium and format, the presence of identification elements (metadata) and the availability of the material, financial and human resources necessary for processing and preservation [COU 14, p. 137]. As for recording, it meets two complementary needs which are the memorization of the record for subsequent uses (consultation, distribution, archiving) and the initiation of a review and validation cycle. It can result in the creation of a digital copy for different uses, either a revisable copy or a broadcast copy. Document naming rules must be put in place [APR 06, p. 12];

– the guarantee of authentic documents, with integrity to guarantee their reliability, complete security to ensure their integrity and perfect legibility (the absence of which is equivalent to the loss, destruction or alteration of documents);

– the communication of these documents to users in a fast, accurate, user-friendly manner with possible levels of access [SOY 09, p. 11].

The dematerialization of information presupposes three essential conditions. Processes must be set up to handle dematerialized information from end to end, hence it is a question of organization. Trust in dematerialized information must be equivalent to that of "paper" information. Information must be delivered with absolute integrity when needed [RIE 10, pp. V–VI]. It requires driving change, as there is a lot of resistance. Individually, this is synonymous with breakdown and questioning and contributes to the loss of one's points of reference and encourages questions about oneself, one's future and one's qualifications. Structural and cyclical causes have an impact on working conditions and working climate. In addition, the organization's value system can be called into question [RIE 10, p. 84]. It can be noted that the migration from paper to electronic records remains a critical issue; the resolution of the transition to the electronic era is not yet a reality. Moreover, digitization programs have yet to be built and the future of analog archives has yet to be decided [SER 16, p. 17].

Dematerialization leads to the implementation of business flows on all the information circuits between each actor in the process, forming complex objects of a new type (files, digital signatures and fingerprints, time and date stamping tokens, business metadata, validations, annotations, status of the documents created). In addition, there are legal issues such as signature value and verification, information structuring, metadata quality and archival strategy [BAN 12a, p. 222].

According to Asterion's white paper on "The 360 Degree Document" published in 2016, there are five main benefits that drive organizations to dematerialize their information:

– to reduce paper processing costs, for 81% of companies. Less time spent handling paper, filing, or franking envelopes;

– to bring documents into compliance: for 47% of companies, it is a means of ensuring compliance with regulations or business legislation;

– to promote the company's brand image that demonstrates its ability to innovate, to ensure its digital transition, and to meet the growing demand of users for multi-channel communication, not to mention the reduction of the ecological footprint thanks to zero paper. This is a motivation for 45% of companies;

– to increase productivity: for 81% of companies, time and resources related to documents must be reduced. Low value-added tasks are automated. Electronic mail management and the dematerialization of work files have become important concerns in order to optimize record access and sharing, make exchanges more fluid and simplify distribution;

– to secure exchanges between companies, administrations and customers, and within the very functioning of companies. Indeed, 72% of companies believe that the traceability and confidentiality of records can minimize the risk of error or fraud and prevent the loss of documents [AST 16, p. 6].

On the obstacle side Asterion notes:

– customer attachment to paper. Around 72% of companies are concerned about confusing their customers who are used to the paper format and for whom the digital format can have negative connotations in terms of reliability and security;

– the legal "vagueness" is a hindrance for 53% of companies, who do not know whether an electronic transmission is legal or not or can be refused by customers;

– resistance to change is recognized by 44% of companies and the willingness not to change work habits is a more latent and hidden obstacle;

– 34% of companies hesitate for fear of reducing the security of exchanges;

– the lack of human resources is a less important obstacle, but cited by 19% of companies [AST 16, p. 6].

However, there are some weaknesses in the management of information assets. IT aims at excellence in the present moment, which can be done at the expense of managing long-term data, information that is useful in the long run. There is also a tendency to favor access to the updating of a note or procedure rather than managing outdated versions that pile up and a number of which could be destroyed. It is also difficult to manage the famous unstructured data. Outside of business applications and rigorous document management projects, their content and value are not really managed. The IT department carries out systematic and blind backups, delegating to users a task for which it is neither tasked nor competent, whereas users tend to think that it is the IT department that takes care of it and shifts their accountability [CHA 18, p. 53].

This is why the increasing complexity of business processes and modes of administration, the exponentially increasing volumes of information, the easy duplication of information and the generalization of digital information have made "a passive attitude that would only process information at the definitive stage and keep only information of high heritage value that would then be described *a posteriori* and made available to requesters" [BAN 12a, p. 218] definitively inoperative.

More than a matter of technology, information management is a matter of method and behavior of the different actors involved. The mandate of records management becomes crucial since it must take charge of all records produced or received by organizations from their creation to their final retention or disposal in order to optimize information management by facilitating access, consultation, distribution and archiving of documents. The main objectives of the information management policy are to enable all the relevant actors in the company to know what they have to do, how and when; to define the role of the actors and their scope of intervention; and to comply with legal and regulatory requirements. Finally, the company must be able to collect, retrieve and preserve its information and avoid the risk of loss, destruction or falsification of evidence [RIE 10, p. 60].

The stakes are high. In the organizational framework, the lack of anticipation can lead to a doubling of processes and work chains, sometimes dedicated to paper documents, sometimes to electronic documents, and therefore a loss of productivity. The inescapable nature of information processing systems imposes a context in which technological developments are very rapid; this requires making choices that will last over time and not giving in to ephemeral tools or fads and taking into account the typology of documents. We must not forget to support the change and ensure good staff training and also take into account digital documents as information heritage to which preservation rules apply [APR 06, p. 6].

This leads us to review information governance from the perspective of responsible long-term management of digital documents and to reflect on good documentary practices to resolve the paradox of transparency in relation to the protection of personal data. Records management falls within the framework of information governance, but it is necessary to differentiate between governance that imposes rules and the management that executes them, and IT governance, which is concerned with the architecture of systems but not with information. The human factor is fundamental, with the need for a culture of management and change in working methods with a unity of purpose and participation, as no single department can achieve all objectives on its own. Collaboration is essential simply because of the multiplicity of participants in the creation, circulation, evaluation and preservation of the information. At its core, information governance is based on the known principles of GRC, that is, governance, risk and compliance with a focus on information management as the fourth driver.

For Jurg Hagmann, information governance is defined as policy decisions about information and information management, with records management becoming one of the decision areas and being managed within the framework of information governance (IM) [HAG 15, p. 18]. He adds that governance is the art of trusted interaction between key stakeholders (IT, business, legal and compliance, RIM, security and privacy). They aspire to converge in order to minimize information risks to the enterprise while maximizing the value of information assets through the construction of desirable behaviors and enable cross-functional decision-making [HAG 15, p. 20]. Information governance cannot be dictated or mandated; it must be part of the way of working and embedded in the culture.

The Gartner firm defines information governance as a specification, a description of the right decisions, an accountability framework that enables the right behavior in the creation, evaluation, storage, use, archiving and disposal of information. It is a set of processes by which the organization has a means of controlling risks, ensuring operational efficiency and integrity of its operations, and identifying all this with good management. This is a global approach that takes into account not only the body of documents, but also all aspects relating to the organization, processes, responsibilities, etc. In reality, information governance is a general concept that tends to define the way in which the company must manage information.

Various studies point out the shortcomings of information governance. For example, Concept Searching estimates that in 2015, 90% of companies do not know what data they have because they do not have the means to search for it. Moreover, half of the time, companies are forced to produce a copy because they cannot find the original. Vanson Bourne in a risk study of 1,350 decision-makers in 11 countries estimates that one in five executives are unaware of their regulatory cyber security obligations in 2017 [CHA 18, pp. 13–14].

In February 2016, a Serda Group survey was conducted among 250 public and private organizations, including a questionnaire of 120 questions administered online. It confirms that digital information governance has become a reality for 66% of the organizations. To date, we can measure a 40% increase over five years, which makes it a priority approach in organizations, to respond as much to the digitization of working methods as to the mandatory economic and legal context [SER 16, p. 4].

Companies want to better understand and process internal and external information in the broadest sense (documents, files, e-mail, all media, data, etc.); this raw material has become a real issue in economic activity and shows the inevitable path of the digital transition. The governance of digital information requires a strategic plan for the organization which must take into account the means, the necessary resources, the information resources concerned, risk management, new uses and new users. However, a balance must be found between methodological tools, technology, and the need for training and awareness raising among employees [SER 16, p. 4].

Structural events serve as accelerators, for example, business restructurings, changes in strategy, head office relocations. They lead to opportunities to change operations and are supported by dematerialization and collaborative function deployment programs [SER 16, p. 6].

The issue that is beginning to take priority is the definition of rules and processes for documentation. We now know what is expected from the governance of digital information, but we are looking for implementation tools and good practices to structure governance (file purging, file naming and version control, filing and retention periods, notifications, etc.) [SER 16, p. 17].

More generally, completion rates for filing and archiving plans remain low. These are known to be two of the essential pivots in the implementation of digitization programs. Priority is given to means of facilitating access to information and documents and to means of protection. Rules and means have yet to be put in place to enable governance to function properly. The filing plan, which is an essential basis for conducting a governance program, remains the primary tool for structuring all the activities concerned and is at the heart of the deployment of electronic record management solutions. New functionalities such as the electronic signature or electronic initials are still lagging behind, despite the strong demand from users and citizens and the fact that technological solutions are mature. This discrepancy can be explained in particular by changes in working methods that are slower to master than the simple commissioning of a tool [SER 16, p. 25].

1.2. The lifecycle of documents

1.2.1. *The concept of the three ages*

The document lifecycle is a document governance aid to determine responsibilities, identify over time the access to information and possible risks and control the traceability of activities. The documents will go through different states which will lead to a specific processing at each stage. This involves the creation of the document, and therefore its capture and validation, its current active utility period, its administrative utility period and its final destination, which results either in the destruction of the document or its permanent archiving. We will therefore focus on the management and conservation of documents produced or received within the framework of an organization's activity from their creation to their final preservation or destruction.

None of the usual standards in records management defines the concept of the lifecycle. The lifecycle of records and archives has been extensively described and commented on since the 1920s. In the archival field, the theory of the three ages has long been used, but its relevance to the electronic world is a matter of debate. The concept of the three ages emerged in 1948 in the report of a Hoover Commission Task Force on the Organization and Functioning of the United States Federal Government. The idea was to reduce the mass of documents produced by modern bureaucracies by scheduling the disposal of documents at the most appropriate times according to their primary and secondary value. According to Theodore Schellenberg, the primary value is the value that the record has based on the business process that gave rise to it. This is the administrative, legal, financial or evidentiary status to decide, act and control decisions and actions taken. It is closely related to the reasons for its creation, existence and use. In contrast, the secondary value is the value that a document acquires for uses other than that for which it was created. It has a scientific and historical utility as well as the character of privileged, authentic and objective testimony or of general information.

In the 1960s, the Frenchman Yves Pérotin divided the life of archives into three ages: an administrative age, an intermediate age, and a historical age from the creation of a document to its final decommissioning. According to this model, in the first age, the documents are active or current and in daily or regular use. For this reason, they are kept with the producing departments for the day-to-day processing of business. This is the administrative age; active files remain operational within the department and are necessary for its proper management. They must be quickly accessible.

Then, semi-active or intermediate documents no longer in common use must be kept temporarily, mainly for administrative or legal purposes. The processing of the file is then completed; the information potential contained in the file has been disseminated and used. However, it can be referred to, for example, as evidence, under the legal time limits. These documents must be grouped together in a common archive room managed by an archive manager in the case of paper documents or in a shared folder for digital documents or in an electronic archive service. Essential records are part of both the first and second archival ages. They are vital for the resumption or maintenance of a business, for carrying out emergency operations during and immediately after a disaster, and for the restoration of the organization's legal, financial and functional responsibilities.

They are then transferred to a historical archive for permanent storage or to an electronic archiving system. Inactive or definitive files are documents whose active and semi-active periods have ended. They are kept without any time limit because of their permanent administrative, legal or historical value. Private organizations may retain them while public organizations must transfer them to national, regional or local archives for permanent preservation or selective retention. Archival records are part of the third age. They are of significant value for administrative, functional, legal, financial, historical, or reference and research purposes. These records are kept on a permanent basis.

This model of the three ages was formalized in France in a decree, following the law of January 3, 1979, on archives. According to this decree, current archives are "documents that are of usual use for the activities of producers"; intermediate archives are "documents that are no longer current archives, but not yet definitive archives". Finally, the definitive archives are "documents to be kept for an unlimited period of time". This regulatory interpretation poses certain problems, as this model is based on subjective frequencies of use and differentiated locations that do not apply to all production contexts, particularly in the electronic system.

In the 1980s, Yves Pérotin believed that for the first age "it is only necessary to get offices to make good archives and to build up files that are not cluttered by uselessness". Forty years later, the "only" is largely obsolete: today, in the digital environment, it is indeed the selection of data to be archived; the identification of the right versions, of documents validated in proper and due form; that poses the most problems. Furthermore, digital media no longer suffer from waiting until their producers no longer need the records before being subject to archival processing: without proper management at the time of creation, authenticity and integrity will be difficult to establish [CHA 12, pp. 7–8].

Active or management archives (1–2 years)	Intermediate or semi-active archives (3–10 years)	Inactive or definitive archives (more than 10 years old)
Administrative age. Records of daily use. Important primary value.	Administrative or legal needs. Records that are less used but need to be quickly accessible. Legal and informational value.	Records kept without time limit because of their permanent administrative, legal and historical value. Significant secondary value.
100% of the mass produced.	80% of the initial mass produced.	10% to 20% of the initial mass produced.
Tools: filing plan, preservation schedule.	Tools: disposal and transfer list, stocktaking plan. Operations: archiving, file cleaning.	Finding aids: guides, digital directories. Operations: destruction of records, identification of backlogs.

Table 1.1. *Table of the three ages of archives*

Thus, explaining the lifecycle of an electronic record on the same principle as that of paper is less relevant, especially since it involves managing the record from the moment it is created, if its integrity is to be easily assessed. Thus, at the current and intermediate stages, the archivist must ensure that reliable records are controlled and created and that authenticity is maintained. At the final stage, the archivist seeks to maintain authenticity and to restore the integrity of the record.

The digital environment challenges the theory of the three ages of archives by suggesting a records lifecycle model closer to that of records management. The moment of records management is radically advanced (at the time of signature, distribution or notification) or even at the time of its creation. The specificity of digital production implies upstream work to guarantee the quality of the data in collaboration with the services that produce them and the management of IT services

[DIS 12, p. 4]. If a document is not managed when it is created, it will be extremely difficult to assess its integrity *a posteriori*. In this sense, the notion of intermediate archiving is no longer relevant. It can be useful if one does not think about age, but about accountability. The issue is no longer one of delimiting the ages of an electronic record, but rather of defining who has accountability for verifying its compliance with the rules required for the proper functioning of an electronic filing system.

The timing of the accession process is radically advanced in order to guarantee the evidentiary form of the document and to preserve legal certainty due to the intrinsic fragility of digital information. In this case, the two essential stages in the lifecycle of the document are validation and the expiry of its legal retention period. The filing process is also advanced since dematerialization makes it possible to automatically retrieve the descriptive elements created as soon as the information is produced, without any interruption in load. Digital files that are to be preserved can be sent to heritage institutions for permanent archiving as soon as they reach the end of their current age, since producers keep a copy for the duration of their administrative utility [BAN 12b, p. 51].

The preservation of archives is a major issue and is posed in terms of preventive conservation. Previously, it was the subject of four successive sequences: collection, evaluation, sorting and preservation. With the digital document, all these sequences are carried forward to the very origin of the documents. The digital form requires the introduction of a whole series of archiving metadata as soon as the records are created. Preventive conservation issues have become a crucial issue with the digital record, not only because of the extreme variety of media, software and their obsolescence, but also because of their physical instability, their mass and especially their content and the need for evidence [DEL 12b, p. 199].

Finally, from a management perspective, the lifecycle has similarities, as the fundamental criterion is the usefulness of the record to the organization. The records lifecycle is therefore punctuated by two stages: its creation and the exhaustion of its primary value, in other words its evidential or asset value. At the end of this second stage, the choice is binary: keep the records for heritage purposes or destroy them [ASS 07, p. 67].

Beyond electronic archiving, the information system as a whole has evolved in recent years from data collection to value generation. User needs are changing along with the possibilities offered by the new tools at their disposal. The Information Lifecycle Management (ILM) or records lifecycle corresponding to a process approach is being taken into account. This reduces the breakdown action and the very notion of transfer appears less and less significant within an organization. It is replaced by the action to be carried out at the moment when a document becomes fixed and when it is absolutely necessary to protect it in order to be able to prove its origin and its integrity in the sense of its information content, and this until the end of its lifecycle [ARN 15, p. 213].

Indeed, while records validation is a step most often relevant in the lifecycle management of electronic documents, the gap between the first and second ages is much less so. Unless there is a particular technical constraint, a transfer of records to the archives during the administrative utility period is not justified. It is more convenient to leave the records online for the user services in the electronic archiving system where they were recorded at the time of their creation and wait until the end of their period of administrative utility. The third age, on the other hand, remains meaningful, since the documents have reached their secondary value and are of less interest to the paying service. However, in a service that keeps its archives from their creation to their unlimited retention, one could envisage having only one electronic archiving system covering the entire records lifecycle. This solution can be envisaged provided that the volume of archived documents does not adversely affect the performance of the system and that search modes and access rights are adapted to the needs of successive users. The first step is to respond first to administrative searches and then to historical searches, but with the confidentiality of the documents being maintained for the required period of time [BUR 13, p. 18].

Asserting the primacy of the current age in the digital environment involves reconsidering the ways in which information is organized and how it is described. The needs of the user take precedence over those of the archivist, whose intellectual logic may be undermined. Indeed, the primary value of information dominates. This observation is reinforced by the staggering growth in the number of data to be archived. The dematerialization of processes relies on computer applications that are often centralized. This contributes to the concentration of the volumes of electronic archives to be processed. Finally, the massive irruption of litigation procedures in our companies also contributes to the increase in document production. Actions and decisions are better documented with a view to gathering up *a priori* evidence to deal with a claim, or even to defend or sue in court. When they are created by computerized means, this evidence is sometimes signed and time-stamped to guarantee its authenticity [BUR 11, p. 76].

The issue is no longer one of delimiting the ages of an electronic document, but rather of defining who is responsible for verifying its compliance with the rules required for the proper functioning of an electronic filing system. Digital technology seems to make the preservation of a document much simpler. However, as in the analog world, the "unnecessary" preservation of thousands of digital documents represents a lower storage cost, but it produces a lot of documentary noise. Furthermore, if we consider only the current active utility period (CUP) with document validation and the administrative utility period (AUP), which is a rule of two ages, we run the risk of obscuring the historical and heritage dimension of the documents produced. It also limits the indispensable role of the records manager and the archivist concerning the added value brought in terms of evaluation and the final fate of the documents after the AUL.

The lifecycle remains a diversity of models and milestones to be identified. It does not matter whether the information is in paper, electronic or any other form of media: the various document flows and systems must be fully integrated to ensure the integrity, authenticity, reliability and usability of the information resource throughout its life. The tools developed to control the lifecycle are the same: a filing plan to structure and have a global vision of the information produced in an organization, a repository of retention rules.

However, the determination of the three lifecycle ages remains operative for personal data protection legislation. For each of the ages, it defines differentiated access rules that become very restricted at the intermediate age, with a possible change of medium making the information less accessible. It is also possible to dispose of certain data in the case of databases before the transition to the intermediate age. This is also effective for access to information which, during the first two ages, must remain the one most familiar to the initial user. For the initial user, the archiving support will be transparent, as he will use his own finding aids to search and access the desired information [BAN 12b, p. 51].

For heritage use, the finding aids will be rethought and reviewed by the records management tools of the heritage services. Finally, this determination remains operative in terms of the responsibilities of the producing service during the first two ages. It remains effective for selection between the files to be kept as heritage and the files to be disposed of. Selection is only carried out at the end of the administrative utility period, even if the functionalities to do so are already in place, when the time comes to create documentary objects of heritage value [BAN 12b, p. 52].

There is also an American lifecycle model developed as early as the 1970s. Unlike the French model, it also integrates data from technological tools. In an article published in 1983, Ira Penn develops the idea that information has a life similar to that of a biological organism. Information is born, which is the creation phase, then it goes through what is the maintenance and use phase before dying which leads to disposal. For Ira Penn, technological tools are only aids to facilitate good management of records, and paper is a technology like any other. In this model, the archive is only one of the possible aspects of the final processing in the prospective vision of the records management professional whereas it does not correspond to the retroactive perspective of the archivist. However, like the three-age model, this cycle model remains linear. It does not allow for backtracking, leapfrogging, subdivision, or simultaneity. Both models will be strongly criticized by proponents of the document-archive continuum [KER 15, p. 52].

1.2.2. The records continuum

Perhaps the greatest detractors of the lifecycles presented above have been the Australians, who see the cycle as too record-centered, while users are forgotten. Archives can have a continuing value that can be historical from the moment they are conceived. A record can serve both organizational and collective memory. The lifecycle unnecessarily distinguishes between responsibilities for managing the active record on the one hand and responsibilities for historical records on the other.

Also, in Australia, Frank Upward proposed in 1996 a more fluid and continuous approach, the Records continuum, which ensures a continuum of responsibilities between records managers and archivists. In this representation, the record must be considered in its four dimensions: a dimension of creation, capture, organization and pluralization along four axes: the evidentiality axis, the transactionality axis, the identity axis and the recordkeeping axis.

Information continuum theory provides the conceptual approach required to manage information resources of business and continuing value in today's environment. There is a lack of differentiation between archival and records management functions, the need to address recordkeeping issues prior to their creation, and the ability of a single information resource to simultaneously occupy multiple positions of information creation, organizational use, accountability and societal use [BAK 11].

Managing records according to their use is important, but the identity of the manager is not. The entity managing the records may be the creator of the records or another institution. The free world of Web 2.0 applications, such as Wikipedia, YouTube or Slideshare, in which the cost of storage and management is not borne by the creator of the information, encourages the storage of huge amounts of information resources. These sites, often proprietary systems, illustrate the total bankruptcy of recordkeeping based on command and control. They complete the decentralization of authority, forcing users to evaluate information content without being able to rely on old forms of authority such as normative publications or institutional affiliation. This lifecycle approach is better suited to the electronic world, as it allows the elements of the document registration system to be made available at any time and to record the evolution of documents in the same system. The document can be used continuously and meets all business, legal and heritage requirements. The continuum metaphor is adapted to the Web 2.0 information culture because it does not need a beginning and does not determine an end. In the continuum, what matters is not the lifecycle of a particular information resource, but the utility of all information resources of business value that are significant, sufficient and sustainable [BAK 11].

The different dimensions of the continuum help us to understand the globality of the ideas represented. The first dimension encompasses the actors, the actions of those actors, and the documents that testify to those actions. The second dimension encompasses the system that records documents in context so that the document can be valued as evidence of the organization's activities. The third dimension brings together the elements that define the organization's business processes. The fourth dimension is the archival dimension which reflects the role of institutions and individuals in the collective social, historical and cultural memory [KER 15, p. 60].

It is a kind of concept map comprising 16 concepts, four dimensions and four axes, that is, 28 elements presented in four concentric circles. It reports on a process that is still in progress. Archives have multiple uses because of their continual value for an individual, an organization or society. We move from a conception of archives as a final product to a conception that emphasizes the never-ending process of archiving. The fourth dimension of the model does not allow us to understand how archives through their use become archives [LEM 15, p. 296].

For the records continuum, there is the identity axis, which concerns the different natural or legal persons involved in the creation and preservation of records. It determines all the players involved, from the creators of archival documents to the centers or institutions responsible for their safekeeping. On the other hand, as soon as the documents are permanently preserved, no mention is made of the identity of the actors involved. However, since it is at the moment of use that archives truly become archives, the chain of actors must be extended to include users and their fields of activity, that is, the frame of reference. This axis makes it possible to consider, rather than the identity of the actors, the various activities with which the documents are associated from their creation to their use. The identity axis then becomes the activity axis with a view to use [LEM 15, p. 297].

The transactionality axis considers the reasons why records are created and then used throughout their existence and reports on the functions performed by the records from their creation to their retention. The transactionality axis would have more to do with the purpose of records than with the fact that they are the product of activities [LEM 15, p. 298].

As for the recordkeeping axis, the use reveals a hidden aspect of the archive. They can only be used because of possible use without the need to satisfy particular conditions of use (object, device, context, public). But how to dispose of a use without context, without a discourse with informational, scientific, patrimonial or artistic content. Nor can it be used without elements of presentation that are more or less formalized or standardized according to context, or without taking advantage of the material characteristics of archival records. Finally, there is no use without the necessarily active role played by the public depending on the manner and environment in which the documents are used [LEM 15, p. 298].

Finally, the evidentiality axis makes it possible to consider the documents in terms of their link with memory, that of traces, of the evidence that the document can provide in a heritage institution (of an individual, company or collective).

With the generalization of management system standards, the lifecycle of records is part of a more global cycle, which is that of the management system. Different granularities of lifecycles are taken into account, depending on whether one is interested in a very short time span, at the level of the business record, or a longer lifespan, at the level of the file or of the institution itself. New models need to be created to take into account metadata, flows and dynamics that are not captured in records management systems, and can be applied to different types of systems, regardless of the archival issues involved. It does not matter how many ages, phases or stages there are in the journey. It is up to each individual to determine what representation they need to carry out their work. The lifecycle is an aid to document governance to determine our responsibilities and identify what the possible points of access to information and risks are, at what point in time, and to control the traceability of activities.

Using the Dublin Core definition of the information science lifecycle, we obtain a description that can be adapted to different contexts, according to the needs of each one. It is then a "sequence of events that mark the development and use of an information resource". The International Council on Archives, for example, has dealt with a three-stage cycle that includes design, where systems are developed and implemented, creation and maintenance of records. The national archives of Great Britain have instead spoken of a five-step approach involving capture, disposition, appraisal, preservation, and transfer/destruction [RAJ 11, p. 82]. In fact, the lifecycle, whatever form it takes, should remain a representation to help define access to information and determine responsibilities in records management, but it should not be seen as a principle and certainly not as an immutable theory. The lifecycle is a means, a concept, a benchmark for identifying document governance, regardless of the information medium (paper, electronic) or system used [KER 15, p. 67].

1.3. Documents in business processes

1.3.1. *Processes*

The ability of organizations to manage and share their information to better exploit it is a major competitive advantage. They need to be able to rely on a policy and information processes that allow them to keep documentary records of the completion of business processes. However, they must deal with individual informational behaviors that may differ from the formal practices recommended by the organization. Document producers actively participate in the creation of documentation solutions by creating the records of the organization's activities that need to be documented for evidentiary, accountability and transparency purposes. Thus, archival documentation processes consist of sets of functions, tools and systems to manage the organization's archives [MAU 10, pp. 102–103].

Information systems act as memory systems by keeping track of activities. It is important to manage the content of these systems as soon as information is created in them. While these systems include some minimal functions for organizing information, they do not fully meet archival requirements. This includes identifying, understanding, and documenting the activities that take place in the conduct of business processes, as well as the genres and types of records and the different types of information practices and information systems in which they are created, organized, and preserved [MAU 10, p. 108].

The process approach is interesting for the continuous improvement of performance. As in any organization, the implementation and management of activities requires the formalization of processes detailing the steps (who, when and how), allowing to control the implementation of these activities [ARN 15, p. 206]. A process can be defined as a set of correlated or interactive activities that transforms input elements into output elements. These elements are either material objects, information, or both [BAI 16, p. 140]. The tasks of creation, management, preservation, and disposition are integrated or must be closely integrated with these processes.

The processes are grouped into three categories: production or service provision, management or steering, and support (human and material resources). "Process" should not be confused with "procedure". The first describes the activities of the company from a transversal viewpoint in relation to its organization, while the second explains how to proceed efficiently in this organization [BAI 16, p. 140].

Business processes can be general or specific, administrative or operational and also functional. The implementation of business processes is supported by a number of information systems that offer sets of functionalities that allow a certain number of tasks to be carried out, while at the same time structuring the information and allowing it to be identified and used by organizational players [MAU 10, p. 103].

A process is a sequence of standardized operations that are performed by people in a business function of an organization to produce a result. Process analysis will be used a lot in records management. It is a tool that will be used at different stages of the implementation of a project with different purposes and granularity. It will be used, for example, to identify the requirements for managing business records, to analyze risks, or to create a filing plan or a management schedule or plan.

This analysis of records management processes articulated with the so-called "business" processes will help to define the right conditions for retention and archiving [ARN 15, p. 207]. A business process can be defined as "a set of operations or activities carried out by actors (employees, customers, suppliers) with and using tools, according to processes and rules for a business purpose. The latter must be able to measure them from both a qualitative and quantitative point of view" [RIE 10, p. 37]. Thus, a business process can be thought of as an orderly sequence of actions designed to produce a result, generating documents and data.

The analysis of processes takes precedence over that of the organization producing the documents, especially since the volatility of structures makes the producing service much less relevant in terms of description than the function, which is perennial. Understanding the processes modelled in information systems becomes essential for analyzing and selecting the data to be archived. It is a question of carrying out a more detailed analysis of business processes than was necessary for the collection of paper archives. The archivist can help to improve documents from business applications or to standardize values in the repositories used by these applications. This approach involves taking into account the needs and constraints of the departments that drive the processes. This prior intervention by the archivist is reinforced by the fact that the indexing, naming and format of files must be defined at the design stage of the IT application to enable them to be preserved in good conditions in the medium and long term [BUR 13 p. 17].

Records management professionals must therefore adapt their methodologies, tools and systems not only to the realities of the digital world, but also to those of business processes. They must deal with the informational behaviors of organizational actors who have a clear preference for accessing information in digital format directly and immediately via their computers. Documentary processes would benefit from being better integrated into information systems from the design stage, in order to support the individual information needs of organizational actors as well as the information needs of organizations as communities. In this way, existing archival processes and systems could be better integrated into the day-to-day reality of organizations [MAU 10, p. 108].

Responsibility for managing corporate memory within the organization should be defined. Everyone, in his or her own way, participates in recording, storing, managing, organizing and making available different components of the organizational memory, without the actions of different departments being unified. This necessarily has consequences, not only on the archiving of corporate memory, but also on its use in business processes [MAU 10, p. 108].

The management of its records must be considered from creation to archiving. To do this, it is necessary to identify which types of documents need to be protected first. One can look at the type of documents that are easily identifiable, which are invoices and contracts. Then, the spectrum of these types of records can be broadened to include more business-specific types of records, for example, through process analysis. This involves taking each business process and interviewing the people involved in those processes, working with them to define the types of deliverables to be retained, the associated metadata, lifecycle information and associated confidentiality. It is important to involve all types of stakeholders in these processes – not only those who produce the records, but also any other type of stakeholder who can provide impetus and support to these processes, such as top management and legal departments, for example.

From a methodological point of view, we list all the actions to be carried out by the actors. For each action, the obligations to preserve evidence, that is, the requirements, are listed. The legal, regulatory and contractual requirements are taken into account and the different types of control required are noted. For each action, the types of documents or records that will be used as evidence are identified in the information systems or in the paper files. For example, whether the medium is the original, native paper or native digital. The result is a database, a dynamic management schedule that is indexed and searchable by process, by action and by type of document. A process is broken down into actions and each action results in a proof, a type of document. Then, we indicate whether the original is paper or from an application and if so, we note which one. The second phase is based on the filing plan, which will indicate in which part of the plan is a particular type of document. The filing plan itself reflects the processes.

1.3.2. Records

In the digital world, records are undergoing an increasing evolution marked by the speed of their production, the increase in their volume, variety, accessibility and rapid transmission. The corollary of this is the vulnerability of digital documents that must be preserved because of organizational negligence, technological and financial limitations, and malicious intent. Because of their fragility from the point of view of the physical medium, these documents need appropriate contextualization for their understanding. Moreover, the value of records in both transactions and overall human activities makes them an essential issue. In this new environment, a document no longer exists as such since the medium and content of the information are now dissociated. Consequently, the display of digital content is the result of a harmony between software, operating systems, hardware and devices, all of which are subject to increasingly similar rates of obsolescence. There is a high risk of loss as soon as data and documents are transmitted in space, with problems relating to the integrity of the information and its security, and in time with the problem of long-term preservation and the obsolescence of data formats [BAN 14, p. 14]. This imposes an integrated management of digital and analog documents. Thus, a publication by Aproged, in 2013, indicates that in organizations, 80% of information is available in unstructured form and comes from the usual office automation tools. Another study reports that 60% of decisions in organizations are made by e-mail and attachments [SER 15, p. 320].

The international standard ISO 15489 defines archival records as "records created, received and preserved, as evidence and information, by a natural or legal person in the performance of legal obligations or the conduct of business". The concept of "document" is central to the Quebec Act, which defines it as follows in section 3: "A document consists of information carried on a medium. The information is delimited and structured, according to the medium used, by tangible or logical features and is intelligible in the form of words, sounds or images. The information may be rendered by any type of writing, including a system of symbols that can be transcribed words, sounds or images or into another system of symbols" [GAG 15, p. 33][1].

Four main functions are proposed for archives that also apply to digital records:

– the evidentiary function: throughout the lifecycle of the digital record, it must be possible to demonstrate a commitment, right, or obligation in light of the evolving legal, regulatory, or legislative context;

– the comprehension function: consulting digital records can help strategic decision-making and a better understanding of the organization's environment;

– the memory function: the creation of knowledge bases from digital records provides a view of the memory of past elements and allows activities to be kept track of;

– the communication function: access to the digital document must make it possible to become aware of its content and context and to disseminate it in order to ensure the communication of information and the visibility of the organization [APR 06, p. 7].

---

1 http://legisquebec.gouv.qc.ca/en/ShowDoc/cs/C-1.1.

ARCHIVES	DOCUMENTATION
A set of records, regardless of date, form or physical medium, produced or received by a person or organization for its needs or the conduct of its business and retained for their general information value.	Set of documents gathered in a voluntarist and subjective way, on a given subject.
Internal information resulting from and reflecting the activities of the organization, they remain grouped according to their origin. They are unique and they have an evidential value that lasts over time.	External information derived from published documents, acquired and not produced by a service for professional purposes. Required to be updated regularly with a quick deletion of outdated documentation.
Evidence: original documents for regulatory obligations.	No legal or confidential value and can be found on any information medium.
Memory: storage and traceability of activities	Available in several places and on several media, it can therefore be disposed of quickly.
Strategy: understanding the facts and helping to make decisions.	Completes the information in a file (approximately 10% of documentation to be retained).
Communication: brand image and transparency of organizations, raw material for researchers.	Constituted according to the value and on a voluntary basis to document a project.

Table 1.2. *Differences between archives and documentation*

The International Electrotechnical Commission Standard 82045-1: 2001 on records management defines a record as "a structured and fixed amount of information that can be managed and interchanged as a unit between users and systems".

We are witnessing the disappearance of the word "archives" in the contemporary administrative environment, which is more sensitive to the notions of information and data, personal or public, than to that of archives. On the other hand, the term archives is increasingly popular in the field of heritage, human sciences and knowledge, where a new epistemology is developing around the word archives, in singular or plural. As for contemporary producers in government or business, they have banished the term archives from their vocabulary[2] [BAN 14, p. 8].

---

2 See in particular MÜLLER, B. , "Archives, documents, données : problèmes et définitions", *La Gazette des archives*, No. 212, "À la découverte des sciences humaines et sociales" Paris, Association des archivistes français, 2008–4, pp. 35–44.

A more comprehensive definition of an archival record is given in the Guide of the International Council on Archives: "Recorded information, produced or received in the initiation, conduct or completion of an institutional or individual activity and that comprises content, context and structure sufficient to provide evidence of the activity" [ICA 05, p. 10][3]. This means that the record is made up of several interrelated elements, namely medium, form, content, identifier, structure and context. The InterPares program distinguishes, according to diplomacy, the four main elements of documentary form, annotations, medium and context.

The digital record is a set composed of content, logical structure, presentation attributes allowing its representation, endowed with a meaning intelligible by man or readable by a machine. Its content is composed of a set of data representing useful information. Its logical structure organizes the elements of its content by assigning them a role in the meaning and possibly includes the electronic signature. The digital document can be created in its native state or obtained by a process of transformation of a physical document, in this case we speak of a digitized document [APR 06, p. 25].

The term "document", associating content with form, remains dominant, followed by the legally more precise term "act", which refers to the official act and the rules of evidence, including in electronic form. The term "data" is not the most widely used, but its progression is dazzling, as it tends to encompass all types of information and is found with the open data movement. This is immediately related to the automated processing of personal data. The term "data" is gradually adopted for the entire field of dissemination and then reuse of data that is now called "public", that is collected or produced, within the framework of its mission, by a public service with public funds [BAN 14, p. 11].

In the terminology of the professional literature on records management, the term "document" is preferred to "information", as a record of a transaction, a case, evidence or information. This is reflected in the official definition of records management as "the organization and control of a process, namely the constitution, selection, preservation and disposal of the records of an administration, business or organization". The term "document" is sufficient in itself, whether it is archived or to be archived. For AFNOR, on the other hand, document is too vague a term in this context and the standardization commission in charge of records management preferred to use the word "record" [BAN 14, p. 12].

There has been an imperceptible shift from document to information, and from information to data, in a context of increasing digital production. In the computer world, the document is being overshadowed by "data", the reference element par

---

3 https://www.ica.org/sites/default/files/ICA_Study-16-Electronic-records_EN.pdf.

excellence. To confine oneself to the State, all recent official publications on information systems refer to data, in the broadest possible sense [BAN 14, p. 12]. The term "data" is increasingly being used, as it tends to encompass all types of information and is found in the open data movement. It is immediately related to the automated processing of personal data. The term "data" appears throughout the field of dissemination and then reuse of data that are now called "public", that is, collected or produced by a public service with public funds within the framework of its mission [BAN 14, p. 11].

In fact, the document is a stable and perennial entity of valuable information. This definition makes it possible to group together the uses of the digital document:

– its form (entity): identification, authenticity, integrity;

– its management (stable and perennial): storage, preservation, lifespan, perpetuation;

– its content (information): intelligibility, readability, accessibility;

– the framework (value) in which it is used: access rights, ownership, control, entitlements [APR 12, p. 10].

The shape of the document means its appearance, colors, dimensions, characters, figures, and header. In the case of analog records, the form is inseparable from the medium, that is, word processing documents, databases, hypertext documents, images, documents produced by spreadsheets, e-mails, voice messages, video documents, etc. [ICA 05, p. 10]. In the digital world, the choice of word processing hardware and software greatly influences the form. In the case of incomplete compatibility, the form will change [KEC 14, p. 111]. The concept of structure refers to how the document is stored in which format and on which medium, for example. The physical structure of an electronic document is variable and depends on the hardware and software used; its logical structure, that is, the relationships between the parts that make it up, renders it intelligible [ICA 05, p. 11].

In the analog world, the medium carries and makes information visible. In the digital world, the document does not physically exist. It is not encased in the materiality of a medium that indissolubly binds the information to its medium. We are faced with structured information whose medium and encoding are transitory, ephemeral. What counts then is the meaningful information and not the encoding or the medium, which only serve to make the information momentarily accessible in a technological context that is constantly evolving [BUR 13, p. 22].

The document can be stored anywhere and on any media and dispersed in multiple files. Bits representing digital information require tools from a hardware, software and environmental interface. To complicate matters, the physical medium is changeable and the elements of the document can be separated from it, an identical copy can be made on another medium, and it can be converted to various standards [KEC 14, pp. 110–111]. As a result, access to the heritage undergoes an upheaval in the status of the document since the preservation of the document is no longer based on the permanence of the physical medium. There is a problem of identity of the document caused by the multiplicity of versions, coupled with a problem of integrity given the absence of content inherence on a stable medium and authenticity, because how can one verify what the document claims to be when it is manipulated and not fixed on a single physical medium [FRE 13, pp. 10–11]?

The difference between the information of a business and the information in a business is one of use and responsibility. On the one hand, documents are a source of information that brings knowledge, allowing one to learn, to reflect, and to continue the activity in a general process of value creation. On the other hand, records are information assets, assets to be preserved and managed according to their own and potential value for the defense of the company's interests [CHA 18, p. 23].

Perhaps one of the greatest impacts of digital technology is to blur the function of saving the written word in favor of a performance objective. The document now aims less at preserving a record of a fact than at responding to a user's day-to-day concerns. As a result, the strategic importance of document use is increasing both in organizations and in society in general [CAR 15, p. 53]. It becomes essential to identify the "document" behind the "content". Content without a date, context or critique is not an archival document. It tells a story, but it does not prove anything; it is not usable or reliable for building evidence. The goal is to contextualize and thus optimize the understanding of a document or information object by placing it in the time and environment of its production; to analyze the formal, intellectual, and material components of a document in order to assess the authenticity of an information object or its reliability to respond to a request for evidence or testimony; and to argue the relevance of its preservation or destruction [CHA 15a, p. 71].

In the digital world, the basic unit is the file, that is the document, or even the data, which can be assimilated, in the paper world, to information within a document. Electronic files can be grouped intellectually into folders. The latter is not a logistical element, it is purely intellectual and becomes completely virtual. The unit to be archived is nevertheless the file or data. The description in the file is unsuitable in the digital world even if computers offer the advantage of structuring information in a very rich way and even have a document that belongs to several files [BUR 13, p. 19].

As for the reference number, which is a convenient sign for locating paper archives in a store, it is no longer relevant to the communication of electronic archives. By simply clicking on its search result, the electronic record is displayed on the screen. In the absence of a reference number in an electronic filing system, the unique identifier of the record can be used as a reference, if necessary [BUR 13, p. 21].

1.3.3. *Files*

Each activity has one or more business processes. Thus, the human resources activity can have the business process recruitment, relations with social partners, or the individual management of staff. Each of these processes produces documents and data that are linked together to form a file. Documents about an employee and his or her career development make up the employee record. A document does not exist in isolation; it is an integral part of a file (project) or a case (customer file). Within the same business process, records are most often subject to the same requirements and retention rules [RIE 10, p. 64].

In the same vein, the file in an electronic archiving system should be seen as a virtual logical envelope of documents, a kind of display device on the screen. As with the filing plan, it is conceivable that a record may be visible in a number of different folders to suit different users' needs or to accommodate distinct business processes but needing to use common information resources. In any case, it is the file that carries the descriptive and management metadata, particularly those relating to its lifecycle and access rights. By attaching business rules to the smallest unit of records, a high degree of flexibility is achieved in terms of access and records management. It also allows for automatic file cleansing, whereby a document that has reached the end of its administrative utility life can be automatically disposed of, while other documents, which have not expired, remain visible in the file [BUR 13, p. 20].

If we return to the definition of a file, Carol Couture considers it to be "a set of documents, papers or even data (sound, image, text), organically constituted by a natural or legal person in the performance of his or her duties, relating to the same matter or object and placed in one or more containers (cassette, cardboard, register, bundle, folder, hard or optical disk)[4]".

---

4 Rousseau J.-Y. and Couture C., *Les fondements de la discipline archivistique*, Québec, Presses de l'Université du Québec, 1994, pp. 121–122.

Louise Gagnon-Arguin and Sabine Mas propose the following definition: "The file is a logical and coherent set of interdependent data and documents, collected during the course of an organization's activities, that can be found in one or more containers, media or places and that are likely to provide complete information on a case, subject, event or activity. It constitutes in itself a unit of information defined by the link between the records it contains" [GAG 11, p. 5]. There is a temporal dimension to the notion of a record. A file is complete only after a certain period of time. It is as the activities of an organization develop that a file is created. A record is complete when the activity or transaction for which it was created is completed [GAG 11, p. 3].

The file is characterized by the interdependence of the documents, which distinguishes it from a collection of items. The documents in the same file explain each other, producing the meaning of the information provided by the file. This relationship provides the evidentiary value of the information. An isolated item does not make sense; it must belong to a whole [GAG 11, p. 5]. A file has only one subject and all documents relate to the same matter, person or activity. It constitutes a unit of documentation on that subject and only becomes meaningful when it is complete [GAG 11, pp. 5–6].

Without records, organizations risk managing stacks of documents – disorganized information crammed onto a hard drive with no retention or knowledge of the context in which it was created and used. The file is therefore a unit of information and not just a physical unit of filing. It has an intellectual dimension, an added value that goes beyond the mere sum of its parts. It supports information. The file is time-dependent. It is built up during the processing of a case, the carrying out of an activity, the holding of an event or the progression of a person through the organization. It is the accumulation of items that will compose it and give it its meaning. It illustrates the stratification on which the constitution of a fonds is based. The file ensures the validity of activities, the interpretation of actions or the memory of facts [GAG 11, pp. 22–23].

The documents in a single file may be scattered and placed in several containers or even stored in several departments for reasons of shared responsibility and compliance with legislation or for preservation practices related to the volume of the file or the particular medium of the documents in a file. For example, the patient record can be considered a "hyperdocument" containing all the information and analyses on a patient. The traditional notion of a single physical record containing all the information necessary for patient follow-up is largely a myth: the information is extremely numerous, on various media (paper, images, digital data) in different places (care units, laboratory) and even in different hospitals [GAG 11, p. 3].

1.4. Data governance

1.4.1. *Data governance issues*

Organizations are sitting on a treasure trove of data without really realizing it. The data is multifaceted, coming from scientific research and its advances, e-administration and social networks. They become the main objective of archiving whether they are structured or not, moving or static, whether they represent a piece of written, sound or visual information.

A single piece of data (name of person, place, date, amount) has no meaning for either the user or the owner, but each grouping of data constitutes a document for the user. Series of data will form binding documents for the owner who has produced or captured names, dates, amounts in the course of his or her business [CHA 18, p. 33]. The improvement of the computer tools used makes it very easy to cross-reference data sets to enrich them. Moreover, the data are increasingly accessible, as is the case on open data portals dedicated to the reuse of data. Enrichment is then possible from a multitude of angles: repositories, addresses, names, values. Any common denominator can be used to repatriate data to complete an existing set [CLI 19, p. 28].

Data governance is becoming essential to build a strategy for data reuse. It can be defined as a system that combines a good knowledge of the applicable rules with a clear statement of the roles and responsibilities of the actors in all the processes that generate data or are directly related to it. Data governance will intervene within the framework of open data policies, the promotion of administrative transparency, the implementation of business intelligence, the creation of new services, and even the redefinition of business models [CLI 19, p. 23].

Initially confined to statistics, accounting and scientific calculations, data processing has now been extended to management, transforming traditional documents and creating new ones. We are gradually moving from an approach of redistributing raw data for commercial purposes, with the sale of data sets, to the reuse and reprocessing of data to invent new uses, such as the production of predictive data [CLI 19, p. 23].

According to IBM, the total data produced by sensors and machines, which represented only 11% of the total data produced in 2005, will increase to 42% in 2020 [DEL 15b, p. 133]. Another indicator shows that the average number of interactions with digital data will rise to 600 in 2020 per person per day. It will exceed 4,700 interactions in 2025, compared to only 85 in 2010[5], a staggering change of scale. The Walmart supermarket chain can process more than one million customer transactions per hour through their cash registers, which allows them to closely manage purchases and supplies in their stores [DEL 15b, p. 131].

In any innovation process involving data, it is first and foremost a question of valuing, characterizing and identifying them. Beginning with an analysis of static data is the first step, involving in particular IT, management control and business players. Once the situation report has been established, it will be necessary to set up a unique and reliable database, which should ideally be fed by dynamic data in real time. A crucial point here is the production of data that must be reliable, exhaustive and interoperable, that is the information systems producing the data must communicate with each other [CLI 19, p. 26].

So a lot of work needs to be done prior. It will be necessary to identify and analyze data sets, qualify, export, process, modify, manipulate, define their lifecycle, understand and apply the regulations relating to the sector of activity, put in place safeguards whatever the scale of data processing, keep the data over time and preserve its legally binding character if necessary. These are all issues that cannot be addressed without a collective effort [CLI 19, p. 23]. The data producer specifies his or her needs, the computer scientist creates the software tool that makes it possible to achieve the objective. The archivist defines the archiving metadata to be taken into account for the management of data over time, the perpetuation and the knowledge of the context that gives meaning to the data from automatic capture protocols [DEL 15b, p. 136].

Understanding how data are produced means looking at the people who produce the data and the context in which they are produced. Records management has never been more necessary, and the skills of archivists have never been more relevant in part to the field of appraisal. Defining how long information should be kept means asking how long it is useful to the producing profession and how long it will be used as evidence for the organization in the event of a dispute. At the end of this period, certain data, now deemed useless, could be disposed of, while others would be kept permanently as a heritage item [CLI 19, p. 23].

Efficient application of the product lifecycle is a competitive advantage for many leading industries. For example, within aerospace firms, data must be retained for up to seventy years between the initiation of a research and development project to design a new aircraft model and its retirement from service. These periods may even be extended to contribute to the analysis of aviation risk or to understand the nature

5 YOOZ, Transformation digitale : why not? Enfin un mode d'emploi, White Paper, p. 7, 2019.

of certain accidents. However, these commitment times are often beyond the projection capacity of organizations. Aside from the archivist, one may wonder who today is capable of organizing data quality in such a distant horizon, where the usual objectives of management see little further than the quarter or the end of the accounting year [CLI 19, p. 25]?

The real problem is the overlapping that has already occurred since document inflation, but whose methods are reversed. It is no longer a question of suppressing data under the argument that it is not useful, that there are too many of them and that we cannot read everything, but of disposing of repetitive and unreliable data. It will be up to archivists to design sophisticated, automated management schedules to control disposals [DEL 15b, p. 137].

The role of governance is to ensure that the data supports current processes, but more importantly that it meets the needs for the future strategic objectives of the structure. Data quality is an ongoing task. If this policy is interrupted, the quality of the data drops drastically and the processes immediately suffer. Examples include the time spent on post-correction, loss of confidence in the information handled, the generalization of manual controls and the decline in efficiency of staff. Data quality must be everyone's business, both in terms of creation and control by the organization's employees. The notion of the "extended enterprise" even allows the reasoning to be broadened to include contributions from suppliers and customers. As producers or consumers of data, they have a say in the quality of the data that concerns them [CLI 19, p. 25].

The traditional task of archivists is to question the quality of data in order to be able to attest that they are dealing with trustworthy "objects". This is of obvious value in the face of dynamic digital resources that are so easy to falsify, intentionally or unintentionally alter, or lose due to ever-increasing technological obsolescence. The archivist brings a holistic understanding of business processes and a focus on the value of the information [BAN 15, p. 41].

Thus, data quality becomes a fundamental issue. The use of quality data repositories makes it possible to objectify political decisions in certain cases, they are a guarantee of administrative transparency through their openness and, finally, they create innovation and wealth through their reuse. Archivists can contribute their achievements and reflections on the authenticity of archives, repositories and contextualization of information (metadata descriptions, thesaurus, filing and evaluation of archives). They can help on the evidential value of digital writing, but also on issues related to the protection of personal data [BAN 15, p. 42].

Exploring data is the most critical activity. This exploration produces a diagnosis that conditions the actions that will then be taken in relation to the data in question:

correcting the data creation process, enriching it, using it to manage or improve an activity, proposing it to other teams or simply deciding not to use the data. The data is represented on numerous graphs, facets and filters and allows you to navigate through the data and bring out its content through visualizations. Users will be able to modify their search scenario and refine their criteria to access the information they are looking for. The other case of widespread use is analysis to identify key facts, actors, themes, developments and to make comparisons as part of decision support. The vision provided is then so different from that offered in a database or Excel file that the user realizes the potential of the data used. He or she involves himself or herself in management based on these data and in the creation of new uses. Moreover, this data exploration is always the moment when false beliefs are discovered, for example, regarding the mechanism that produced the dataset. This facilitates the improvement of the data creation process upstream [CLI 19, p. 28]. The data must be provided with metadata, context, meaning, and preservation. In this way, they give them the added value attached to archiving, which reduces conservation costs and facilitates their use by the producer.

1.4.2. Big data

The first wave of the digital revolution first introduced electronic documents into companies and organizations, leading to significant productivity gains and lower management costs. The second wave, with the Internet, revolutionized the way businesses operate and saw the deployment of portals and blogs, e-commerce, social networks and mobility [CHA 15c, p. 374].

The third wave of the digital revolution is underway. The combination of the explosion in the number of connected users, the data flows they generate, the globalization of the economy, the competition it induces and the advances in computing capabilities has meant that data analysis has extended its field from business intelligence to data science. It induces the need for real-time analysis and the fact that it no longer only takes into account structured data, but also unstructured or semi-structured data [CHA 15c, p. 380].

The term "big data" is believed to have emerged in the late 1990s within the Association for Computing Machinery. This multifaceted phenomenon has developed gradually over more than 30 years, stimulated by the growth of computer data storage and processing capacities. Scientific research, particularly in the field of astronomy, was the first to store large amounts of data from sky observation. Companies followed suit, increasingly computerizing their internal data and processes. But it was with the advent of the Internet and especially Web 2.0 that the phenomenon took off most, when every Internet user was able to become an information producer themself. The amount of data will increase further with the

Internet of Things. The digital universe is doubling every two years. It poses the complexity of a new world: by 2020, it could have up to 80 billion connected objects and weigh 44,000 billion gigabytes [CHA 15c, p. 375].

Big data is governed by the 4V rule according to the White Paper published by the Digital Information and Communication Strategy Committee in November 2013:

– the volume corresponds to the considerable amount of data to be taken into account according to the given context. A rural municipality has a different vision of big data with regard to the data of its citizens than that of an international online sales site for example. For an online photo and video sharing site, the published content represents both a considerable amount of storage but a reduced amount of information. On the other hand, the data relating to these files, that is descriptive metadata, data relating to publication transactions, or even data produced by *a posteriori* digital analysis processing of the contents, represent a considerable volume of individual data for a much smaller storage volume [CHA 15c, p. 376]. Massive data taken separately may seem uninteresting but are worthwhile when combined. In 2013, humanity produced over 2 trillion gigabytes of new digital data on the Internet. This data is used to offer new products, but also to predict consumer or citizen behavior [JUN 15, p. 13];

– the variety consists of processing any type and structure of data: texts, sensor data, recordings, maps, sound, images, videos, related data from social networks, computer files and more. An image, video, telephone conversation or text can now be processed almost as easily as a table of numbers was once processed. The variety of data includes their form, but also over time as new flows appear or evolve over time. Efforts will be made to broaden the scope of the flows to increase the number of data to be interpreted and to vary the scope over time and exclude sources that are not proven reliable [CHA 15c, p. 377]. The diversity and multiplicity of sources are now easily accessible. They can be found in companies' internal data, data from sensors that are multiplying with the Internet of Things, data from the Web and social media. Processing makes it possible to generate information with high added value for the whole company. The aim is to assist in decision-making, in a context where information has become the major strategic asset of companies [HUO 15, p.15];

– velocity characterizes the speed with which information is generated, delivered, stored and finally removed or erased. It is measured in the ability to allow decisions to be made in real or near real time, which appears necessary to allow organizations to be flexible. Thus 6,000 tweets are written every second. With big data, we aim at a considerably reduced processing time compared to the existing situation. However, the detection of epidemics by analysis of social network flows will not meet the same time requirements as those relating to the dynamic management of road traffic in cities [CHA 15c, p. 377];

– veracity refers to the quality, accuracy and credibility of the data that govern the ability to make decisions with certainty in a context of selectivity between different sources of data acquisition [HUO 15, p. 12].

The concept of big data refers to the possibility of mass production or collection of data. The term is used when the amount of data that an organization needs to manage reaches a critical size that requires new technological approaches to its storage, processing and use. And it is a trend in information management to move away from the use of intermediaries, messaging, collaborative tools, EDM or electronic archiving systems. It is important to ensure that aspects related to the creation and lifecycle of data can be included in the big data, since it is not only a question of being able to search for information, but also of being able to parameterize the way it is produced.

The real wealth of a Big Data project is to cross heterogeneous data in real time and to imagine possible combinations and correlations. Using these data increases tolerance to inaccuracies, but above all allows us to move from the search for "causes" to the search for "correlations". For example, by placing censors on certain mechanical parts, it is possible to predict the imminence of a failure before it occurs [BAI 15, p. 25].

In Canada, by analyzing information on the health status of premature babies in real time with diagnostic software, infections were detected 24 hours before visible symptoms appeared. The use of big data in predictive analysis is based on the processing of data from the past to detect the most influential variables and apply them to present data to learn from them such as in crime control [JUN 15, p. 13]. But this approach can become very intrusive, hence the interest in preventing possible abuse and guaranteeing the ethical use of data, their controlled storage and their safe disposal when the time comes.

Companies want to better control and conquer their market or better understand their customers' expectations. Information becomes a strategic asset. Big data is a creator of wealth, with companies focusing on activities of data collection, verification, processing, use, archiving. Thus, implementing a big data approach is a competitiveness issue with the possibility of generating new profits and positioning themselves in new activities.

For public players, it means having the capacity to optimize their operations and offer new services to citizens. For citizens, it is an opportunity to be conscious actors in the massive data ecosystem, and to benefit from new services that will improve their quality of life. This presupposes an understanding and a mastery of the value of data, of what can and cannot be shared, with issues relating to intellectual property and knowledge of the regulations, particularly in the area of personal data [HUO 15, p. 16].

Several obstacles appear. The most serious is the creation of new monopolies. The big digital players such as Google, Apple, LinkedIn, Facebook, Amazon, all American, offer companies direct access to the general public's data and sometimes even to their own data. The risk for traditional players who need the tools offered by these providers to develop is that these large players use this asset and their dominant position to interfere in customer relations, since they seek to impose their own services on them, for example, in insurance and credit [HUO 15, p.17]. On the other hand, isn't the notion of owner outdated by that of user? In any case, we can no longer speak of the sole ownership of data. In social networks such as Facebook or Google, we only talk about use, because it seems to be taken for granted from the point of view of these companies that they own the data. Data ownership is therefore a crucial issue in our society [HUO 15, p. 39].

LinkedIn, despite its relatively small size of 700 employees, relies on more than 100 data scientists. The company has implemented new unified big-database search capabilities to predict what content might be of interest to the user and to optimize the presentation of results. Its People You May Know functionality (Project PYMK) has been the greatest source of value for the company. It provides LinkedIn members with a list of other members they may wish to connect with. The system uses a multi-factor approach to identify possible new connections, particularly schools, workplaces, relationships and common geographical locations. The messages triggered 30% more clicks than the other invitations sent out, prompting users to return to the site and allowing the company to grow [DAV 14, p. 25].

Heathrow has implemented a semi-authorized flight management system (Airport Collaborative Decision Making, A-CDM). It creates and co-ordinates all the operations involved in the rotation of a flight, when the aircraft lands and arrives at its gate, how much baggage to unload, when to refuel, when the next crew arrives, when to board the passengers and when the aircraft takes off. The departure punctuality rate immediately increased from 60 to 85% [FAD 14, pp. 158–159].

Similarly, UPS has equipped more than 46,000 of its vehicles with telematics sensors. In 2011, this initiative saved more than 30 million liters of fuel by reducing the number of kilometers travelled by 1.3 billion. By reducing driver travel by only 3 km per day, it saved $30 million [DAV 14, p. 186].

Another problem is data control. Companies are aware of the importance of the data they hold. But the strategic nature may prohibit the sharing of this data. This intrinsically limits their use in a context of massive data because it increases the risk of information leakage. When data can be shared, it raises the question of operating licenses and the associated intellectual property, as well as the traceability of its use. The notions of rights to use data also lead to questions of non-repudiation. The issue of traceability of data and processing is all the more important in a context of open data. This concerns in particular the use of cultural data and research data and leads to the identification of authors or researchers. For public actors, the issue of intellectual property may derive from the acceptance of users and operators to deliver data in a public storage facility [HUO 15, p. 17].

Finally, the handling of personal data leads to questions about anonymization processes and raises the issue of their non-reversible encryption. The respect of conditions relating to personal data must be thought out prior to the implementation of the system. This process allows personal information to be irreversibly altered, so that the bearer of this personal information cannot be directly or indirectly identified, whether by an automaton processing the personal information alone or in collaboration with any other device [HUO 15, p. 11].

In terms of data processing, the issues at stake include:

– the definition of repositories (metadata) to facilitate exploitation and categorization, filtering and source reconciliation, deposit, aggregation and cleansing of data, ontologies by business;

– traceability of the operations carried out on the data;

– intellectual property and user acceptance to deliver data into a storage facility;

– the interoperability of the systems and their modularity (to be able to easily and quickly change solutions and to be able to pool different information that is retrieved by different solutions) [HUO 15, p. 34];

– the image risk can be important for some actors because of "Big Brother" effects and derivatives.

The legal issues and associated user rights are of importance for companies wishing to establish quality processes in a long-term setting. Data, as soon as it circulates, is copied and transformed, becomes an object of exchange. If it has or gains value, then it becomes important to know its owner. Is it the producer of the data or the owner of the infrastructure that produces it? Is it the one who operates the infrastructure that produces the data? Is it the person who distributes copies? Is it the one who transforms it? Once disseminated, does the owner retain ownership of the data? Can one piece of data have multiple owners? [HUO 15, p. 38]

It is also a question of respecting certain principles such as the quality of the information, the specificity of the purposes, the limitation of use, the guarantees of security, transparency, the simplicity of exercising the right of access and the principle of responsibility. Thus, data are collected and processed fairly and lawfully for specified, explicit and legitimate purposes. They are adequate, relevant and not excessive in relation to the purposes; they are accurate, complete and up to date. They shall be kept in a form which permits identification of data subjects for no longer than is necessary for the purposes for which the data were collected and processed [HUO 15, p. 56].

Mass data will also accelerate the artificial intelligence revolution. In the 1980s and 1990s, researchers Geoffrey Hinton, Yann LeCun and Yoshua Bengio laid the foundation for deep learning. The advantage of this approach is that it allows the system to learn by itself complex tasks that would otherwise be difficult to program from start to finish. It wasn't until 2010 that data became the fuel for artificial intelligence, as previously there was a lack of computing power and mass of data. These big data are used to improve the training of intelligent systems. At the same time, the development of graphics processors is exploding the processing power of computers. The general principle is to let the computer discover for itself the optimal strategy for solving a problem. If the computer is supplied with a massive amount of data (sound, images or text) and the result expected from it, the computer gradually adjusts its internal parameters. It can then perform the learned task such as translating a document or describing an image. By giving sufficient examples and using the learning algorithms, the computer is able to generate its own intuitive understanding from the data it has been trained with.

During the training phase, the computer discovers by itself, from thousands of tagged images and through its neural network, the simple and complex patterns that make up the object. Once trained, it can then recognize the object in any image. In 2012, thanks to the ImageNet competition, deep learning gained the esteem of the scientific community around the world. The competition challenged researchers from around the world to create an intelligent system capable of classifying hundreds of thousands of images into hundreds of categories. At that time, the best results from computer vision systems had error rates of more than 25%. Geoffrey Hinton and his students, building on the work of his colleagues Yann LeCun and Yoshua Bengio, achieved an error rate of less than 16% thanks to deep learning that reveals its full potential. From that point on, there was a renewed interest in the development of artificial intelligence. The new challenge now facing researchers is to describe scenes on video. Again, using various methods derived from deep learning, the aim is to detect both the objects in the image and the relationship between them, and even to anticipate certain movements before they occur. This ability to predict future action is particularly important for the control system of an autonomous car. Providing a complete view of dynamic scenes, in real time, to the control system of the autonomous car is a huge challenge. The autonomous car must have the ability to decode the intentions of other vehicles in its environment and act accordingly. At the moment, its most astonishing capabilities are associated with specialized tasks, in the health sector among others[6].

6 André Bernard, *La révolution de l'intelligence artificielle*, Découverte, Radio-Canada, February 2017.

1.4.3. *Open data*

The term "open data" first appeared in the 1970s in agreements signed by NASA with partner countries to share satellite data. The concept developed in the 2000s in English-speaking countries. It is linked to the concept of open government, promoted following the election of President Obama in 2008. To fill a lack of communication of democratic institutions, it was thought to open some of the public data to citizens to bring more transparency. A more economic aspect consisted in imagining that the processing of these data by companies would offer them an added value [GUY 15a, p. 385]. Data are often referred to as the "black gold of the 21st Century". The economic development argument is important, because open data is seen as a potential for innovation and the creation of new services, as in the tourism, transport or energy sectors. Administrations and businesses alike can thus bring a new ecosystem into being, based on private, public or citizen initiatives. It is also a response to demands for transparency in democratic controls (budgetary choices, allocation of subsidies, public procurement procedures, etc.), but also to more consumerist aspects such as Open food facts. It is a database of food products made by everyone, for everyone. It allows more informed choices to be made, and because the data is open, anyone can use it for any purpose [CLI 19, p. 31].

In fact, the principle is to open up public data that are collected, retained and used by public bodies and make them available for access and re-use by citizens and businesses. This is a response to the need for user confidence and transparency in public services. Public authorities also want to open up decision-making processes to build a culture of accountability. In addition, a digital revolution in public administration tends to share information resources, which any active, informed and autonomous civil society demands to develop [MAD 15b, p. 153].

The definition given in the *Vade-mecum sur l'ouverture et le partage des données publiques* published by the Etalab mission is as follows: public data is "information or data produced or received by an administrative authority in the context of its public service mission, published by an administrative authority or communicable to any person requesting it. This information must be presented in a format that allows its automated processing and re-use"[7]. The *open data* movement to facilitate access initially left aside the requirements related in particular to data quality, not wanting to hinder the participation of organizations in this movement [CLI 19, p. 30].

---

7 Etalab, *Vade-mecum sur l'ouverture et le partage des données publiques,* French General secretariat for the modernization of public action, French Government, September 2013, p. 4, online: 61618-vade-mecum-sur-l-ouverture-et-le-partage-des-donnees-publiques.pdf.

Private data, or personal data protected by legislation, does not normally enter the world of open data. Government data is public data that can potentially be disseminated. Other data is data held by companies or individuals that can potentially be offered as open data. To this can be added the voluminous publicly or privately managed data that includes open data, but also a multitude of micro-data collected by all computer applications mainly on the Internet [GUY 15a, p. 286].

The administration proposes a proactive approach. Rather than responding to a one-off request, it anticipates this demand by publishing public datasets. The individual no longer makes a request for access to information, but it is the administration that makes information available by publishing it on the Internet [GUY 15c, p. 107].

If at the beginning, we may have had a very technophile and idealistic vision of the opening of data, thinking that it was enough to create computer tools, we had to admit that extracting and exposing data to the public presupposes a new organization of work. Any open data approach must inevitably go through a first phase of mapping the organization's information production. Having a good knowledge of the data held and produced is essential in order to then study what can be opened or not, and under what conditions. Thus, we sometimes observe, by ease, the automatic exclusion of personal data from the field of data to be opened, whereas processing methods such as pseudonymization can allow their availability if their context of use justifies it [CLI 19, p. 31].

Information governance brings greater robustness to open data. Indeed, if we want users to create new wealth from open data, we must give them a certain number of guarantees: data origin, authenticity, freshness, technical reusability, etc. Otherwise, the development of new activities or services will be, if not impossible, far too fragile and unsustainable [CLI 19, p. 31].

Finally, the obligation of openness brings new arguments to data managers. Indeed, the dialogue with the editors of IT solutions is not always simple when it comes to negotiating the extraction of data and metadata from the tool concerned. Negotiating the obligations of public authorities from a legal perspective has already borne fruit. The open data approach brings a definite qualitative gain. It provides legal security for decision-makers and producers who are sometimes reluctant to release the data produced. Open data must therefore be seen as a specific version of a general information management project [CLI 19, p. 31].

Beyond the stated principle of openness of public data, it is indeed essential that the data published are of high quality. Quality data is data documented by contextualizing data and documents throughout their lifecycle, from their creation and during their preservation process [GUY 15c, p. 110]. The principle of access to public data remains a dead letter if the conditions of production of the data are not able to ensure their quality, that is, their authenticity, reliability, integrity and readability [MAD 15b, p. 158].

The 10 principles for "Open Government Information" were defined by a group of experts at the Sebastopol meeting in California in December 2007 and completed in the article published by the Sunlight Foundation. In practice, they come up against significant technical constraints. The data accumulated by the administrative services were not accumulated for publication. The vast majority have not been subject to quality analysis, which limits their openness, since administrations are reluctant to disseminate data whose quality of interpretation cannot be guaranteed. The absence of the notion of data reliability is a gap in the principles and calls into question their reliability [GUY 15a, p. 387].

The data must be complete even if the notion of completeness cannot be general. It must relate to a specific field of activity or to the fact that part of the original data set has not been removed [GUY 15a, p. 387].

The data must be primary, in other words raw, which is a naive view. It presupposes that the data is the reflection of an abstract objective reality, whereas it is the object from its origin of a manufacturing process that is only cognizable by the addition of metadata that documents its source [GUY 15a, p. 388]. These relevant and standardized metadata will provide the added value necessary for the reuse of the data which are thus contextualized.

The data must be updated, which implies a constraint of relevance over time. Ideally, this would require that each piece of data be "dated" in order to be usable in the long term, which is rarely the case [GUY 15a, p. 388].

The data must be accessible and machine-readable. This is a *sine qua non* for their reusability and a major obstacle to the publication of data in tabular form as a document [GUY 15a, p. 388].

The data must be accessible without discrimination in order to meet the requirement of transparency which initially applies to documents. This implies a technical and intellectual capacity to process them. To be publishable, the data must be in open and non-proprietary formats and the datasets must be described using metadata [GUY 15a, p. 388].

Data must be accessible in a perennial way online, which implies electronic data archiving, which is still far from being generalized. Either the data have a short lifespan and are not intended to be kept over time, or the data must be archived and the tools put in place by the archive centers should also allow their publication in open data mode. This involves first describing the data to be published using a set of metadata and then transferring the data and their metadata to a dedicated platform [GUY 15a, p. 390].

The data must be free of charge, that is, the price of making it available must not exceed the cost of production. The debate is far from over as to the nature of the licenses attached to open data and the nature of the cost of making public data available [GUY 15a, p. 389].

In short, it is comprehensive, interoperable, royalty-free data, free to reuse and non-proprietary in format. It excludes personal or private data that could lead to the identification of a person or individual[8], or data subject to national defense secrets, or commercial transactions [MAD 15b, p. 152].

However, the openness of the data gives much more importance to access and dissemination than to contextualization, which is essential. A dataset whose source, production conditions or primary uses are unknown is not of value, because the interpretation will be distorted from the outset [MAD 15b, p. 160]. Thus, if datasets whose composition is based on nomenclatures that are not supplied with them, they will only form a list of unusable characters [CLI 19, p. 31].

The identification and contextualization of the data will be done by associating descriptive, management and technical metadata with the data produced. Unfortunately, the data sets are produced by systems, potentially useful for an opening, but which require a much greater processing effort than that allowed by the means of the administrations. As a result, the selection of the data that can be opened is received rather than chosen. This is why Charlotte Maday suggests using a data evaluation and selection process based on records management methods. For example, process analysis, as described in the ISO 26122 standard, could be integrated into data governance as a method for identifying authentic information eligible for open data from its creation and for selecting data through automated processes developed for this purpose. This would facilitate the capture of metadata needed to authenticate the author, the day and time of the link to the process, and the use of open format and the addition of metadata if not produced by a compatible application [MAD 15b, p. 163].

---

8 It is possible to anonymize sets of personal data in order to promote their re-use, in particular for health data produced by hospitals or social security bodies.

1.4.4. The paradox of access to and protection of personal data

Paul Otlet in his 1934 treatise on documentation already dreamed of easier access to books and secondary sources, but technology had not yet been able to meet this desire to embrace all human knowledge. Yet he could already see the possibilities for the future, and it was precisely in the field of documentation that the first attempts at computerization were made. Here is an excerpt from this prophetic text:

> Here, the work desk is no longer loaded with books. In their place is a screen and a telephone within reach. Over there in the distance, in a huge building, are all the books and information, with all the space required for their registration and handling, with all the apparatus of its catalogues, bibliographies and indexes... From there, the page to be read for the answers to questions asked by telephone, wired or wireless, appears on the screen. A screen would be double, quadruple or tenfold if the texts and documents to be confronted simultaneously were to be multiplied: there would be a loudspeaker if sight were to be aided by hearing, if vision were to be supplemented by hearing. Such a hypothesis is a utopia today because it does not yet exist anywhere, but it could well become tomorrow's reality as long as our methods and instrumentation are further perfected. [OTL 34]

Access to information is a positive concept concerning all those who need information and the purpose of any information management. Indeed, the user often sees preservation through access. It refers to an active approach, an advantage as opposed to security, which is perceived as a constraint. Access is first the right to access the information and then the actual process by which it can be accessed [CHA 18, pp. 46–47]. There is a desire for quick access or to restrict access to certain individuals or to access documents at a later date. One needs to know that the information exists and be able to access the medium to read the document or file that contains the information. The two must be managed in parallel for the required length of time, which implies knowing it [CHA 18, p. 12].

Access to information has expanded thanks to new means of communication that influence research uses. Even if one may question the reliable and exhaustive nature of the results obtained on the Internet, which depends on the quality of online content and its referencing, we have all nevertheless adopted these research tools for their intuitive, simple and effective nature. The same is true for the user of the archives, who expects the same tools and the same level of service to which he/she is now accustomed in his/her daily life. If the access rights are compliant, the document sought is displayed on screen without using the reference number to link the description to the document, which could lead to the progressive development of online reading rooms. To do this, electronic archiving systems must offer acceptable restitution methods in terms of time, volume and reliability [BUR 11, pp. 78–79]. In the example of building and public works, when the building has been delivered and the reserves lifted, the builder provides the client with the list of the works executed, the volume of which may exceed 1 m³ of paper. By entering this set into an electronic archiving system, it will be possible to return to it 10 years later with a withdrawal time of one hour, which is widely acceptable [AGE 16, p. 6].

The challenge of access is also to ensure that freedoms are respected and to facilitate the reuse of public data. The traditional balances of openness and secrecy are being called into question. Rules that used to apply smoothly to paper no longer work in an interconnected digital environment that can threaten privacy and individual freedoms. Each document, taken in isolation, may have its own time limit for disclosure without damage, but all documents put and cross-referenced together may negate the protective effect of particular time limits. This is what happens when documents are put online that are physically dispersed. Thus, in France, the 75-year time limit for communicating civil status documents on paper has been extended to 100 years for the same documents consulted online [DEL 12b, p. 201]. Databases and open data risk being a false illusion for the population and over a certain period of time.

Search engines rank by popularity, not truth. Their algorithms build hierarchies of sites resulting from a keyword search according to the concept of *PageRank,* which indicates the most relevant pages or sites in relation to the keywords searched for. The PageRank level is obtained by taking into account factors such as the age of the site, the frequency of updates, the relevance to the content of a page, the number of visitors. The two main criteria are the number of links from other sites that link to the site in question and the weight of these external links [FRE 13, p. 92]. This method is comparable to an election where only those who have a Web page are eligible to vote. The votes do not have the same value, the most popular pages will express through their links, votes of major value [FRE 13, pp. 92–93].

The user builds connections, but the work of selecting and organizing the data in a hierarchy is left to the search engines, which operate in such a way as to give visibility to everything that is typical, popular and standard. Rather than organizing heterogeneity, the web's internal filtering mechanisms normalize it [FRE 13, pp. 100–101].

The Facebook network is identical where the most popular profiles and groups are those with more friends. Likewise, the enhancement of the document, its patrimonial being, is a function of a system that makes what is already memorable. This tendency to set aside the minor, the unusual or the deviant from the popular also applies to individuals. If two different users search for the same information on Google, they will get different results. We think we are looking at a shared encyclopedia when it is cross-referenced according to our preferences. Google confirms our view of the world by telling us only what we know or think we know [FRE 13, pp. 95–96]. For now, we remain obsessed with the declining quality of answers to our questions, not with the problem of poor-quality education and diminished ability to think critically.

Moreover, the archival heritage on physical media will never be entirely online and a whole range of archives will disappear from the panorama of researchers because they will not appear online [DUN 15, p. 185]. Thus in 2006, the public archives of France counted 29 million online civil status pages, and six times as many in 2010, to reach 174 million. This represents only one to two thousandths of the 3,000 linear kilometers of paper documents kept in public archives. Only the most valuable and fragile records, as well as the records most used by researchers, will be available online, accounting for more than 80% of the consultations [DEL 12b, p. 193]. Let us not forget the need for identity and recognition linked to the instability of families. In France, 25% of young people between the ages of 17 and 25 have completed their genealogy [DEL 12b p. 196].

However, there is also a trend towards new digital scholarship. Archives are being visited to consult original documents that cannot be found elsewhere. They are once again becoming repositories for the preservation and development of finding aids that may lead to the digitization or online availability of archival series that are widely consulted by the general public, leading to a silent democratization of access [DEL 12b, p. 194].

In addition to the document manager who has a transversal and generalist view, teams with multiple skills must be considered. This is necessary in order to establish partnerships with the producers of digital documents who master the content and with the heads of the information system concerned who manage the system. The communication and appraisal of archives must be based on collaborative work to enhance the value of disused archives, a work that has proved its worth with wikis and genealogists. "Everyone contributes what they know and can do. Everyone values what they know and is valued by what they bring" [DEL 12b, p. 202].

According to Michel Duchein, privacy is a principle for which there is no universal legal definition, so that access to archives depends more on the interpretation of nominative information and its more or less personal and intimate nature. These are documents whose content makes an appraisal or value judgment about a named or easily identifiable natural person.

Carol Couture shows the sensitivity levels in different countries. For some, the focus is on family relationships and the honor of families or individuals (Italy, Russia, Senegal), adoption files (Ontario, Quebec) and curatorship files. Others are more sensitive to the intimacy of people's sexual lives (France, Italy), to statistical data showing private behavior (France), and to information on the adoption of criminal measures (Italy, Denmark). On the other hand, many countries protect information of a medical, genetic or psychiatric nature (France, Italy, Canada [Ontario, Quebec]) [COU 14, p. 74].

Confidentiality raises the question of access rights to archived documents, all the more so if it concerns personal data or sensitive data (arms bills, health data, bank data, specific pay slips, technical plans for nuclear power plants, etc.). Confidentiality reserves access to an archived document to authorized users only, managing their rights of use and keeping track of the use they have made of it. The ISO 27001 standard on Information Security Management identifies it as a security criterion in the same way as integrity [AGE 16, p. 5].

In fact, confidentiality has both the notion of secrecy and of dissemination restricted to a small number of people. It represents a property that ensures that, under the conditions normally provided for, only authorized or entitled users have access to the information concerned. The main limitation of confidentiality is that a person cannot be held responsible for any disclosure if the material revealed was already in the public domain or if he or she already knew about it or could obtain it from third parties by legitimate means [CAP 07, p. 21].

In the context of information assets, confidential information is obviously important and generally quite few in number: medical confidentiality (person with HIV, etc.), confidentiality of bank card codes, personal passwords for physical and/or logical access control in the company. It may be wise to anticipate the situation where unauthorized persons would nevertheless manage to access the information system. In the latter case, however, the confidentiality of the data can be preserved through the implementation of an encryption system. The main feature of such a system is to make the data unreadable by anyone who does not have the key to decrypt it. However, knowledge of and access to this key can be very difficult, especially after many years [CAP 07, p. 21].

Information assets obviously involve much more data than personal data, and we can also cite customer databases, business process databases, supplier directories, databases of sensitive archives, litigation, cash flow, tax aspects, accounting audits, etc. Data confidentiality is also a commercial issue. Indeed, in the context of major markets, knowledge of the conditions offered by the competition can make it possible to win a market or, on the contrary, to lose it [CAP 07, p. 22].

Knowledge can be a public good, that is, a non-rivalled good that can easily be exchanged over the network, but which can also become a source of profit for the digital giants. Economist Yann Moulier-Boutang says that Google has become the emblem of cognitive capitalism because it has invented a new economic model based on the controlled development of collective intelligence networks. "You work for Google! Every second, 15 million people click and feed Google with data," he explains. Google sells a meta-service, which depends on everyone's contribution. For him, human activity is comparable to the worker bee that pollinates Google's economy.

In 2016, several cases of theft of personal data from Yahoo!, Dropbox, MySpace, LinkedIn and Tumblr made headlines. Before them, Orange, Sony, Ashley Madison and eBay were involved in similar cases. In a world that is more connected than ever, customer data can quickly fall into the wrong hands. It's at the heart of today's business strategies. It is an invaluable resource and a key lever for the development of the digital economy. However, this is only possible if we know how to use and protect them, because they affect the privacy and fundamental rights and freedoms of individuals [SER 17, p. 3].

Thus, a European regulation, the General Data Protection Regulation (GDPR), which came into force on May 25, 2018, intends to put an end to the use of personal data without the consent of Internet users, but the weak link remains human behavior. It aims to standardize data protection throughout the European Union and update European law. Indeed, the law previously was based on Directive 95/46/EC of 1995, the date of the beginning of the Internet. As a result, it did not take into account the rise of search engines, social networks, connected objects or cloud computing and mass data. The GDPR aims to strengthen the control of European citizens over the use of their personal data, while simplifying the regulation for organizations [SER 17, p. 4].

The general scope of the GDPR is binding in its entirety and directly applicable in all Member States. A maximum period of two years is proposed for compliance by the entities concerned (Art. 171). It defines "personal data" as follows:

– data actively and consciously declared by the data subject, such as data provided to create an online account (e-mail address, username, age, etc.);

– data generated by the activity of the data subject, when using a service or device (purchases, search history, bank statements, e-mails sent or received, etc.).

Article 20 of the GDPR deals with the new right to data portability. This allows a person to retrieve the data he or she has provided, in an easily reusable form, and, where appropriate, to subsequently transfer it to a third party or store it on a device or in a cloud, for example. He or she can manage personal data (e.g. transcripts for students) more easily and on his or her own. On the other hand, personal data that are derived, calculated or inferred from data provided by the data subject, such as a user profile created through the analysis of raw data produced by a "smart" meter, are excluded from the right of portability, insofar as they are not provided by the data subject, but created by the organization.

The right of portability applies to personal data which are limited to those provided by the data subject. Paper files are not taken into account, but automated data processing is done on the basis of the prior consent of the person. Its exercise must not infringe the rights and freedoms of third parties, whose data would be included in the data transmitted following a portability request. Users must be informed of the use of their data and must in principle give their consent to the processing of their data or be able to object to it. The burden of proof of consent lies with the data controller.

One of the other main principles of the text is "privacy by design". The data controller integrates privacy protection from the design of a service or product from the collection of data to its deletion. To this end, the organization undertakes to take the appropriate technical and organizational measures. In particular, it may resort to pseudonymization of data, which consists of replacing one attribute with another in order to avoid the direct identification of an individual. It should be borne in mind that anonymization of data hampers investigations of hereditary diseases, for example, but also any research on political, social and cultural history, and acts as a barrier to studies involving individuals or families as subjects. Since in a computerized environment, data can be anonymized or deleted at the touch of a few buttons, and some people will not hesitate to press the button, we can expect carnage [KEC 14, p. 66].

The principle of "privacy by default" complements and reinforces the precedent. The security measures are natively integrated in the service or application, but the data controller ensures by default the highest level of confidentiality by guaranteeing that it only processes the information necessary for the purpose for which it is intended. The controller must, moreover, obtain the explicit and informed consent of the data subjects and systematically destroy the data once the purpose has been achieved. There are exceptions for data kept for historical, scientific or statistical purposes. The notion of privacy must be shared by all actors: staff should be trained on the new obligations introduced by the GDPR, a simple Excel file containing contacts constituting a processing of personal data.

The GDPR also reinforces the right to comprehensive information in clear, intelligible language that is easily accessible to data subjects in relation to data processing operations.

It is the responsibility of the entity to take all measures and to demonstrate this at all times by keeping an up-to-date register of all its processing operations, the actions and documents carried out at each stage having to be reviewed and updated regularly to ensure continuous data protection.

There are steps to follow to comply with the GDPR regulations:

– appoint a Data Protection Officer (DPO). His/her mission is to identify the collections of personal data and their purpose in order to analyze their compliance with the GDPR. He or she is the regulator of the personal data protection policy, involving all stakeholders (agents, students, etc.). It is subject to professional secrecy and an obligation of confidentiality. This function can be "outsourced" and a service contract can then be concluded in this sense with a person or even a body whose purpose is to perform such functions. The DPO must meet certain requirements in order to perform his/her duties. He or she must have legal expertise, an understanding of the processing operations that he or she is required to supervise, and an understanding of information technology and data security. The DPO must be able to raise awareness of data protection issues among staff;

– map the processing operations by reviewing all personal data processing, whether computerized or not (paper records). This involves identifying the processes concerned and then calculating their level of compliance by subjecting them to a Privacy Impact Assessment (PIA);

– establish a plan of action. Computer work is being undertaken to secure the most critical data, either by anonymization or encryption. It is also a question of reviewing the modalities for exercising the rights of the individuals concerned, the collection of consent, and the right to be forgotten, which is no longer certain. What has been disseminated, even fleetingly at a given moment, may remain accessible and be disseminated indefinitely even if it is removed from its original site. In some cases, there is no longer any critical sorting [DEL 15a, p. 283].

The purpose of each processing operation and the length of time the data are kept must be established, which involves a thorough revision of the privacy policy. Compliance with the privacy policy does indeed imply that personal data should not be kept beyond a certain period of time (usually the applicable prescription period). This is in fact the respect of the "right to forget". It is possible to ask for a link to be removed from a search engine or for information to be deleted if it infringes on the privacy of the person concerned.

Furthermore, compliance also concerns subcontractors. Contractually, the latter undertake to implement adequate protection measures and to alert the data controller in the event of data leakage. The GDPR now provides for a "right to an effective judicial remedy" and a "right to compensation". It lays down rules on the jurisdiction of courts replacing the rules of private international law of the Member States and determines the fines to be issued by the national supervisory authorities.

Depending on the category of the infringement, fines may be as high as €20 million or, in the case of a company, from 2% to 4% of its annual worldwide turnover (whichever is the higher). Infringement of the provisions of the GDPR is subject to an administrative fine of up to €10 million, which is doubled in the event of a repeat offence. The authority may also withdraw the certification issued or order the certification body to withdraw certification related to new compliance tools used by the organization [SER 17, p. 12].

1.5. Conclusion

Archives respond to the vital need of institutions and individuals alike to have long-term access to the information necessary for their activities and the preservation of their heritage and history. However, the digital revolution is disrupting document management, which must intervene much earlier to contextualize the document in order to restore its full understanding and promote its dissemination. In these turbulent and unstable times, when the association between content and media is breaking down, information is subject to multiple decompositions and recompositions. Records management can therefore provide better information governance through the processing and reliable preservation of digital documents, which are still information recorded on a medium, whether it is directly native to a computer or is the result of digitization. It has the responsibility to ensure the organization and preservation of huge masses of documents by identifying and protecting them in a changing world that demands rapid and transparent access to information.

Data is the backbone of digital information, but digital technology places a priority on instant access and use, which underpins its performance and ignores the fundamental issues of long-term preservation and use. The digital world also creates the impression that data are directly and freely accessible without a mediator. This is an illusion, because putting data online and, above all, making it sustainable requires a great deal of work; otherwise there is a risk of losing important information. It is paradoxical that the beginnings of the information society are in reality very poorly documented, as the data do not withstand the first migrations. Moreover, they pose certain problems in terms of confidentiality, for the protection of medical, business or security confidentiality, in the field of intellectual property or in the context of market research to target specific audiences. From this point of view, the massive accumulation of data presupposes an ethical awareness to prevent abuse of the expected purposes and effective management of their processing and dissemination.

2

Managing Records

Standards are voluntary in nature and derive their legitimacy from the community that contributes to their development. Standards are usually developed within an organization or a small group of organizations and then elevated to a standard by a lobby group. Technical areas need them to speak a common language and use common units of measurement in order to adopt practices for effective exchange. This is different in the area of records management and archiving, where standards can quickly become an intellectual straitjacket if applied too rigidly, since the needs and resources of organizations are not all the same. However, since 2001, standards have been in existence that define the broad areas of records policy and requirements for the provision of authentic, integrity, reliable and usable records. Processes such as electronic signatures and digital fingerprints can help to validate records, but metadata is also essential.

The judicialization of activities has invaded all areas of the economy and society and led to the creation of new fields of activity consisting of information security and risk management. The preservation of evidence and the prevention of legal risk, in addition to compliance, traceability and transparency requirements, are now an integral part of a records policy. With digital technology, archives are becoming a memory and evidence issue. It includes analog records, information systems and networks, and user practices that may pose risks to the organization. Digital records are more likely to suffer computer breakdowns, due to malicious or accidental breakdowns, causing service disruptions or leaks of confidential records. In addition, the dissemination of information and the decentralization of activities in organizations result in a loss of control over practices, some of which may jeopardize the integrity of information.

Easy to use and available on both personal and professional computer equipment, electronic messaging has become an indispensable tool for sending and receiving messages as well as for storing information. As a result, strategic information is increasingly concentrated in them. Instead of administrative notes, messages are now used to convey decision-making at all levels of organizations. E-mail can be engaging and requires good management and storage to meet regulatory obligations and organizational needs.

2.1. Record management standards

2.1.1. The ISO 15489 standard for records management

According to the definition of ISO/IEC Guide 2: 2004, in article 3.2, a standard is a "record, established by consensus and approved by a recognized body, which provides, for common and repeated use, rules, guidelines or characteristics for activities or their results, ensuring an optimum level of order in a given context". Standards should be based on the combined achievements of science, technology and experience and aimed at the optimum benefit of the community.

The number of standards is very important in the electronic archiving sector. Their recommendations are well adapted to the sector from which they originate, but not necessarily relevant to other areas. Their scope and purpose should be identified and their relevance and limitations to the issue in question should be assessed. Reading the standards is nevertheless useful for creating ideas and developing methods, but they should be approached with a critical spirit and by favoring a documentary analysis specific to each project that is being carried out [BUR 13, p. 18].

Organizations are required to produce many records, whether in their relations with customers, shareholders or public authorities. For this reason, the creation of a records system within the framework of quality management systems is relevant. There are strategic records related to the general policy of the company, records specifying all the procedures put in place to describe the structure of the company. Then, there are records dealing with the company's know-how: work instructions, operating procedures, which will be precise in their definition and make all the company's know-how legible. Finally, there are binding records that will demonstrate the correct implementation and application of the documentation. The records will have to meet the requirements of internal customers, employees, shareholders, actors in the process, partners and suppliers [NES 15a].

The ISO 15489 standard Information and documentation – "Records management" – is part of this normative trend. It is based on AS 4390 "Records management", adopted in 1996 by the Australian government. It was on the occasion of the presentation of the Australian standard to ISO that subcommittee 11 was created within TC 46, with its French correspondent, Commission de normalization 11 (CN 11), whose first draft was ISO 15489.

Although it was proposed to ISO as an international standard, it was not unanimously approved when it was published in English in 2001 and then in French in 2002, particularly in the French-speaking world. It differed too much from their practices, particularly for the ages of archives and integrated management, whereas it is divided in English-speaking culture. However, following the Enron and Andersen cases, which revealed serious manipulation of information and destruction of evidence, the United States adopted, in 2002, the so-called "Sarbanes-Oxley" Act, which includes, among other things, the obligation to exercise internal control. This led to risk management, the formalization of processes, the identification of traces to be kept and their rigorous management, making ISO 15489 a highly relevant standard.

The ISO 15489 standard complements, on a technical level, the ISO 9001 standard on quality management systems and ISO 14001 on environmental management. Yet, ISO 15489 has long been the sole records management standard.

ISO 9001: 2015 requires 22 documented pieces of information that include both the term "procedure" and "registration". This checklist will be both a procedure and a record, since it is both a rule and evidence. All records that are deemed relevant to the risk analysis and control are taken into account in order to aim for the effectiveness of the management system.

The requirements of ISO 9001: 2015 are:

– identification of records, with the implementation of a system that avoids confusion between two records, and allows everyone to know which record they are using;

– a good format, which ensures that the records are easy to read;

– a review that validates the consistency of the records system, and an approval of the relevance and adequacy;

– an approval that is a commitment to implement the documentation and have sufficient resources.

There are rules for record control and potentially record retention. There must be rapid availability and good protection of records with rules for distribution and access authorizations. Storage involves preserving the readability and quality of records. Change control is mandatory. It is necessary to know the current version, the modifications that have taken place and the traceability of these modifications in relation to the previous version. Finally, it is necessary to have a sustainable method of storage and disposal, to assess the disposition and risks associated with disposals. Very long-term preservation is also considered to retain available information [NES 15a].

The standard specifies that documented information of external origin, which is not produced by the company but is necessary for its proper functioning, should also be managed. The way in which these records are received will be introduced into the record management procedures, if the requirements are integrated into the company's records system. We are going to make sure that the transposition has been carried out in good conditions, and that there is no gap between what the supplier requires, the specifications required by the customer, and what is actually implemented in the company. The records system will have to be evaluated in order to have an efficient system so as not to be an obstacle to innovation or represent an administrative burden [NES 15a].

The analysis determines whether the record is understandable and readable, whether the information is easy to find and within an acceptable time frame. We will make sure that there is a consensus with all concerned. The record must be useful; if it has not been modified in the last five years, it means that it is not being used, that it has not been updated, and therefore that it has no interest or added value. A diagnosis can be made to check whether the records system is relevant. The analysis is done within each of the business processes: is there a list of records? Has the list been updated? Is there a procedure for removing obsolete records? Are the modes of dissemination clarified? If the answer is negative, corrective action should be taken to validate the availability of the information. If a record list is not available at the time of filing or organization of the archive, it will not be known which records need to be preserved [NES 15a].

However, while this 9001 standard contains requirements for the production of so-called "quality" records to attest and testify to an organization's activities, it does not contain any specifics on what a "quality record" is.

These details are contained in the ISO 15489 standard, which aims at implementing standards of quality and excellence in the management of routine and intermediate archives in organizations of all categories. It responds to the need to standardize information management practices at a time when records are multiplying and when information technology plays a predominant role in the creation, processing, archiving and preservation of records. In summary, ISO 15489 defines the fundamental aspects of records management (concepts, terminology, principles, metadata) and provides a conceptual and normative framework for structuring a project or a records policy.

It also brings new dimensions, including the taking into account of an extended lifecycle upstream of archiving, the exclusion of the dimension of definitive archives, which represents an aspect more specific to the Anglo-Saxon world, and the notion of working in project mode. It clarifies the notion of requirement which implies that professionals must perceive this standard not as a "manual" or a "directive", but as a guide to conform their practices and their system [COT 16].

The ISO 15489 standard provides a procedure to follow. It reminds us of the importance of consensus and management buy-in. It requires a systematization of processes as well as a reflection on the issues related to this type of implementation. It adds credibility to archival interventions, especially with professionals used to working with standards[1]. Because of its general nature, it is intended for a large number of organizations and stakeholders, whether they are leaders, records managers, computer specialists or anyone who finds a records management model that integrates with quality management standards. The ISO 15489 standard makes stakeholders more accountable by proposing a uniform definition of information quality. It is intended for decision-makers and organizational managers alike. It defines the rules of governance of record management by specifying the records management policy to be followed. It proposes the development of specifications for record management systems, the definition of record management procedures, the determination of requirements for evidence management, business continuity, the assignment of responsibilities and job profiles [ASS 07, p. 73].

This record management policy should serve as evidence, manage risk, ensure the security of records and enable business continuity in the event of a disaster, facilitate the management and retention of records or their disposal, and generate savings[2]. It is about identifying records that are considered essential to support an organization's accountability to the law, employees, partners, customers and competitors. The goal is to organize the traceability of records by meeting quality

---

1 However, it should be remembered that the standard contains a method for implementing a records management system and that the archivist must refer to other standards to develop its various parts, according to his or her needs. In particular, the archivist may refer to ISO standards in the field of information management and archives such as ISO 11108 – Archival paper – Requirements for permanence and durability; ISO 11179 – Metadata registers; ISO 18921 – Compact discs (CD-ROM) – Method for estimating life expectancy based on the effects of temperature and relative humidity; ISO 23081 – Metadata for records; ISO 19005 – Records management. File format of electronic records for long-term preservation – Part 1: Use of PDF 1.4 (PDF/A-1); ISO/IEC 27001:2005, Information security, etc.; ISO/IEC 27001:2005, Information security, etc.; ISO/IEC 27001:2005, Information security.

2 The cost of record management is estimated at between 1 and 3% of company turnover (see TEXIER, B. "Politique globale de gouvernance, y'a-t-il un pilote pour l'info?" *Archimag*, No. 242, p. 19, March 2011).

standards as well as to determine the needs for consultation and retention periods according to legal rules. In other words, the purpose of records management is all the records that the organization has decided to preserve as evidence or because of their informational value. These are records that are essential or useful in the conduct of its business. The standard is not concerned with definitive records. Records management considers the record in a completed, unalterable version, validated and signed as necessary [ASS 05, p. 107].

This standard is intended for decision-makers and management. It introduces the term records, which it defines as follows: "records created, received and preserved as evidence and information by a natural or legal person in the exercise of its legal obligations or in the conduct of its business." Furthermore, according to the French translation, records management (RM) covers the "field of organization and management responsible for the effective and systematic control of the creation, receipt, conservation, use and disposition of records, including methods of fixing and preserving evidence and information related to the form of records". For Marie-Anne Chabin, the translation of this definition is the "function responsible for the rigorous and systematic control of the production, reception, conservation, use and final disposition of binding records, as well as of the processes for capturing and maintaining evidentiary and documented traces of the activity of a company or organization" [CHA 12, p. 9].

The standard also suggests the integration of methods into work processes through the development of an approach to the general validity of information, through the establishment of principles, measurement methods, strategic and organizational procedures and techniques applicable to records management. Given the relative complexity and costs associated with a project to develop a management system for current and intermediate archives, it is essential to target the interventions, both in terms of the records to be considered and the units or ways of proceeding, so as to obtain maximum tangible and beneficial results as quickly as possible.

In fact, records management is not intended to follow the lifecycle of the record beyond its administrative utility period. This is why it has no use for non-probative records, without legal value such as drafts, working records without validation sign, documentation. This is the role of a common workspace where archivists do not have to intervene directly. As for the patrimonial development of records, and therefore their use for scientific purposes, it is up to the electronic archiving system (EAS) to ensure processes for the perpetuation of records, even if records management ensures standardized production, which is a prerequisite for these processes [HAS 13, p. 27].

The challenges of records management are also of an economic nature. Cost control and cost reduction are essential in times of crisis, in both paper and digital environments where the use of service providers and the volume of data represent significant expenses. Finally, records management is a pillar of social responsibility and transparency. Throughout society, sustainable development requires that citizens and civil society have access to public data and their personal data so that good and transparent governance can be exercised everywhere.

Records management is a reliable record of the administrative and political action of organizations. It represents a decision-making aid and allows a precise and quick justification of actions and rights in order to ensure the control of legal risk. By avoiding confusion linked to duplicates and different versions, it also allows a gain in productivity. Prior to final archiving, records management is a sluice and a filter. Useful information is filtered and structured and the volume of information is limited and regularized [HAS 13, p. 27].

Its purpose is to ensure that the record exists, if necessary, create it for each type of activity and ensure that the essential information is contained in it, that it is known where to find it, that it is accessible, traceable, authentic, reliable, honest and usable. This system keeps the record in context or in connection with the record, ensures that records are retained and returned in a timely manner and in appropriate media according to the associated access rights [ASS 05, pp. 107–108]. It also involves deciding in what form and structure records should be produced and archived, and what technologies should be used; assessing the risks associated with the unavailability of evidentiary records; and identifying opportunities to improve the cost-effectiveness, efficiency and quality of the methods, decisions and operations involved in the creation, organization or management of records [CHA 12, p. 10].

The standard includes general statements to establish the fundamental principles of records management and to identify the benefits of records management (Chapter 4). It also emphasizes the need for organizations to identify the regulatory environment in which they operate to ensure that they respond appropriately (Chapter 5). It includes a section setting out the policies and responsibilities within the organization for records management (Chapter 6) and the requirements for outlining a program for managing routine and intermediate records. Emphasis is placed on metadata to ensure the authenticity, reliability, integrity and usability of records (Chapter 7). The principles of records system design and implementation follow (Chapter 8). This is followed by procedures for selecting records, defining retention periods, integrating and recording records into the system, filing, storage, access, traceability and finally the final disposition of records (Chapter 9). Finally, the organizations are invited to set up means of control and verification as well as to ensure the training of the various stakeholders (Chapters 10 and 11).

Part 1 of ISO 15489 "Guiding principles" is the standard and provides the framework for the management of routine and intermediate archives. It defines the responsibilities of organizations with respect to their records and presents the policies, procedures and methods required for the design and implementation of a system for managing day-to-day and intermediate records, while emphasizing the need for stable identification of the environment in which the organization operates. It is a comprehensive plan for the integrated management of records, covering the creation, preservation, organization and retrieval of records in all forms and media. The standard is intended for use by agency heads, records management and information technology professionals, all agency staff, and anyone with responsibility for creating and maintaining records.

Part 2 of ISO 15489 is an implementation guide to the standard that provides a methodology to facilitate the work of those responsible for setting up routine and interim records management systems. It provides a general overview of the processes and factors to be considered in organizations wishing to comply with the standard. In particular, it provides additional information on the policies, procedures and types of responsibilities that need to be defined in the development of a records management system. It essentially reiterates the principles set out in the standard, specifying the processes, factors to be considered, methods and means to achieve the objectives set out in Part 1.

This second part proposes an eight-step implementation method:

1) Conduct a preliminary investigation to describe the role and purpose of the organization, its structure, legal, regulatory, economic and political environment.

2) Starting from this perimeter, identify and document all of the producer's activities (missions, attributions and procedures) and prioritize them in an activity classification plan, accompanied, for each activity, by a list of the resulting records.

3) For each record, determine the archival retention requirements based on the legal environment, the information needs of teams and the risk of not producing or retaining that record.

4) At the same time, conduct an assessment of existing systems for information management and archiving.

5) Build an archival strategy to meet the identified requirements.

6) This strategy enables the design of a comprehensive records management system.

7) Implement the system.

8) Regularly check and audit the system after implementation to ensure that it meets the needs of the services it provides. [ASS 07, p. 79]

The standard describes the requirements for records management, which consists of:

– define the records that should be kept within an organization;

– specify in what form and with what structure the records and the technologies to be used to preserve them should be collected, produced and archived;

– design what metadata should be associated with these records and how this metadata should be managed over time;

– identify research and record use needs;

– determine retention periods that correspond to legal and user needs;

– assess the risks to the unavailability of records;

– ensure that records are stored in a secure environment;

– identify and evaluate opportunities to improve the efficiency and quality of records management methods and organization to ensure the best possible archiving of records [RIE 10, p. 235].

Records management requires that processes and procedures be put in place to systematize the methods of producing and preserving records. Processes and procedures must be clear and applied by all. The steps in the records management process are important. Each record, each file identified must be identified in relation to the context in which it was created: each assignment is broken down into several specific responsibilities, carried out by one or more departments, and sometimes by several organizations; each responsibility is broken down into a certain number of procedures; each stage of a procedure results in the creation of one or more records. ISO 15489 uses the terms "function", "activities" and "process". Beyond the vocabulary, the important point of this approach is a description of the activity of services in three hierarchical levels [ASS 07, p. 83].

The organization defines the Records management policy, that is, the main principles and guidelines. This policy must be known and implemented at all hierarchical levels of the organization. It must take into account the legislative and regulatory context, the economic and organizational environment of the organization, as well as internal rules and constraints. It must be integrated into the organization's overall policy and be consistent with its other policies: information system, security, risk management, investment, equipment and quality policies [ASS 05, p. 108].

Levels	Examples
1) Mission	Implementation of the heritage protection policy.
2) Attribution	Attribution of a grant for the safeguarding of heritage buildings.
3) Procedure	Instruction of a grant application file.
Steps in the procedure	Receipt of the request, drafting and sending of an acknowledgment of receipt, drafting of a summary report and transmission to the deliberative body for decision, drafting and notification of the order to the association.
Folders and files	Grant file, application form, supporting records, acknowledgment of receipt (copy), packing slips, report (copy or original), grant order (original or amendment), notification of the order to the association, notification letter (copy).

Table 2.1. *Example of a description of service activity in three hierarchical levels and records produced according to ISO 15489 (source: [ASS 07, p. 83])*

Records management and, more broadly, that of current and intermediate archives, is based on the office automation tools existing in the organization: mail registration, electronic record management, etc. It also relies on specific tools, the most common of which are the filing plan and the retention period calendar or the retention reference system. Some or all of these tools and procedures may be grouped together in a single record, often referred to as a "records management charter" or "records management charter" [ASS 07, p. 87]. It is a reference record that describes the objectives and policies implemented to achieve them. It incorporates rules and tools. All decisions in the records management charter are documented and maintained [ASS 05, p. 114].

The approach to designing a records management system follows the classic approach to designing an information system. The main steps are as follows: the constitution of a group of people representative of management, entities and users, to follow the project and make decisions. Then, preliminary studies are carried out on the organization, its missions and objectives, its structure, then the study of the project (the stakes for the organization), the study of its context (existing information systems, regulatory environment), the study of the constraints (financial, technical, organizational, human resources, etc.), the study of the needs and practices of the users [ASS 05, p. 114].

The recommended methodology consists of:

– designating a person in charge to act as a referent for the deployment;

– making an analysis of the existing situation;

– implementing a records policy validated by the hierarchy, including procedures (authorizations, payment, filing, consultation, destruction), a preservation reference system and legal references;

– establishing a retention program for vital records;

– preparing for change management by training in archiving and records management;

– deploying IT, hardware or software solutions dedicated to records management;

– reviewing the policy and periodically auditing the monitoring of procedures and the change program;

– implementing the Continuous Improvement Plan [ARN 12b, p. 162].

Record management tools and procedures are then formalized by:

– the definition of a function-based file plan to identify and link records together. The analysis and classification of the record produced or received is mandatory. This allows for the identification of the classification heading in the activity classification plan and the identification of the category of the record;

– the implementation of naming and indexing rules and rules to ensure the management of the perennial identification of records;

– perennial identification of the origin and ownership of records;

– the development of appropriate retention periods for records and the establishment of a destruction authority;

– the definition of appropriate security and protection for records and the establishment of adequate access authorizations [ARN 12b, p. 168].

How can managers and staff be convinced to implement a documentation policy?

1) Understanding the situation

– Difficulty in getting people interested in the project by asking them to commit time and resources when they will not get the benefit of their investment until later.

– Often, the problem identified may hide larger dysfunctions: lack of protection of contracts, records that are misidentified or lost, difficult after-sales service, excessive information flow, lack of managers or procedures.

– The record does not think, but the person who manages or retains it must have procedures in place.

– The speaker is there to reassure and provide solutions, not new problems. To propose change, the user must be convinced to participate in the implementation of the system.

2) Establishing a strategy

– Consultation with management and memorandum essential to inform the services, validate visits and check that the memoranda are read properly. Without the validation of the management which delegates the intervention and provides the means, the project is not viable.

– Set objectives and set priorities.

– Appointment of an interface at a high level of hierarchy between management, services and the stakeholder to facilitate and empower interventions.

– Target the contacts to be met.

– We can't do everything at once. We have to find a logic and plan the operations. You have to see the emergencies, prioritize the issues that are of interest to management and have an overview.

3) Preparing for meetings

– It is mandatory to see the head of department and ask to meet with a contact person.

– Do not exceed one hour of interview (10 people per day and 3 services maximum).

– Write a model sheet to keep track of important points that will be used for reporting to standardize the results (flow of information, frequency of access to records, identification and protection of essential records, confidentiality measures in place, previous disposals or losses of records, locations of records outside the institution, filing and retrieval difficulties, existing finding aids, procedures, forms used, costs of purchasing equipment, computer memory and space).

4) Profiles of the people met

– Decision-makers. Get them to talk about their department, their project; get them to delegate a resource person.

– Overworked. They need to show that they are essential in their department and that they have little time. They are often anxious and need to be reassured and show that they exist. They need to be convinced that a good procedure will diminish their work and may enhance their creativity.

– The gray eminences. They do not necessarily appear in the organization chart as responsible, but have a strong hold on their colleagues who appreciate them and often call on their knowledge. They must be made an ally so as not to undermine the credibility of the intervention (in the case of administrative assistants, for example, offer them the opportunity to become responsible for the filing plan).

– The buyers. They are not inclined to help, but they want the means, the space, a person dedicated to record management. We will have to try to meet their requirements by a commitment on their part as well, but we must be careful not to promise what we cannot deliver.

– The aggressive ones. They refute our arguments, seek the fight to make us doubt ourselves. Sometimes we have to press for validation from management and if necessary exclude them from the system in the first instance so as not to discourage others. Neutralize them.

– The silencers. They are attentive and want first to be convinced of the merits of the measure. On the other hand, those who always say yes rarely move the project forward. They are often hard to convince and need proposals that reassure them; their reactions are studied.

– The elders. They possess the knowledge of the organism and are the memory. In order to convince them without frightening them, it is necessary to propose they become responsible for the good functioning of the system and to integrate them in the implementation of procedures.

– It can be difficult to get to know the people who create and use archives well. We will study their functioning, their habits and attitudes, their place in the administrative structure, their leadership, their information needs.

– Do not forget that in order to set up a system you need to surround yourself with people with whom you have sympathy and who are constructive. A pilot service can be a good way to choose a team that you can move forward with.

– To identify the personnel assigned to the management of the archives, their attitude and degree of motivation, their professional qualifications.

5) Conduct of maintenance

– The speaker should be punchy and diplomatic; let people talk and expose problems.

– Do not be overly directive or make rash promises, but remain optimistic.

– Do not psychologically miss the interview, reinforce your brand image, show your skills while insisting on the need for collaboration. An interview that goes badly can lead to the erection of barriers in the project.

– To move forward in stages, to make suggestions, but without giving a quick solution, to propose several options, to take into account means and human resources.

6) Technical support and coaching

– Be an ally and avoid making judgments, do not hesitate to come back and coach for the implementation of procedures, be available when needed.

– Begin work with resource people who can in turn coach the service agents.

– There is no set policy. Tools and proposals must be adapted to the situation encountered. Record management is not ready-to-wear, but requires customization.

In conclusion, it is necessary to adapt one's responses according to needs and resources, and to propose several options. Always evaluate the time and means to be implemented, propose different solutions according to the achievements requested; even in the event of a catastrophic situation, make proposals and be positive, seek allies and convince opponents through a more efficient system.

Records management is becoming indispensable in today's changing digital world. The idea of entirety that it wants to control the whole of an organization's conclusive production does not always resist the limited resources and above all the investment in time and quality that it takes to intervene on information systems. We must not overlook the resistance linked to habitual change and a poor perception of agents' needs. These are underestimated constraints in the world now equipped with Web 2.0 tools, which are used by agents outside the scope of their organization and their IT department [BAN 12b, p. 54]. Therefore, it is necessary to collaborate and dialogue with the IT department responsible for the maintenance and development of the management tool as well as the software publisher if necessary. Maintenance is also the ideal framework for the process of explanation and awareness that must accompany any company that organizes and manages archives rationally, and is part of the archivist's expertise [ASS 07, p. 82].

Collaboration with the IT department and users of information systems allows archivists to focus on a number of stages in the record lifecycle:

– the creation of new computer applications: these must be able to identify records of enduring value and ensure their long-term preservation and accessibility;

– the operation of existing applications: archivists must ensure that all parts of an archival record, such as the record itself, its metadata, and documentation describing the operation of the application, are properly maintained and that no changes to the application affect the archival quality of the records;

– modifications, updates, migrations and other changes to the computer application do not affect the authenticity and integrity of the records;

– the capacity of the system to preserve the records, and the capacity of the producing or archival services to provide long-term access to the records;

– shutting down computer applications or removing archival records from those applications [ICA 05, p. 19].

In hindsight, the ability to integrate requirements into records being created will probably have been one of the most important developments for many professionals accustomed to applying filing, analysis, or other techniques to existing holdings [COT16].

The revision of ISO 15489 in 2016 covers several topics:

– the consideration of the digital records environment is not very present in the 1st version;

– risk management that goes beyond the asset value of records alone;

– alignment with the new standards, including terminology, which have emerged, in particular ISO 23081 for metadata.

While retaining the fundamental concepts, there are three examples of new approaches. First, the concept of records: it relates to metadata to ensure transactional value. The notion of metadata is addressed through requirements to create sets that respond to a given context. Then the notion of appraisal to determine what records should be produced, and how they should be managed until their disposition. Also, the records system can be understood as a tool or a group of tools (GED, records retention system). Finally, the process approach, which encompasses the creation, capture, filing and other processing of records up to their disposition [COT 16].

With this revision, record management professionals have a normative tool with new principles and the ambition to intervene in the lifecycle as early as possible. Interoperability with other standards will also be another way of using ISO 15489. It is part of the globalization of exchanges in digital form and meets the interoperability needs of many businesses in terms of security, traceability, integrity and transparency.

2.1.2. The ISO 30300 series of standards for the records management system

In the current context of the rapid and globalized development of the digital economy and the dematerialization of information carriers, the ISO 30300 series of standards aims to define a general framework for good governance. This series of standards developed from 2008 onwards has made it possible to draw up records to access standards aimed at certification. This makes the entire process of decisions related to records management transparent. These standards find their place among management system standards in the same way as those related to quality management, environmental management or risk management. They complement the ISO 15489 standard by providing the highest level of organizations with the necessary elements for the formalization of a records policy as part of their strategy. They address management by describing the processes relating to the lifecycle of records from a quality perspective and therefore the continuous improvement of the system's performance [COT 14, p. 2].

ISO 15489 was too general a technical standard and did not address the issue of certification. ISO has therefore embarked on a series of management standards which includes five fascicles devoted to records management systems. The first two were published in 2011 following a unanimous vote by committee members. They deal with fundamentals, vocabulary and requirements. ISO 30302 is an implementation guide published in 2015. Two other publications are expected: ISO 30303 for requirements for auditing and certification and ISO 30304 offering an assessment guide. ISO 30301 has an annex containing a "self-assessment checklist".

The 30300 series of standards are high-level standards, known as management system standards (MSS). They emphasize the responsibility and leadership of the directorates-general in charge of the records policy and they transfer to the operational levels the modalities of implementation of this policy[3]. They describe the records management process by giving it a general framework for good governance. As Michel Cottin points out, "This framework is special because it allows us to work on requirements for results, and not requirements for means. It defines the goals to be achieved, and in no case does it impose modalities for implementation. Consequently, they are not standards that are instructions for use, but standards that make it possible to describe what will be implemented, which will be carried out from a technical point of view, in other texts". They are sometimes

---

3 The 30300 series of standards describes the processes for designing, implementing and controlling a management system for records that meets the characteristics described in ISO 15489. These standards are therefore very much oriented towards self-assessment, continuous improvement of the system, auditing and, ultimately, certification, all of which are intended to guarantee the reliability of the system. Thus, ISO 15489 and the ISO 30300 family of standards should be used in conjunction with each other and also take into account related standards already published, such as ISO 23081-1:2017 and 23081-2:2009 concerning metadata or ISO 26122:2008 concerning process analysis of records. These standards are intended for the leaders of organizations for the implementation of the DMS and those responsible for risk management, audit, records, information systems and information security. They are therefore related to ISO 9001:2008 Quality management systems, ISO 14001:2004, ISO 19011:2018 Systems auditing, ISO/IEC 27001:2005 Information technology, information security.

misunderstood because they relate to a set of requirements that have been developed in a consistent manner [COT 15].

The management system for records is therefore one that:

– formalizes and documents practices (business processes, operating procedures, etc.);

– conducts checks to verify the conformity of what is done in relation to what is described and expected (e.g. internal audits);

– analysis of the results, monitors through objective measurements the efficiency and thus the performance of the system;

– and finally, makes the necessary adjustments and corrective actions [COT 14, p. 7].

These standards are constructed as a result of three doctrinal developments:

– the prioritization of the ISO 30300 series of record policy standards on the one hand, and technical implementation standards on the other, such as ISO 15489. The former have a strategic scope, while the latter are an indispensable component in the implementation of good governance;

– the process-based vision of the management of record activities with their modeling offering audit and certification modalities. A process is an organized system of activities that uses resources (personnel, equipment, materials and machinery, raw material and information) to transform input elements into output elements whose expected end result is a product (source ISO 9001). For human resources, filling positions is a process. It can be broken down into a series of sub-processes, the first of which is recruitment. For each one, we distinguish an input, actions, information, records and output the expected result. The quality managers define standard record models which have their own lifecycle. This understanding of the organization's activities should determine the impact of legislation, regulations, standards and good practice on the creation of records relevant to the activities by taking into account the organizational and economic environment and by carrying out regular reviews. Attention should be paid to the present and future needs of the organization's customers and the expectations of other stakeholders [ARN 12a, p. 111];

– the introduction, through evaluation methods and a metric, of the notion of continuous improvement of the service rendered inherent in quality management [COT 14, pp. 4–5].

These standards are referred to as generic because they are intended for any organization, regardless of its size, whether it is a commercial enterprise, a public administration or a government structure. They are also generic insofar as they also address and cascade to the top management that report to the directorate general and to the services over which they have authority. The ISO 30300 and ISO 30301 standards must take into account the bodies of records specified by their counterparts dealing with quality, the environment or risk. This point is particularly interesting to develop, as it underlines the specificity of ISO 30300-30301 in terms of interoperability with other management system standards. It positions it as a point of articulation with the other major processes of organizations related to quality, information security, risk management, the environment, etc. In fact, with the inclusion of records management, these management standards no longer position the latter solely on technical aspects and at the operational level of organizations, but on system management aspects, at the level of the management of these same organizations [COT 14, p. 17].

As a result, an organization may need to implement several system management standards and ensure their interoperability. This refers to the ability of a product or system, whose interfaces are fully known, to work with other existing or future products or systems without restriction of access or implementation. This is an essential factor for consistency and economic optimization. From this perspective, the positioning of information and therefore records within an organization is a major issue. It appears to be the point of articulation for ensuring their interoperability [COT 14, p. 17].

The concept of interoperability of information systems has become central to the ability of partners to interact using standardized data formats. Standards help to link other management systems within organizations in terms of information needs even if not all are designed with interoperability in mind and may sometimes compete for international status. This is why the integration of the ISO 30300 series of management standards is a first step towards interoperability of management systems. It promotes collaborative synergies between these different systems to better understand the constraints, better formalize objectives and better identify levers for improvement. However, it is still a delicate point to define, based on three aspects. On the one hand, there are the records that make up the standard models that enter into the functioning of the organization's business processes or operating methods. On the other hand, there are the recorded records produced and received in the context of the organization's activities and which constitute the corpus of documentation as well as the documentation produced in the context of the implementation of other management systems such as quality or information security. For this interoperability to be effective, the standard models for records must be clear, intelligible and correspond to the needs of users. In addition, registered records must provide tangible proof that their reliability, integrity and durability are unfailing. They are managed and made available to users through easy, fast, and secure access for as long as necessary. Finally, the drafting of the documentation of the different management systems needs to be shared to avoid simultaneous or superimposed drafting preventing the exchange of information, the ideal being to ensure a common drafting of the same documentation for all systems. It is useful to be able to implement interoperability in the data capture processes, in the implementation of metadata repositories, in the filtering and information extraction processes and in the restitution of results.

In other words, records management must be interoperable with other policies in the organization. It must be based on a corporate responsibility policy that is based on principles and values set out in a charter of ethics, rules of governance for performance and quality of service and an innovation strategy for a better balance between economic competitiveness and social progress [ARN 12b, p. 156].

To ensure the successful implementation of the records management system, several principles must be respected:

– a focus on the present and future needs of the organization's clients and other stakeholders;

– an ability to lead and provide strong leadership in defining the purpose, direction and governance ethic of the organization. Individuals must understand and be encouraged to adopt good records management practices consistent with the organization's objectives and to meet its accountability obligations. Chapter 5.2 describes the policy that should always be linked to the organization's purpose and high-level strategies to enable the creation and control of all records. This policy must allow for management commitment, which is a central element in the implementation of a project. One never starts a management system for records project without having a decision or a mission letter, the forms of which are different according to the cultures of the organizations. Communication aspects are included at all levels, even that of the partners, because everyone is concerned by record systems [COT 15];

– evidence-based decision-making therefore the ability to organize the creation of digital records and what allows us to anticipate risks. The implementation of the IMS requires management commitment and, at the operational level, the creation, integration and control of reliable and authentic records. With the example of leadership, which is an important requirement in this standard, management sets objectives and delineates roles and responsibilities. As required by the standard, the leader must prepare performance reports, including proposals for improvement. The designated records manager must report to all stakeholders, with indicators, and lead a reflection of each one to improve dysfunctions. For example, he or she establishes dashboards to evaluate the flow of records. The use of this standard is particular because it sets requirements that must be answered with questions and then evidence;

– involvement of the staff. Responsibilities for the control of records shall be clearly defined and appropriate training shall be provided to all employees of an organization who create, handle or use records. This applies to contractors, other stakeholders and staff of other organizations sharing business processes and associated information and records. Where resources are scarce, investment and the implementation of training actions are essential. Setting up a management system for records is essentially a matter of increasing the skills of teams of employees. For example, if we read the following requirement: "everyone must recognize for their job the impact of a possible drift in the proper functioning of records management", we will have to provide proof of this. In this implementation example, job description sheets are available: if each employee has job description sheet specifications relating to records management, they will be able to recognize the impacts of records management and, as a result, Requirement 7.3 is met [COT 15];

– a process approach. The management of the organization's activities and programs must be carried out in the form of processes in which activities for the creation and management of records are integrated. This makes it possible to improve the efficiency of all activities, both operational and informational;

– a systemic approach and management system modeling. The integration of records management within the business must be part of a broader management system that includes the analysis of requirements and plans, and the organization, correction and improvement of policies and procedures on a regular basis;

– continuous improvement. The regular monitoring, review and continuous improvement of the overall performance of the management system for records should feed into the review and improvement of the organization's overall management system. It is a question of ensuring the necessary adaptations and corrective actions. It implements the continuous improvement principle of the "Deming wheel" so that each process and sub-process is planned, implemented and maintained, monitored, audited and reviewed and improved. This is done with a view to continuously improving performance while meeting the needs of all stakeholders in the organizations [COT 14, p. 7]. In Chapter 6.2, governance according to ISO 30301, implies that measures for monitoring and analyzing performance indicators are put in place, such as record reuse. Then, this review of governance makes it possible to ensure responses that are adapted to the needs of users in particular, and to integrate areas for improvement: for example, in terms of ergonomics, ease of access, record search. The evaluation of efficiency can be audited and lead to certifications. These standards are voluntary: it is not essential to apply all the requirements, except where certification is envisaged. What is special about these standards is that organizations can choose from among all the requirements those that seem to represent the best source of continuous improvement in their performance [COT 15].

The IMS is considered reliable if it is able to be the primary source of information on the organization's activities. It must enable the integration, classification and immediate identification of all records produced or received by the organization in the course of its activities and their metadata. It shall protect records and metadata against improper alteration or disposal. It must ensure the protection of records essential to the smooth functioning and survival of the organization in the event of a disaster, and control the circulation of and access to records [ARN 12a, p. 107].

Launching governance in a management system for records can start, for example, with an inventory of the existing system, that is, how records are created and how their retention and final disposition is organized. One can estimate the stakes and the possibility of achieving the organization's objectives: an organization that has a production system, for example, that has information and records system flaws. We will be able to measure the consequences of these shortcomings on the quality of production. It is important, when embarking on a management system for records approach, to ensure that the decision-making, start-up or non-start-up phase of a governance approach is well framed. Finally, another important element is to always be able to communicate on the decision-making process.

These are the main points that meet the normative requirements to ensure good governance:

– decisions supported by relevant sources;

– effective capitalization of knowledge;

– lower development costs through good record lifecycle management;

– the ability to contribute to innovation through a process of record acquisition and processing;

– contributing to increased collective confidence through transparency on how records are created;

– rapid disaster response with easy access to vital records that will facilitate business resumption and reduce risk factors [COT 15].

2.2. Criteria and requirements of the digital record

2.2.1. Evidence

Relations between people are becoming more complex with the pace of globalization, leading to disputes in commercial and private life and, as a result, the multiplication of contracts and litigation. Also, corporate information that produces engaging records requires rigorous management. Wherever these records are located, they support the original information useful for the proper functioning of activities and proof of the organization's compliance and good law. They must be well managed in space and time [CHA 18, p. 41].

Paradoxically, it is the individual who becomes the lowest common denominator of a globalizing society. He has access to everything, he can know everything and challenge everything, but at the same time he is the most threatened. He is the object of rumors and solicitations while he is not prepared to master this complexity. The consideration of human rights and legislation is not a fashion, but the response to the growing fragility of the individual, faced with institutions, companies, and special interests that ignore them, hence the strengthening of regulations and laws [DEL 12b, p. 196].

With the development of technology, the rules of the law of evidence have been adapted. It is no longer true that only writing, testimony and other means of evidence can be used to establish the mutual consent of the parties to be bound by a contract, because now a person can express his or her willingness to be bound by contract with a simple "click" of the mouse [GAG 15, p. 1].

Several countries, including France, in a context of rapid development of commercial transactions, have put an end to the supremacy of the written word with evidential force over the paper medium. Thus, French law no. 2000-230 of March 13, 2000, adapts the law of evidence to information technology, which modifies the Civil Code in article 1316-1: "A writing in electronic form is admitted in evidence in the same way as a writing on paper, provided that the person from whom it emanates can be duly identified, and that it is established and preserved in conditions that guarantee its integrity." This text enshrines the generalization of the dematerialization of information at source. Similarly, section 31.1 of the Canada Evidence Act of 1985, as amended in 2000, states that "the onus is on the person seeking to admit an electronic record into evidence to establish its authenticity by means of evidence from which it can be concluded that the record is what it appears to be" (2000, c. 5, s. 56). Until then, the principle of the indivisibility of a durable physical medium and the information it carries was the basis for the quality of evidence, and in particular for pre-constituted evidence of a juridical act. For the first time, a functional definition of writing is given, making it independent of its medium: "Literal evidence, or evidence in writing, results from a series of letters, characters, numbers or any other signs or symbols with an intelligible meaning, whatever their medium and mode of transmission" (CC, art. 1316) [BAN 09, p. 31].

The first condition for the admissibility of a legal act whose terms are recorded on a computer medium is that it must therefore be intelligible. This element of intelligibility is defined in its usual meaning of a record which can be read directly, that is to say, in the sense of a record which can be understood, which is accessible and clear. Thus, a record on which appears a language that can be understood by a machine only could not constitute an intelligible record [GAG 15, p. 8].

The legal system in place makes it possible to dematerialize the information produced and exchanged progressively throughout the chain. The notions of authentication and integrity are central and it is public key cryptography technologies that are used to meet these requirements. Infrastructures have been set up to secure exchanges, transactions and data flows: platforms use signature and time-stamping services, known as third-party certifiers and third-party time-stampers [BAN 09, p. 33].

The Court of Cassation recalls that the copy must be faithful, which implies that it must be visually presented as the original, with the indications on the letterhead and the signature of the sender. Technically, this can result in the creation of a PDF-type digital record of the original signed letter, which will be time-stamped and, if necessary, secured by a hash calculation to ensure that no modification can be made to it subsequently and, above all, preserved by a system that guarantees the traceability of all operations carried out on the record after its creation [RIE 10, p. 293].

Similarly, the notion of interoperability is becoming fundamental so that partners' information systems can dialogue using standardized data formats, for example XML, which has become essential in this environment. The European Telecommunications Standards Institute (ETSI) distinguishes four layers of interoperability:

– technical interoperability is associated with hardware/software components, systems and platforms that enable machine/machine communication. This layer focuses on the communication protocols and the infrastructure needed to operate these protocols;

– syntactic interoperability is associated with s-formats and data representation models;

– semantic interoperability is associated with the meaning of content, and therefore concerns the human interpretation of content and not that of machines. There needs to be a common understanding of the meaning of the exchanged content;

– operational interoperability is associated with the ability of organizations to communicate effectively. It builds on the three previous layers [ROB 15, p. 371].

However, issues related to the retention periods of data and records, the implementation processes related to their lifecycle and their medium- and long-term sustainability have not been taken into account in the legislation.

2.2.2. *Authenticity*

Authenticity is defined as the persistence over time of the original characteristics of the record with regard to its context, structure and content, which means that the record is what it claims to be. To preserve integrity, the identity of the author must be attested and the record must not be corrupted or altered. It is a question of verifying the plausibility of the validation of the record by its author as well as the date of this validation, that is, it was created or sent on the date indicated by the designated author. The means of analysis are the study of the record itself, which may present inconsistencies, the study of its routing and traceability and the comparative study of other records by the same author [CHA 18, p. 31].

In fact, the record collected is indeed the one that was produced. The known author of the record is not questionable. The record does reflect the action it purports to relate to, whether it was produced or received by the person claiming to have produced or received it, at the time it is believed to have been produced or received.

Authenticity qualifies a well-produced record, with the identification of the issuer, the date, the validation. For this record to remain authentic over time, it must not undergo any change in issuer, date or validation, in other words, it must remain intact. If it is false at the beginning, it will remain false on arrival. The authenticity of a record must be verified upon receipt and then its integrity must be continuously traced if it is to be proven that it has not been falsified [CHA 18, p. 32].

For records embedded in electronic systems, asserting authenticity means proving that the record is what it is intended to be without having undergone substantial change or corruption when it has been transmitted across space (between people, systems, applications) or time (when it is no longer online and has been archived, when management or maintenance hardware or software is updated or replaced). Whoever keeps it must be able to establish its identity and demonstrate its integrity by observing that certain requirements are met [DUR 03, p. 610].

Identifying someone consists of establishing the person's identity, that is, its permanent and fundamental character, whereas authenticating is certifying the accuracy of the person's identity. Authentication is the degree to which data are accurate, correct, truthful or adequate. The duality of these two concepts of identification and authentication is important in access control to authenticate the individual after identifying him or her [CAP 07, p. 17].

Identity refers to the attributes of a record that characterize and distinguish it from other records. These attributes include the names of the persons involved in the formation of the record (author, recipient, writer, host [e-mail address holder]); the date(s) of its creation and transmission; an indication of the purpose or action in which it is involved; the expression of its archival links; and an indication of attached records [DUR 03, p. 609].

Documented control policies and procedures should be established and documented for the creation, receipt, transmission, preservation and disposition of records. These procedures ensure that the creators of records are authorized and identified as such, and that records are protected against unauthorized additions, deletions, alterations and concealment. This refers to the notion of accountability, that is, the ability to attribute, with the required level of confidence, an action on an item of information to a specific person. It also leads to non-repudiation, that is, the impossibility for a person to deny his or her participation in an exchange of information, since this participation may concern both the origin of the information and its content [FLE 12, p. 182].

Authenticity is often confused in everyday language with truthfulness and authentication. Authenticity is used to characterize the condition of a record, that is, what it is meant to be without having been altered or corrupted. Thus defined, authenticity is distinguished from the truthfulness that characterizes the assertions contained in the record, but also from authenticity in its old diplomatic sense, which designates the record provided with signs of validation, the record whose authenticity is affirmed by the producer, by the addition of a declaration or other element that would fall under the scope of authentication. Authenticity is a property of the record that accompanies it throughout its life, while authentication is a means of proving, at some point in time, that the record is what it purports to be [DUR 03, p. 609].

In reality, the term authentication applies only to objects and there is regular talk, for example, of authenticating a work of art. Thus, the use of this term in computer science is often misused to mean "identification". The origin of this error comes from an Anglicism linked to the English term authentication, false friend which means both "identification" and "authentication". But in French, only the term "identification" is appropriate to determine whether an object or entity is indeed the person concerned. This is a true identity check. Conversely, authentication will determine whether an object, and not a person, has the claimed characteristics. The principle is generally to identify the person by means of a system of identification (login) with a password. However, there is no certainty that it is the right person. In summary, the authentication of a person is based on at least one of the following three criteria: what the person knows (a password), what the person has (a token or electronic certificate), what the person is (biometrics) [CAP 07, pp. 17–18].

The combination of integrity and traceability ensures the authenticity of the record. Traceability is a procedure for automatically following an object from its birth to its final preservation or destruction. The simple fact of constituting a sequential journal and thus tracing the various operations carried out, for example on an electronic archiving system, offers a real guarantee. It will indeed become extremely difficult, if not impossible, for a third party to question the system. Traceability also allows control over the reality of the actions carried out on an object and the traceability of these operations. Thus, the record may be retained as evidence by a judge [CAP 07, p. 25].

Traceability is a fundamental element of proof, as one can prove the state of the record at a time "t" by presenting the history of the processing carried out on a record throughout its lifecycle. Traceability specifies all the events that occurred in the archiving system. It is possible to know who was connected to the archiving system, at the time the record was consulted, if migration operations were carried out. The traceability will be able to be used in case of audit while respecting the management of personal data. When the auditor has to verify a record, it will be presented to the auditor with its associated metadata, or with other records, such as an invoice and purchase order.

Traces of conformity, like traces of authenticity, take two forms. They are either metadata or records, such as event logs or reports verifying the validity of an electronic signature, for example. The collection of these traces is essential, since any user needs to be able to trust the image of a record he or she is viewing on his or her screen [GUY 15c, p. 107].

The robustness of indirect digital evidence can be enhanced by metadata that records the exact date and time any record was sent or received, which computer created it and which computer received it. A statement made by an expert relying on the reliability of the record and the procedures controlling it is recognized as valid authentication. It is indirect evidence that the system is performing its function without deterioration and that it is free from any unauthorized manipulation of the system whether intentional or accidental. Biometric identification systems and cryptography are not considered by digital forensics to be the most reliable means of authentication [DUR 12, p. 122].

In this sense, it seems preferable to focus on the internal characteristics of digital records, that is, the content of the information, rather than their technical characteristics, which are necessarily changing due to the rapid obsolescence of formats, media and operating systems. From this point of view, basing the authenticity of a record on purely technical characteristics (fingerprinting, time stamping, cryptography) would be risky, even illusory, especially since a technical failure is always possible. The analysis of the consistency of internal characters (date of place and time, name, function and organization of the issuer, etc.) remains relevant. In addition, some technical devices are not permanent and their renewal represents a significant cost [BUR 13, p. 22].

Preservation of the documentary context is essential, as is the evidentiary value of the record, which must be admissible in court and functionally equivalent to paper records in transactions. Contextual information also helps to strengthen the proof of authenticity, reliability and integrity of records. This is of particular importance for electronic records. The business processes, functions and system for the creation and maintenance of records in a records producing organization are part of the context of those records. Context may be preserved by elements internal to the records (for example, attachments, appendices, links, reference numbers and codes) or by external elements such as metadata [ICA 05, p. 12].

Copies of the same record may exist throughout the organization. It is vital for the organization to know which is the "official" record, especially since each transmission of the same record inevitably has the quality of a copy, not an original. The only true "original" record in electronic systems is the first actual and complete record to be received or stored on a file in the system if it is transmitted over time, a status that ceases after the record is first stored. As soon as it is recalled, the stored entity assumes the copy status.

The same applies to the draft or working record: even if it remains in spirit the draft of the final record, it will never appear as a copy, simple or figurative, of the preparatory state stored beforehand. The official copy of each record can only ever be identified, and must be subject to control procedures that will take the place of a kind of authentication. Technology-based authentications are used only for records transmitted across space, as they usually constitute an obstacle to the maintenance of the record to which they are linked. Of course, when the official record is identified, the office with the formal authority to manage it is known. It shares the same classification and period of custody. The advantage of this operation is that it reduces duplication of responsibilities and makes it possible to determine who is responsible for the records [DUR 03, p. 617].

When the record is removed from the electronic system, the creator must have implemented procedures to decide which documentation should be transferred to the records manager along with the records themselves. This documentation includes all the information needed to access the records, establish their identity, and demonstrate their integrity [DUR 03, pp. 617–618].

Once the authenticity of the transferred records has been presumed or verified, the authenticity of the transferred records must be maintained. The custodian must produce authentic copies of the records concerned, which is the only way to ensure their preservation, a requirement that stems from the nature of electronic records, the physical and intellectual parts of which do not necessarily coincide. It is strictly impossible to preserve an electronic record, because in fact only the ability to reproduce it is preserved [DUR 03, p. 618].

The verification shall be certified by the person responsible for archiving, duly authorized to do so himself. Such a certificate guarantees that the copy thus produced conforms to the record reproduced, until proven otherwise [DUR 03, p. 619].

All copying activity must also be documented, including the date of copying and the name of the custodian, the relationship between the record received from the creator and the copies produced by the custodian. This includes the impact of the reproduction process on their form, content, accessibility and use. This documentation is essential to ensure that the custodian plays its role as a trustworthy guardian, so that the user can access the history of the reproduction of the record, which becomes an integral part of the history of the record [DUR 03, p. 620].

The importance of the Interpares (The International Research on Permanent Authentic Records in Electronic Systems) project, launched in 1999, which has gone through three phases over 13 years, should be stressed here. The project began with conceptual observation and continued with testing with the full diversity of digital records, gradually moving towards the application of these results in the reality of organizations. The research work was organized into four areas of inquiry:

– the first was to formulate the conceptual conditions necessary for the preservation of authentic electronic records;

– the second was to develop evaluation criteria and selection methods for authentic electronic records;

– the third was to define the methods and responsibilities of conservation;

– the fourth was to develop a framework for defining policies, strategies and standards in this area [DUR 03, p. 608].

Interpares in Phase 1 focused on the authentic preservation of administrative and legal records created and maintained in databases and records management systems. Phase 2 focused on developing theory and methods to ensure the reliability, accuracy and authenticity of electronic records from their creation to their disposal or throughout their long-term preservation. Phase 3 aimed to implement the findings of the first two phases of the project in archives with limited resources. Interpares produced a set of *requirements for* assessing and maintaining the authenticity of electronic archives. Phase 2 proposed guidelines for creators of records created using dynamic and interactive systems [COU 14, p. 125].

Interpares' results have determined the conditions that a digital record must meet:

– be fixed on a specific medium or support;

– have a stable content with unchanged data and message in the record and without modifications;

– having a fixed form, the records are kept in such a way that they are represented in the same way as on the screen;

– have explicit (or archival) links to other records within or outside the records system of which it is a part;

– have five people involved in its creation: the author, the writer, the initiator, the recipient and the creator;

– be linked to a specific action;

– have six contexts of creation: legal, administrative, procedural, documentary, technological and provenance.

2.2.3. The electronic signature

In the digital environment, the electronic signature is one of the technical means to guarantee the authenticity of a record. Event logging, on the other hand, is a means of recording all the actions performed on a record so that it can be considered authentic. It allows all traces to be recorded in an XML file type file, which will contain all the events. This log will itself be signed, time-stamped and archived in the archiving system.

In the case of an office record, it will contain a title, an author, a date and even a company logo in the record template. This information, whether it is present in the content of the record or in the associated metadata, can be easily modified and deleted. One reliable process is the electronic signature process. Beware, scanning the handwritten signature and inserting it into the record has no value.

To ensure the authenticity and integrity of the records, the archiving system can integrate digital signature and timestamp functions during capture. Signing a record consists of encrypting its digital fingerprint using the signer's private key, which constitutes a seal. As for the timestamp, time information is added to the fingerprint and the result is signed, that is, it is encrypted. This constitutes a timestamp token that can be provided by trusted third parties. To verify the authenticity, the fingerprint of the record is then generated using the same algorithm as the one used when it was captured and compared with the fingerprint stored in the secure archiving system. Identical fingerprints confirm the record's compliance [LEP 11, p. 16].

The electronic signature provides a response to the legal requirement to identify the author of an electronic record and his or her accountability. This requires proof of the validity of this signature in the event of use of the signed record. This validity then requires verification of the signature both in terms of the integrity of the signed record and the validity of the certificate used to make the signature. Given the obsolescence of cryptographic processes and the need to preserve the means of this verification over time, another solution consists of using a trusted third party (Evidence Management Authority – EMA) to perform this signature verification as soon as possible and then keep a record of this verification associated with the original record [RIE 10, p. 84].

A digital signature mechanism must have the following properties: it must allow the reader of a record to identify the person or organization that has signed it and guarantee that the record has not been altered between the time the author signed it and the time the reader consults it. The signature cannot be falsified and is not reusable. A signed record is unalterable; it cannot be altered. For this reason, it differs from the "simple" signature, which is only made up of a sequence of characters [SOY 09, p. 56].

The two main functions of the signature are both to identify the person signing in an unquestionable manner and also to manifest that person's will in a certain manner. So this amended article 1316-4 of the Civil Code specifies that, in fact, "it must be based on a reliable identification process which guarantees the link with the act. The reliability of the process is presumed when the signature is created, the identity of the signatory is assured, and the integrity of the act is guaranteed". The identity of the link with the act is the timestamp.

Time stamping gives electronic writing its full probative value. It must be possible to demonstrate the origin of the record, that the record has been kept under conditions that guarantee its integrity, and the date the record was created. It will not be sufficient to recover the file that has remained stored on a backup tape to provide this proof [FLE 12, p. 187].

The electronic signature refers to two distinct actions: the electronic signature is a technological (cryptographic) process that allows consent to be given to a written record as an asset of its authenticity (equivalent to a handwritten signature). The same technical process can be used by a third party to "seal" a file in order to guarantee its integrity. Other simpler processes exist, such as e-mail to give consent to a record. However, inserting an image of a handwritten signature into an office file is not an electronic signature [CHA 18, p. 52].

The electronic signature is a code that identifies an individual and expresses consent to be bound. It is therefore a personal code by which the author of a record signifies to third parties that he or she is indeed the one from whom the record or other acceptance emanates and which, conversely, assures third parties that the original record is indeed from the issuer. In practice, the electronic signature serves the same purpose as a handwritten or traditional signature and, like the latter, is a personal and distinctive mark. However, unlike a handwritten signature, it requires the intervention of a third party, whether it is a software developer, a network operator or a company specializing in setting up an electronic signature system, which will act primarily at the level of generating the signature. In other words, in order to be able to sign a record electronically, one must be granted a personal electronic signature by a third party, whereas a handwritten signature is a creation of the signatory [GAG 15, p. 14].

The electronic signature does not, like the handwritten signature, provide an immediately identifiable graphic element that is sufficient to identify and recognize the signatory. A visualization tool is used to identify the presence of an electronic signature and ensure its validity. It allows the user to consult a number of authenticity criteria attached to the content: name of the signatory/author of the record, name of the certification authority, date of the signature/stamp, and name of the timestamping authority. These elements are displayed in a "signatures" block. However, the link between these marks and the content is broken if the electronically signed record is printed for distribution, for example [GUY 15c, p. 84].

In addition, in order to support and reassure users in their transition to the digital world, the project owners propose to make the authenticity marks visible. This visibility is achieved through a mechanism for tattooing the record with the addition of a form of authenticity cartridge. In this cartridge, the attributes of date, non-alteration of the content and origin of the record are materialized, as much metadata registered in the properties of the electronic signature. The electronic signature and the timestamp token are then given a visible form by the addition, on the record, of a cartridge with the reference of the signature certificate, the result of the printing of the electronically signed record, the scanned signature, the dates and times of the signature [GUY 15c, p. 85].

The use of the electronic signature is likely to generate media breaks, which are sometimes complex to manage, in particular because of the multiplication of similar copies of the record on different media. The only qualifier used to characterize a digital record is its version. However, the version of a record does not account for the uses of the record, which may be informative, legal, or patrimonial, focusing on the criterion of chronology of production of the record.

Céline Guyon from the *Archives départementales de l'Aube*, gives an example of an interesting practice in the context of the results of analyses carried out by the veterinary and food diagnostic laboratory of the Aube department. These are signed electronically by authorized technicians and the certificates are acquired from a certified authority. The analysis results, in their original and original form, are on digital media. They are also entrusted, in this form, to the department's electronic archiving service. With the use of electronic signatures, the break in the dematerialization chain has been postponed until the results are distributed to the people concerned (veterinarians, farmers, departmental veterinary services directorate). The copy sent to the client is always the copy on which the authenticity cartridge has been affixed, which qualifies it as an authentic copy. However, the coexistence of several copies of the same record, possibly on different media, makes it necessary and indispensable to identify and qualify the reference copy. This reference copy is the copy qualified as an original, that is the original record signed electronically and kept by the department's Electronic Archiving Service. An "evidentiary agreement" clause has been included in the Laboratory's contracts with its customers so that each party recognizes that the copy admitted as evidence is the reference copy [GUY 15c, p. 87].

When talking about electronic signatures, the following conditions must be met: authenticity marked by the identity of the signatory, which must be traceable with certainty, and the signature cannot be forged or re-used; it must be part of the signed record and not be moved to another record. It must also be unalterable and irrevocable (the person who signed cannot deny it). The electronic signature with asymmetric cryptography is currently considered to be one of the most secure systems and especially one of the most widespread for signing in the electronic environment [SOY 09, p. 22].

This technique is based on a triangular relationship between the signatory, the recipient of the message and a certification authority. In practice, any person wishing to sign electronically must first ask the certification authority to issue a private, secret key held exclusively by the signatory. At the same time, the certification authority must create a public key complementary to the private key. The private key encrypts the written record, the public key decrypts it. The signatory can therefore, if he wishes to send a signed message to the recipient, apply the private key to the message. The message (usually only the hash fingerprint of the message obtained by a "hash" function) will then be encrypted according to the private key algorithm. When the message is received by the recipient, the recipient will attempt to decrypt the message using the public key of the theoretical sender of the message. If these two keys match, the message can be decrypted and the recipient can be sure that the message was signed by the sender's private key. However, if decryption fails, the message has not been signed with the presumed originator's private key [SOY 09, p. 22].

Since it is impossible to replay an electronic signature over time, due to the life of the certificate which is only a few years and much shorter than the retention period of the record, mechanisms to verify the validity of the signature and to record the results of the verification in a report are implemented. The inextricable link between the electronically signed record and the verification report is ensured by, among other things, the fingerprint of the record that is recorded in the verification report and in the record metadata. However, this link is not timeless, and care must be taken to ensure that the verification report does not become detached from the record during format conversion [GUY 15c, p. 93].

During decryption, the public key checks whether the record was actually created by the person who has the private key and whether the record has been altered after signing. The electronic signature is not indecipherable or eternal. Encryption algorithms will be decipherable in five to ten years. Keys must be renewed and signed records must be re-encrypted periodically. Retention of encrypted records involves a risk of accessibility [KEC 14, p. 141].

The strength of the symmetric signature depends on two things: the algorithm used and the length of the key. The longer the key is (number of bits), the longer it will take to break it. The principle of asymmetric encryption (also called public key encryption) appeared in 1976 with a public key that is used only to encrypt data and identify you to the recipient, and a private key that is used only to decrypt data that has been encrypted with your public key. Thus, in a public key encryption system, users choose a random key that only they know (this is the private key). From this key, they each automatically derive an algorithm (this is the public key). Users exchange this public key through an unsecured channel. When a user wishes to send a message to another user, he simply encrypts the message to be sent using the recipient's public key. The latter will be able to decrypt the message using his private key (which only he knows).

As an image, a user randomly creates a small metal key (the private key) and then makes a large number of padlocks (the public key) that he or she places in a locker accessible to everyone (the locker acts as an unsecured channel). To send him a record, each user can take a padlock (open), close a briefcase containing the record thanks to this padlock, then send the briefcase to the owner of the public key (the owner of the padlock). Only the owner will then be able to open the case with his private key.

A cheaper technique based on the implementation of a cryptographic hash system for each stored record may be preferred. Authenticity is ensured by the historization of metadata to trace the origin of each record [FLE 12, p. 186].

The Public Record Office in Victoria, Australia, "wraps" records with metadata after conversion, then electronically signs the "envelopes" and repeats these operations after each subsequent alteration. Interpares recommends that electronic signatures be removed and that the metadata on them be retained, documenting that the electronic signature has taken place [KEC 14, p. 141].

2.2.4. Integrity

Integrity defines the whole and healthy state of a record; a record has the attribute of integrity when it has remained intact and free of corruption, in other words, when the message it is supposed to convey in order to fulfil its function remains unaltered. It is complete and has not been altered in its essential aspects or falsified and the message communicated has not been altered in its transmission or communication. The message is immutable, unalterable, and its use traced.

According to the Quebec Act respecting the legal framework for information technology (RLRQ c C-1.1, ss. 5 and 6), the integrity of the record is ensured when it can be verified that the information is not altered and that it is maintained in its entirety, and that the medium carrying the information provides it with the desired stability and durability. The integrity of the record must be maintained throughout its lifecycle, from its creation, through its transfer, consultation and transmission, to its preservation, including archiving or destruction. Account is taken, in particular, of the security measures taken to protect the record during its lifecycle [DEM 15, p. 131].

Therefore, in order for a technology-based record to be admissible in evidence, it will be necessary to demonstrate that the medium using the new technologies makes it possible to preserve the information contained in the record in its entirety. Thus, a technology-based record could have integrity without demonstrating the veracity of the record's content [GAG 15, p. 38].

In the digital environment, the format or media migration operation generally causes an integrity flaw. The bitstreams are no longer exactly the same without the message being impacted. Integrity can be demonstrated by evidence found in the record, in metadata linked to it, or in one or more of its creation and management contexts (documentary, procedural, technological, provenance context, legal-administrative context) [DUR 03, p. 610]. Integrity does not mean that files and metadata remain intact, as maintaining fixity would require retaining the original software and would not be appropriate for dynamic records. Integrity should be viewed as completeness, retaining all the essential elements of the record. The content, identifier, structure and context must be kept unaltered because they carry the coherence of the record [KEC 14, p. 133].

This does not mean that the record must be the same as it was at the time of its creation for its integrity to exist and be proven if we consider the fragility of the medium and the obsolescence of the technology. When we refer to the electronic record, we consider it complete and unaltered, if the message it is supposed to communicate to accomplish its purpose is unaltered, which does not prevent changing software versions or media forms. Finally, a record must be usable and therefore easily locatable and communicable [LEP 11, p. 10].

In order to be able to demonstrate that a record has not been altered or corrupted, a fingerprint calculation is performed. This mechanism consists of producing a string of characters obtained using a hash function specific to each record and checking it regularly. If a single comma in the record is changed, the fingerprint is changed and integrity is no longer guaranteed. The fingerprint is sealed with an electronic stamp and then time-stamped. A secure log is used to record this payment and all subsequent operations relating to the record. This log ensures the traceability of operations. It is the timestamp of the events recorded in the log that makes it possible to establish the date and time of the events (moving the archive, consultation, etc.) in order to prove them afterwards [AGE 16, p. 5].

Reading a sealed file whose seal is broken corrupts the technical integrity of an archive. Legally, if the migration and manipulation are traced, they do not jeopardize the integrity of the information. Integrity is thus preserved, as the information remains authentic and reliable [FLE 12, p. 183].

Conversely, integrity in the legal sense of a record consists of retaining the meaning of the information it contains without necessarily attaching to the form. Thus, changing an accent in a text will not fundamentally change its meaning, but it will be enough to cause it to lose its technical integrity. In order to provide a solution to this difficulty of interpretation, the Internet Rights Forum and the Digital Economy Mission recommended in their 2006 report that the notion of record integrity as provided for in Article 1316-1 of the Civil Code be ensured by the combined respect of the following three criteria: legibility of the record, stability of the information content and traceability of operations on the record [CAP 07, p. 13].

In general, breaches of integrity are of malicious origin. Cases of accidents or errors are much rarer. According to the French *Club de la Sécurité des Systèmes d'Information*, over a period of more than 10 years, malevolence has increased by nearly 15% per year, mainly to the detriment of data integrity and processing.

The loss of integrity can present vital dangers, such as mutations of blood group data in a shared medical record stored in a medical records center or of a patient identifier. Moreover, the issue is also a legal one, insofar as the company must guarantee the integrity of its processing and the flow of information it creates, at the risk of being condemned [CAP 07, p. 14].

If we consider the security criterion relating to the integrity of a record, several solutions are possible. First of all, a software solution that consists of calculating the record's fingerprint. The fingerprint is recalculated on a regular basis or when the record is queried to verify that it has not been altered and is verified against the original fingerprint. Then a storage strategy such as CAS (content access storage) type solutions automatically manages the integrity check on a regular or *ad hoc* basis depending on the settings selected. Finally, an organizational solution, where, according to the new European regulation, it provides a presumption of integrity to any record time-stamped by a qualified trusted service provider (PSCO). As a result, the storage service will only have to worry about the durability of the record. A secure log is kept of the deposit operation and then of all operations concerning the archived record. However, if an alteration occurs on a record, the system will be able to detect it, but will be unable to restore the original record. It will be important to distinguish between purely security aspects and more common aspects of service quality and performance, such as availability and response times [ARN 15, pp. 213–214].

It is recommended that controls be put in place over the right of access, user identity, right of disposal, alteration or improper movement of records to prevent unauthorized use of the system. Integrity shall be verified by means of continuous and contradictory control based on the making of integrity fingerprints or signatures on the records. This check is carried out and the result is recorded in the event log. Each day, the log is sealed, time-stamped and archived [FLE 12, p. 183].

As part of the implementation of an electronic records management system, which must be able to provide proof that the files entrusted to it have not been altered over time, it is necessary to put in place a mechanism for sealing records and an electronic safe. In order to ensure the integrity of a record entrusted to the safe, an imprint of the record must be taken when the file is stored. The fingerprint cannot be used to reconstruct the record, but it must be kept in the vault with the archived record [SOY 09, p. 48].

2.2.5. Reliability

A record is reliable when the recording, preservation and reproduction of the data have taken place in circumstances that allow the judge to conclude that the record is likely to reproduce the legal act. Thus, reliability refers to the quality of an archival record that can be relied upon because it meets the requirements of completeness of form and control over the process of its creation.

For a record to be reliable, its contents must be capable of being regarded as a complete and accurate representation of the activities or transactions it describes, so that subsequent reference to it will make it possible to understand how the transaction it describes was carried out. In general, the record should contain sufficient information to enable the same operation as that described to be carried out and the same result to be achieved. The record should be created at the time of the operation, by the persons who carried it out or who have a good knowledge of it.

This requirement applies to many debit card transactions such as deposits, bill payments or purchases. It is a simple presumption that can, for example, be overturned when it is shown that the company's computer system was experiencing difficulties at the time the record in question was created. Furthermore, the prohibition against contradicting by testimony the terms of a contract evidenced in writing does not apply to computerized entries. Consequently, it is easier to contest such a record than a private deed or a notarial deed [GAG 15, p. 9].

Reliability of records and records systems is ensured if records are collected in a way that is at least routine, if not automatic; if records are collected immediately or shortly after the action that produced them; and if the system includes tools for ongoing monitoring, capable of detecting any malfunction and allowing the recovery of elements of all data related to a particular record or operation [ICA 05, p. 30].

According to the ISO15489 standard, records produced in the course of an activity must be created in such a way as to be the preferred source of information. Access to records and their metadata must be immediate. They must reflect the operations of the producer, in order to retain as much information as possible about the context in which they were produced. Finally, the system must be able to evolve according to the needs of the organization without affecting the characteristics of the records.

2.2.6. Usability

Usability is defined as the ability of the record to be located, retrieved, communicated and interpreted. Contextual links in records should carry information relevant to an understanding of the operations that created and used them [FLE 12, p. 183]. The links between the record and other records related to it should be known and maintained, as well as their place in the organization's chain of activities. Finally, the format or medium in which it is kept should allow for its reuse for as long as possible. Usability is the fact that the record can continue to be used after it has been produced and that it remains usable. For a record to remain usable, it is necessary to associate metadata to it and manage the migration of media and formats in order to maintain its usability. Exploitation takes place under conditions of creation and preservation of documentary heritage.

Retained holdings may be complete and authentic, and will remain useless if they cannot be accessed or understood. Records must be accessible and understandable. This means that there is always some kind of technology, both hardware and software, that makes it possible to find records of interest and then translate them into a form that is accessible to the human senses. This understanding may require the use of other information, also included in the archival system, but not every record considered in isolation is required to be meaningful [ICA 05, p. 40].

Records may be accessible even if the hardware or software originally used to produce them is no longer available. All that is required is that there be a means of making the records human-readable, even if the records do not have all the properties conferred by the software that created them. For example, records are created by software that allows them to be modified and presented in different ways; it is conceivable to provide long-term access to these records, using a program that will only allow them to be viewed and in one form [ICA 05, p. 40].

Records may be understandable on their own if they are accessible, but other types of records may require additional information to be understandable. One may be confronted with records relating to an agricultural survey, which uses a coding system to indicate the category of land or the type of soil on each plot. The coding system can have a unique character, either a number or a letter, for each type of land or soil. Obviously, records coded in this way are not intelligible since these codes have no intrinsic meaning. But if we also keep the coding system with the records, then they become understandable. Also, the coding system is an integral part of the record, but in many computer systems it is separate from it. It may exist only in paper form, or as part of the instructions given to the users of the system [ICA 05, p. 40].

Care is taken to ensure that the computer record is kept in machine-readable form, that information and explanations of the coding system are kept in accessible form, and that the link between these two elements is always maintained [ICA 05, p. 40].

2.3. Risk management

2.3.1. Documentary risks

Risk is the effect of uncertainty on the achievement of the objective and may prevent the achievement of expected results. Risk control consists of the systematic application of preventive and curative measures predefined in the management system. With digital records, the risks are accentuated, therefore the lack of management and control of these digital records can lead to the impossibility to secure access, to fulfil legal obligations, to make decisions on reliable information, to guarantee transparency when making data available to the public.

Risk management is old, but it has developed strongly since the 1990s. In the banking sector, the Basel recommendations (1988) have made it possible to guarantee a minimum level of capital in order to ensure the financial soundness of each institution. The CRBF Regulation was introduced in 1997 to provide a framework for internal control with a set of obligations for credit institutions and investment firms. This trend has been reinforced and the regulations have been supplemented and now concern all sectors. The Enron affair in 2001 and the Andersen case in 2002 showed culpable practices of information manipulation, forgery and destruction of evidence. In 2002, the United States passed the Sarbanes-Oxley Act, named after its promoters, which includes, in addition to provisions concerning senior management, the obligation to implement internal control. This led to *risk management*, the formalization of processes, the identification of traces to be kept and their rigorous management. This law has had an international impact, with multinationals listed in the United States having to apply it. In France, the Financial Security Act of 2003 imposes new obligations on companies in terms of transparency and accuracy of accounts. This has led to the development of internal control, with audits and inspections and cost control. Each department is called upon to justify its activities, optimize its processes, measure its performance and reduce project completion times [HOL 15, p. 110].

In litigation in the United States, e-discovery is a formal process that allows both parties to a dispute to exchange information about the evidence to be presented at trial. It allows each party to review the other party's records in order to understand the thought process and anticipate what might happen at trial. A written request, called a *subpoena* through the court, is made by one party to ask the other party for certain information to prepare for the trial. The subpoena may require the CEO to attend the trial to talk about the litigation or to request all e-mails sent by the CEO on a particular date, about a specific product, or about certain information about the litigation [SAM 15].

E-discovery concerns records in electronic format. The information that the opposing party wishes to receive about the company could come from social networks, be provided in the traditional form of e-mail, or be stored in an external or internal cloud or on employees' devices. Information can come from anywhere, which implies knowing what records exist and where they are stored [SAM 15].

E-discovery became a legal term after its inclusion in the Federal Code of Civil Procedure in 2006. There is a section of the Federal Code of Civil Procedure that governs the production of electronic information, and how to communicate it to the opposing party. The Federal Code emphasizes both the preservation of information and the production of electronic information. Preservation does not only mean the preservation of an e-mail in its original format, but also the preservation of metadata such as the date of creation, the original IP address of the e-mail, possibly the date and the person responsible for deletion, all information that may be relevant in the context of litigation. The Federal Code of Civil Procedure imposes a very short deadline of 30 days from the date of receipt of the subpoena by the company to respond to an e-discovery request [SAM 15].

With digital records and the dematerialization of processes, the tools for managing records for operational use and as archives tend to be common. In the industrial field for large-scale construction projects, companies contract records to be delivered alongside physical deliveries, under threat of significant penalties. We then see the emergence of the Document Controller profession, also called a "technical documentation manager", who will monitor the delivery of records throughout the activity and ensure their management within the allotted time. Thus, the people who produce and share records will have them validated and distributed on a given date. The Document Controller intervenes well upstream and even before the records are created. It must optimize and improve the quality of this information to reduce the risks associated with poor record management. The risks are, for example, to work on a bad version of a record, an outdated, refused or non-validated version, or even worse, to be unable to access the information. The role of the Document Controller is to guarantee the correct respect of the procedures that he applies and that he makes apply to all the actors of the project. It ensures the quality of the record base so that all records are available, well identified, validated and that we have the traceability associated with these records always in a logic of litigation. The goal is not only to protect the company, but also to help the operational teams in their daily missions [DEC 15].

The Document Controller will check that all records correspond to the required model, with the right logos, and that all the coding elements at the bottom of the record ID card are filled in, thus guaranteeing the uniqueness of the record. If a single element is not good, the record is refused. At the end of the project, if the control methodology has been respected, all the records are complete, original, available and usable. They are all organized, classified according to the filing plan defined by the customer and all available validation certificates. This provides confirmation that all records have been approved, that they have been executed in accordance with the approval and, above all, that they will be handed over to the customer on time. This saves money and improves the client's image [DEC 15].

Record management is one of the vectors of risk control; the dematerialization of processes requires a precise management of the lifecycle of records and an ability to manage more and more digital records. Records management is more and more dependent on employees who must create, distribute and ensure the preservation of records useful to their activities in a context of information overload [HOL 15, p. 117].

The protection and enhancement of the information heritage, considered as all the data and valuable or historical knowledge of a natural or legal person, must be guaranteed throughout the lifecycle of the information. Indeed, it must be possible to be sure that it is indeed the authenticated person who is at the origin of the data sending and thus ensure data traceability. The information must also be available, with a guarantee of access without interruption or degradation and only to authorized persons. Finally, the value of information depends not only on its integrity over time, but also on its accuracy, relevance and validity [CAP 07, p. 8].

The ISO 15489 standard considers records management as part of the control of the risks of non-availability of information over time. Disclosure is the opposite danger, highlighted by information security policies. These risks are all the more numerous as information is abundant and on multiple media, as exchanges develop through networks that are difficult to control, and as the pressure of audits or the threat of litigation increases [CHA 12, p. 19].

The risk of not retrieving a record may be related to mismanagement because it was not archived or misidentified, or it was disposed of too quickly due to a lack of retention periods. On July 27, 2001, Reuters reported the case of University of Southern California neurobiologist Joseph Miller, who had asked NASA for access to some old data sent from Mars by the Viking probes in the mid-1970s. The 25-year-old tapes were in an unreadable format and the programmers who knew the software were long dead. Joseph Miller was looking for evidence of microbial life on Mars in this data, traces that had originally been classified as signs of "uninteresting chemical activity". He had to make do with the printed records that the NASA team at the time had saved, which contained only one-third of the original digital data.

The record may have remained in the cupboard or in the messaging system of its author or recipient, but it may also be because the record was never produced, because it was decided during a telephone conversation and was not traced, for example. Without a sufficient description, the record is drowned in the mass and escapes search. Changes made to the records may remove the evidential value of the archived record. This has become a concern with the digital and malleability of uncontrolled data. Not changing the records is both a matter of media and format quality and of controlling write access after the record has been put into the records management system. However, beware of records that have been kept for too long, which may turn out to be a burden when they could have been safely destroyed: an overly chatty e-mail about a questionable agreement or a report that mentions a probable manufacturing defect are examples that are not fiction [CHA 12, p. 20].

The causes of the non-availability of information include the disappearance or destruction of its support, poor identification or indexing, data corruption and lack of accessibility. The storage of obsolete records or outdated confidential records or even versions that are no longer up to date leads to additional costs and increases search problems. Some software publishers or hosting providers offer referencing, but during the migration of a tool or a new search engine, one can still access this data [CHA 18, p. 17].

Availability is defined as the ability of an information system to be available for use at any time and to keep up with expected performance. It has an impact on many professions, whether in the continuity of medical and hospital care, air traffic control, stock exchange trading rooms or industrial processes. For employees, high availability implies an immediate back-up site in the event of a disaster, including a new information system loaded with backups to quickly restart production in the disaster-stricken company [CAP 07, p. 10].

If you only want to ensure the continuity of a service, it will suffice to be able to host the IT team at a third party to temporarily restart the information system at the latter's premises with the *ad hoc* hardware and software. On the other hand, business continuity implies taking into account the continuity of IT and telecommunications services and hosting users to continue their activity. For example, a trading room must be rebuilt within four hours of the disaster.

The service or business continuity plan consists of a set of procedures, planning and directories (of staff and suppliers) for the restart of activity after a disaster at the information processing center or the building housing it. This requires good backups (backup copies), a functioning two-way telecommunications network, and a pre-tested back-up computer system that is compatible with the damaged system [CAP 07, p. 11].

The main purpose of security is to protect data from an external or internal threat that would lead to the destruction, corruption and disclosure of corporate information. It also prevents any unfortunate or accidental compromise of the integrity of corporate data. It therefore involves securing the record or file itself by means of electronic signature, encryption, anonymization and pseudonymization. The storage environment is protected by the electronic safe, biometric access to the storage rooms, and connection logs. However, it is necessary to remain reasonable as to the security measures, but ensure that the completeness of the secure perimeter is controlled. One does not seek perfection, but rather adequacy for the environment by understanding all of the risks and costs associated with decisions [CHA 18, pp. 42–43].

There are many threats to information. For example, the White House website was completely erased when George Bush became president. All speeches and official communications of the Clinton administration disappeared overnight. Much of this content had been backed up by the National Archives and Records Administration (NARA), which archived several versions of the site throughout the years of the Clinton presidency, but a large number of web links to this content hosted on other sites were broken.

Most often, the risk is linked to an event that has not yet occurred; it is a deferred risk that leads to considering archiving as an insurance. However, if this risk is not covered by a retention rule at the time of creation of the record, which is an easily identifiable moment, it is more difficult to do so *a posteriori*. How can we be sure that the record has not undergone changes that would call into question its authenticity and reliability if it has not been under control from the outset? If we wait until the managers of the record no longer need to consult it for day-to-day business to decide its future, there is a good chance that it will escape rigorous lifecycle management, or even be forgotten until the cabinet is moved or the workstation replaced [CHA 18, p. 122].

Files exchanged over computer networks may present an immediate risk of disclosure. This risk stems on the one hand from the confidential nature of certain records, and on the other hand from the possibility of distortion or misinterpretation of incomplete, imprecise or decontextualized information. This risk is multiplied tenfold by the malleability of digital material [CHA 18, p. 123].

We can focus on three major risk and cost issues. The lack of security, which requires us to check the capabilities of tools whose functional administration is not or only poorly coordinated at the global level of the company, such as office automation, messaging, collaborative spaces, smartphones. For paper volumes, care must be taken to avoid material damage due to water, fire or disclosure. For digital media, care must be taken to ensure appropriate media migration [CHA 18, p. 157]. The risks of data corruption and non-readability are higher for data encoding formats. The average durability of the formats is shorter than that of the carriers, which experts estimate at about five years. The variety of formats is extremely wide and not very standardized and they evolve very quickly. Audiovisual or 3D encoding formats are sometimes difficult to sustain. The lack of organization is due to the somewhat anarchic nature of the production of records resulting from certain activities that are less structured than others, with processes and operating methods divided into several geographical teams [CHA 18, p. 158].

From an IT point of view, the cost of storing redundant data is minor in relation to this security. However, it has disadvantages in that it increases the risk of disclosure if the confidentiality of the information is not managed. Similarly, the deletion and destruction of data that no longer need to be kept will be more delicate insofar as destroying the committing record by leaving copies of the same information accessible is not satisfactory. There is no substitute for human vigilance in the production of data and the proper qualification of files from the moment they are created [CHA 18, p. 160].

On the other hand, the human factor is a major risk, as it is often the cause of theft, breakdowns, operating errors, misdemeanors or malicious acts. The charter for the use of electronic communications is a functional compendium of the rules applicable to employees and external service providers when they use the computer resources and networks made available to them by the company. Emphasis should be placed on copyright, but also on the ban on communicating confidential data forming part of the company's information assets to other persons. This charter should include elements enabling the administration of evidence and computer traces which largely condition the relevance and effectiveness of the company's legal remedies, even for evidentiary purposes to exonerate it from liability. The charter may also include issues relating to the retention of connection data and the management of access to workstations and networks. In 2005, a Chinese trainee working for an automotive supplier was accused of copying data to her hard disk, which she took home with her. The IT administrator noticed an abnormal download of files and issued an alert. The company filed a complaint based on fraudulent access to an automated data system. However, the trainee justified her complaint by stating that a copy of the data was necessary for her internship report and that the data was fully accessible on the company's intranet [CAP 07, p. 35]. It is therefore understandable that it is important to integrate user awareness and accountability for the use of information resources at all levels. Security measures must be proportionate to the company's purpose. The company must ensure this change through awareness-raising and training actions. The charter must be enforceable against all employees and for this purpose it is essential to include it as an appendix to the employees' employment contract or to the company's internal regulations. Employee representative bodies must be consulted and informed of the decisions and technical means for monitoring employee activity [CAP 07, p. 34].

There are several ways to assess risk and identify the dangerousness of cases. For example, the New Brunswick provincial government uses four levels of security classification for the disclosure or loss of information and assets:

– unclassified records that have no effect on the business and whose disclosure may be beneficial to the public and the organization;

– records classified at a low level that have little impact and should not be released to the public;

– records classified at the medium level which may cause harm in particular to individuals concerning their private life or financial losses, or harm relations between partners and therefore need to be protected and must not be disclosed;

– highly classified records causing serious harm to citizens, corporations or employees, and could harm relationships between organizations and individuals that require special measures to be adequately protected. Disclosure is prohibited [APN 13, p. 28].

To adopt a good risk management policy, its probability and intensity will be assessed. When we talk about probability, there is a chance that it will happen. Losing information is more frequent than a fire starting in an archive storage room, for example. Intensity consists of evaluating the impact of the dangerous situation. It can be a loss of information caused by an employee or a malicious act. The intensity will be higher for the second case. Each company has a different vulnerability depending on its fragility in the face of the situation and the control it has to avoid the risks. The consequences may directly concern the company or its partners. The absence of an analysis report may present a difficulty for a client, but this will be less serious than not being able to provide proof of operation during a tax audit. The company's ability to reconstruct the missing information is also analyzed [NES 15b].

Risk analysis is a decision-making aid. It makes it possible to evaluate risks based on the information at the time of its possible disappearance and the consequences for the overall performance of the organization. It is carried out in several stages. First of all, the context of the situation is studied in relation to customer and regulatory requirements. We then move on to the processing of the risk, studying how to control it by implementing actions to respond either to the frequency or the intensity of the risk. All the actors directly concerned participate in the work and sometimes even the process pilots and not only the records management service [NES 15b].

A list of possible hazardous situations is listed, along with the causes and reasons why the objectives are not being met. A clear and comprehensible summary is then provided for all stakeholders to analyze at each stage whether the risk may or may not occur, whether it is serious or not, and whether it is frequent or not. All this information is rated according to severity and probability. We will use scales that must be discriminating so that there is no lack of decision. By prioritizing the criticality of risks, we check whether the risk is significant and almost certain, and conversely, whether a minor risk is insignificant and rare. For example, for the ability to have relevant information, three causes have been defined: not finding a record in the system, an absence of the record in the system and finally, no access to the system when outside the company. We will be able to assess the impact and seriousness of the situation [NES 15b].

Probability/Occurrence	Impact/Severity			
1 Almost certain	High	High	Review	Review
2 Probable	Moderate	High	Review	Review
3 Unlikely	Minor	Minor	High	High
4 Rare	Minor	Minor	High	High
	1 Not significant	2 Minor	3 Major	4 Very significant

Table 2.2. *Risk assessment for records management (source: [NES 15b])*

You can have significant criticality because of severe and immediate consequences on the functioning and performance of the organism, but you can also have significant criticality on a problem that will be a little less important in terms of intrinsic severity, but it occurs on a daily basis. A significant criticality will exist for an impact that is not the most important, but which has a very frequent, even systematic probability of occurrence and which requires the implementation of preventive or curative measures essential to prevent the occurrence of this risk [NES 15b].

We must plan how to correct the situation should this risk ever arise. Decisions are made to ensure technical control with an automatic backup as well as human control by having someone intervene as a backup every weekend. It is recognized that the residual risk will be greater with human control because naturally individuals may have a greater source of failure than the technique [NES 15b].

2.3.2. Technological dependence

Access to information presupposes the proper preservation of records, but also their restitution in digital form from technological systems which sometimes have long periods on their scale due to the rapid obsolescence of the materials. The problem of technological dependence linked to the reversibility of data is a crucial point which must be taken into account, otherwise the information will not be able to be restored. Thus, dissemination includes the notion of reversibility, that is, restitution with a view to reintegration into another preservation system [APR 06, p. 16].

According to ISO 27.001, security is the "preservation of the confidentiality, integrity and availability of information". Since information security is concerned with the continuity of services, it must ensure the reversibility of data over time [DEM 15, p. 118].

Companies need to be able to migrate their records from one system to another. "Reversibility" can be defined as the ability to return retained records and the data necessary to ensure the integrity and authenticity of records to their owners in a secure manner [VER 15, p. 17].

In the context of the retention of electronic records over time, "the risk of non-reversibility means, on the one hand, the inability of a system to restore records and, on the other hand, the inability to restore them in a way that guarantees their integrity and authenticity". This is a dependency that can lead to financial risk and loss of information [DEM 15, p. 122].

The non-reversibility of a system makes it necessary to keep it running regardless of its cost. If this is not possible, it will no longer be possible to have access to the integrity and authenticity of records or to use them to assert one's rights in the event of litigation. The company places this documentary risk at a high level of danger, since it may prevent the continuation of its activities [DEM 15, p. 122].

Faced with a non-reversible system, the company is faced with three choices: maintain an unsuitable or obsolete system, develop tools that make it possible to exit with partial losses, and accept the loss of records [VER 15, p. 17]. It is possible to combine palliative solutions, for example, by maintaining the system for several years to minimize the risk of records not being disposed of, or by developing tools only for records identified as major. However, these choices cannot be a satisfactory solution. To avoid finding ourselves in such a situation, it is essential to anticipate the risk of non-reversibility at each phase of an information system project [VER 15, p. 17].

In the event of a dispute, it is important to be able to return an electronic record in a readable form that is preserved from any alteration. A lawsuit may be lost, or a less favorable judgment obtained, if the records are lost or illegible or unconvincing or have lost their integrity. A record may also be void for lack of form or deemed to be non-existent if it has not been prepared in accordance with certain rules of validity, including electronic signatures. These form requirements must be met when the record is created and remain unaltered throughout its lifecycle [DEM 15, p. 123].

In addition to litigation before the courts, companies must regularly provide records in the context of controls or investigations carried out by a competent authority in the fields of taxation, social law, hygiene and the environment. A tax adjustment is to be feared if supporting records, in particular invoices, used to establish the tax base are not kept or if their integrity and authenticity are questioned. The supervisory authority may also have the power to impose criminal or administrative fines if the records required by law have not been kept [DEM 15, p. 123].

Thus, reversibility in which standardization work is yet to be done implies a proactive organization consisting of permanently ensuring the extraction capacity in a secure environment. The risks usually encountered concern data from a GED, a human resources system or an electronic archiving system; they are *a priori* the following:

– a loss of records, metadata or research indexes;

– the impossibility of re-reading the format of the record due to encryption or missing font or duplication of extracted records, because several indexes point to a record;

– risks to the integrity of the record in a file;

– a breach in confidentiality of access related to the record;

– high costs and long migration time.

These risks must also be covered contractually with suppliers and partners with clearly defined obligations and expected service levels. Record retrieval requires the elements necessary for their exploitation: the metadata of the records, which describe the context, history and documentation of the system where they are kept; the history and documentation of the migration out of the system; the links between all the records and data restored to make all the information usable [DEM 15, p. 125].

It should also be noted that the reversibility operated with a third party archiver may involve the communication by the latter of information that it has itself generated from the data, as well as documentation on its internal procedures (migration, security, etc.). The service provider may hold rights to this information, which is part of its know-how and which it may be reluctant to communicate, especially if the data is going to be entrusted to a competitor. It is particularly important to anticipate reversibility when a contract is concluded with a third party, whether it is to collaborate in the installation of an internal electronic archiving system (EAS) or to provide a third-party archiving service. In order to guarantee and preserve the legal value of a record, it is therefore necessary to ensure that quality records are maintained with an EAS that preserves their integrity and authenticity, which also implies ensuring the reversibility of data. It is also crucial to record transfers and to keep this information with the electronic records [DEM 15, pp. 126–127].

The attention paid to reversibility when negotiating with a third party archiver may also have a preventive effect, encouraging the provider not to make light-hearted promises about the reversibility of the system. The contract should clearly stipulate who is the owner of the stored data. It seems relatively obvious that the retained records remain the property of the client who has entrusted them to the provider, but it is preferable to specify in the contract that the provider has no right of retention of the data and must return them at the end of the contract, in the manner provided for, whatever the reason. The contract should also specify the elements to be returned, first of all the records and their metadata, but also all the data which make it possible to guarantee the integrity and authenticity of the records [DEM 15, p. 134].

Once the transfer has been completed, it is important to allow time to check that the records and all the data provided by the customer have been returned and that all the necessary information is present. In addition, the service provider is required to destroy all copies of records in his possession within a specified period of time and to provide a certificate of destruction. In addition, it is estimated that the average time to change service providers in order to obtain better offers is about five years. The contractual framework for such a situation may make it difficult to define the responsibilities of successive providers in the event of the system not being reversible [DEM 15, p. 135].

It is imperative to have complete and accurate documentation of the system, otherwise the authenticity and integrity of the records and the understanding of the system and thus the events that occurred will be lost. Furthermore, it is also the system documentation that will help to understand the information architecture and to predict precisely what should be implemented for a successful migration [DEM 15, p. 137].

As part of the technical and functional evaluation of solutions, the first requirement is to check with the supplier whether the solution envisaged is reversible. If the answer is negative, the solution must be discarded even if it meets the company's business needs in a positive way; otherwise it is exposed to risks [DEM 15, p. 138].

The second requirement is the assignment of a unique identifier to each record and batch of records. Assigned in the form of metadata, these identifiers must be returned with the record when it leaves the system. It should also be checked that the solution is based on the unique identifiers to track each event. The absence of the use of unique identifiers means that the solution is, in fact, not reversible and should be discarded [DEM 15, p. 138].

Next, it should be checked whether the system is capable of retrieving the desired elements, including the records, their metadata, logs of every event and development that has occurred in the records themselves and in the operation of the system, and system documentation. If one of its elements is not retrievable, this also amounts to a lack of reversibility [DEM 15, p. 138].

Finally, restitution formats must be open and documented and correspond to the expected s-formats before or after migration to ensure their sustainability [DEM 15, p. 139].

Once the information to meet these four requirements has been collected, it is advisable to check that it is correct. The first step is to check the system documentation or the proposal received, making sure that the technical descriptions correspond to the recommendations of the cited norms and standards. The second step is to test the ability to return the elements [DEM 15, p. 139].

The test must be conducted using data rich enough to verify the correct restitution of elements in cases where the metadata of the records has been modified during the lifecycle, signed records, time-stamped records, consulted records, format migration and system evolutions [DEM 15, p. 140].

A system is not immutable and can evolve. They have several origins, including technological developments at the functional or technical layer; applications; legal or regulatory developments; the integration of new services; and an evolution of the use of the system compared to the initial intended use [DEM 15, p. 141].

Great care must be taken during system setup, system life and system output to benefit from better reversibility. Certain factors will guarantee an adequate system:

– knowledge of technical and functional evolutions such as the use of PDF/A, or XML formats; adoption of a system based on the OAIS standard;

– the adequacy between the evolutions and the use of the system. The documentary perimeter must be absolutely clear so as not to deal with records that are outside this perimeter or forget about them;

– a balance between risk control and costs: it is absolutely necessary to manage a risk picture;

– throughout the life of the solution, monitor the technological and economic developments that are affected by the solution.

Provision should be made for documenting each stage of the migration and for ensuring that each operation is carried out correctly by means of tests to verify that what is recovered corresponds to what was to be recovered, while maintaining the appropriate level of security. Be careful not to restore records that can be deleted during a migration, as there is a risk of possibly recovering records that have been deleted. It is also necessary to define the conditions for testing the migration as well as the conditions for the destruction of the elements after migration to the old system and to the intermediate system if this solution has been chosen [DEM 15, p. 143].

In short, migration will be managed as a project in its own right. The needs analysis and the specifications will have to integrate the issue of reversibility and the migration plan will have to define at least the elements to be retrieved (records, metadata, links, etc.); the restitution modalities (the attribution of a unique identifier to the migration batch, the physical security conditions, etc.); and the migration plan will have to define at least the following: the elements to be retrieved (records, metadata, links, etc.); the restitution modalities (the attribution of a unique identifier to the migration batch, the physical security conditions, etc.); and the migration plan will have to define at least the following elements: the elements to be retrieved (records, metadata, links, etc.); the destruction procedures; the procedures for transfer to the new system (recovery of all metadata, history of past events, etc.); and the test procedures (checking that everything is transferred before destruction, and then destroyed) [VER 15, p. 18].

2.4. The management and conservation of e-mails

According to the Radicati Group's estimates in its statistical report, 2015–2019, the number of e-mails sent and received per day is 205 billion and businesspeople send or receive an average of 122 messages per day, compared to no more than 33 messages per day in 2011. In relation to the role they play, organizations do not always give them the necessary attention despite the importance of the information they contain, as can be seen from the scandals and trials in the Enron and Wikileaks cases that have been the subject of e-mails sent or updated.

After these cases, the American legislator concluded that it was necessary to archive electronic mail. When Enron, one of the largest American companies by market capitalization in the natural gas sector, went bankrupt in December 2001, the reason was related to heavy losses caused by speculative transactions and account make-up. The former CEO of Enron was sentenced to 24 years in prison, which were eventually reduced to 14 years. At the time of the investigation by the US government, hundreds of thousands of e-mails, written by about 100 employees from 1998 and 2002, were analyzed and made public. As a result, the Sarbanes-Oxley Act requires companies not only to archive all e-mails, but also to have a specific standardized tool that allows authorized government officials to consult and search any e-mail. This has been introduced in Europe by US software companies under the term "legal" archiving, but in fact this archiving is only mandatory and legal for US companies or those listed on a US stock exchange. UK law has also chosen the same path as US law.

In business or commercial law, the evidence is free. Most of the records produced by lawyers before judges are e-mails or records consisting of printed office or business computer files that can themselves be attached to e-mails. This shows the importance of the proper preservation for their evidential value of the records established by the computer systems whatever they may be and first and foremost the messages and their attached records.

Validation is the act that completes a record and freezes it at a given point in time. It can be a handwritten or electronic signature or simple initials. Posting a record on a website, a supplier platform or an intranet is also a means of validating information for the recipients even if it leaves no trace on the record itself. An electronic message sent to a customer or supplier by an employee who does not have the authority or authorization to do so may bind the company through the domain name in the issuer's electronic address [CHA 18, p. 30]. If the e-mail is created and maintained by the central server, if the indication of certain metadata is mandatory, if the e-mail account refers to the employee's function and not to his or her name (Directeur-General@EnergieNB.ca) the successor will inherit it.

In fact, the conditions for validation concern only legal acts in civil law, subject to the legal evidence regime, and not legal facts, for which the evidence remains free, which explains recent case law accepting as evidence e-mails that are not electronically signed. In areas of law other than civil law, the evidence is also free [MES 15, p. 144]. Thus, e-mail may be admissible as evidence in certain circumstances. The contents of e-mails could be disclosed to the opposing party in litigation and be highly prejudicial to the author or the author's employer. For example, the production of an e-mail in cross-examination could show that the witness made prior inconsistent statements [GAG 15, p. 19].

E-mail has always come from a particular context, and is often the hallmark of a transaction. E-mails interact with each other, and can interact with other records: we will find links, attachments. E-mails have metadata, information that is external to the record, but which paradoxically is part of it, which describes them and which can sometimes give them evidentiary value: a date or a name, for example.

E-mails have a higher legal value than scanned paper mail that is only a scanned image. Its content is not analyzed; the actual date, author and place of filing of the paper record are only known if they have been the subject of a specific seizure. It is necessary to add control data during scanning to ensure a link with the original record, which is not always simple. An e-mail is a record that is created and transmitted directly in digital form, but during the creation and transmission of this record, data is added that is not all directly visible, but which helps to guarantee its integrity, authenticity and traceability. These are the metadata, in particular: date and time linked to the record (start of creation, sending, passage through the various routing servers, reception, opening of the record), unalterable order number, control key enabling the detection of alterations to the text transmitted and to the metadata, identification of the stations and the sending and receiving servers. Under these conditions, a simple e-mail is more convincing than ordinary mail, or even registered mail.

Some of the advantages of e-mail include the speed of real-time message traffic; the ability to send a message even if the recipient is not logged in and for the recipient to view the message based on its availability; ease of use and operation on virtually any type of device; free to users; the ability to set up mailing lists; the ability to track messages and send attachments; and the ability to reuse messages in messaging or other systems [BIS 13, p. 81].

However, messaging has considerably amplified the phenomenon of information overload. Processing is often time-consuming, it can be difficult to prioritize, and it is not always the best means of communication. Employees can abuse messages by multiplying the number of exchanges and interlocutors copied. Controlling the volume of information processed by each employee is one of the major concerns of companies, for technical, economic and social reasons [MIN 13, p. 24]. Moreover, e-mail is the first and main vector for the spread of computer viruses.

The overabundance of e-mail causes significant time loss when searching for information and the risk of stress increases, even leading to the loss of spatial and temporal reference points and a paradoxical decrease in productivity. According to columnist Olivier Schmouker, in an article in the November 2011 issue of *Les Affaires*, "Sixty-four seconds is the average time it takes to get back to your train of thought when you are interrupted by the arrival of a message". That's why turning off notifications of new audio and visual messages helps concentration. Approximately 65% of employees say they check their e-mail inbox every hour, but in reality it's more like every five minutes. In order to be more efficient in their work, users plan one to three time slots devoted to consulting and processing messages. If you are absent from the office for more than two days, it is advisable to activate the office absence manager [BIS 13, p. 83].

Unnecessary duplication of the same record sent to many users requires double management and takes up storage space. Identical e-mails are kept by multiple employees in different locations and on multiple media (file servers, mail system, SD cards, USB sticks, DVDs, CDs, hard drives on desktop and laptop computers, physical folders, etc.) [BIS 13, p. 80].

Although most e-mails are of ephemeral interest, when e-mails are left in mailboxes rather than in a common space, only the recipients can view them. Information or additional information is then not known or accessible to others. This can hamper collaboration and lead to the loss of crucial information such as contracts or answers to a customer. In addition, in the event of a change in personnel, such as the departure of an employee, there is a considerable increase in the risk of losing information and knowledge [BIS 13, p. 79].

Data confidentiality is random. We often compare an e-mail with a postcard where the postman or other people can read it because nothing is hidden. Confidential data stored in e-mail spaces is exposed and is at risk of being lost or exploited in an ill-intentioned manner. As Quebec law states, information must be destroyed once the purpose for which it was collected has expired. "Every person carrying on an enterprise must take security measures to ensure the protection of personal information that is collected, used, communicated, retained or destroyed and that are reasonable in light of, among other things, its sensitivity, the purpose for which it is used, its quantity, distribution and medium" (RLRQ, chapter P-39.1, art 10).

The right to privacy may, however, be subject to limitations that are only acceptable if certain principles are respected. In order to be legal, the interference must be provided for by a standard. It must be clear, precise and accessible. A regulation or an employment contract may suffice. Consent may in some cases be required, and data may not be disclosed without specific justification. Case law has clarified that privacy in the workplace includes respect for the secrecy of correspondence and its inviolability. Messages exchanged between colleagues may be recognized as private and therefore be covered by the principle of secrecy of correspondence, in particular in the event of denigration of a superior [MIN 13, p. 18].

The purpose must also have a legitimate aim such as the prevention of offenses, respect for morals or respect for the rights and freedoms of others. A charter aimed at preventing fraud and corruption of a computer system may be considered legitimate, the purpose being compliance with legislation on archives. The measure must be proportionate to the aim pursued and limited to what is strictly necessary. It must be verified whether the aim pursued by the interference cannot be achieved by non-intrusive measures. Case law emphasizes that the employer's control over its employees' mailboxes must be proportionate to the aim pursued. The employer may thus exercise control only when confronted with suspicious behavior on the part of his employee [MIN 13, p. 19].

Finally, the principle of transparency insists on the fact that, in the event of a dispute with one of its employees, the employer can only resort to evidence obtained through processes made known to its employees. The collection of personal data in the context of control operations cannot take place without the employee's knowledge. Otherwise, the company is liable for failure to comply with the obligation of transparency [MIN 13, p. 18]. Similarly, any person may have access to the archives concerning him or her and may also correct, modify or delete any erroneous or false information concerning him or her [MIN 13, p. 21].

The real difficulties often lie in finding the relevant information to be archived and selecting it in the midst of what most often looks like bulk information with no internal organization. Any e-mail retention program must be based on a solid understanding of user preferences and behaviors. The professional literature agrees that personal messages; spam; broadcast discussions or e-mail; messages received for information; copies or excerpts of broadcast records that do not lead to follow-up by the organization; notices that are not related to a professional activity; so-called transitory messages and drafts should not be archived. Only messages, sent and received, that have informational and/or legal value for the organization should be retained [MIN 13, p. 32].

E-mails with ephemeral administrative primary value constitute the majority of an organization's internal e-mails. It relates to records generated in the day-to-day operations of the organization, such as routine correspondence. We also find: a request for a copy of a record; an appointment, an invitation; an internal memorandum and memorandum, except those related to specific files; copies of e-mails, including those received as a certified copy and those generated by transfers to other recipients; and bulletins or circulars received[4].

E-mails generated and received with a primary administrative, financial and legal value as well as a potential secondary value are stored and archived. These records must be kept for a longer period of time given the needs of the organization, the laws governing these records, or the legacy dimension they may have in the future. General evaluation criteria will include e-mail elements that document the organization's decision-making and activities. They support the organization's reporting, results and accountability requirements [BIS 13, p. 87].

These are therefore e-mails that reflect official positions and actions, decision-making, business transactions, and measures adopted by the organization. They provide evidence of rights and obligations. They document and contain information about the organization's projects, policies and transactions. They provide information on the development and implementation of reports, studies, and

---

4 Bibliothèque et Archives nationales du Québec, *Orientations pour la gestion documentaire des courriels au gouvernement du Québec*, January 2009, available at: https://www.banq.qc.ca/documents/archives/archivistique_ged/publications/Orientations_Gestion_courriels_gouv_Quebec.pdf.

position papers. They acknowledge receipt of a report or information under a regulation (Bibliothèque et Archives nationales du Québec, 2009).

We can have rules that set out how long individual e-mails must be kept. Depending on the time considered, the archiving system will contain various messages and, over time, the number of these messages will decrease. As long as it can be demonstrated that the deleted messages have been deleted in accordance with the organization's policy and that no messages, which did not originally exist, are in the system, the completeness of the system has been demonstrated [ICA 05, p. 40].

As far as e-mail management is concerned, simple solutions are possible by using good practices, but this requires the collaboration of people who need to be aware of the right procedures. These good practices assist in the removal of unnecessary records and the management of the record lifecycle, thus contributing to easier and more efficient retrieval of information. It is important to define a policy on e-mail management in collaboration with managers, since their support is essential to establish the credibility of the procedures put in place.

When replying or resending a message, do not hesitate to change the subject to make it more relevant and thus avoid being filtered by spam. Avoid subjects with overly general headings such as "Signing of contract", "Agenda for the meeting", "To be read immediately". A more complete object makes it easier to file and decide whether or not to keep it, such as "Report: Student Recruitment Record Management 2019–20, Final Version" or "Board of Directors: Agenda 2012-05-16". When several topics are mentioned, it is preferable to write several e-mails to facilitate their filing rather than integrating several topics in the same e-mail [BIS 13, p. 90].

To avoid	What to do
Legal basis estimated by the Board	Legal basis on the height of the front steps estimated by the Caraquet town council.
Signature record	Signing of the 2019–2020 snow removal contract.
Agenda for the meeting	Agenda of the Board of Directors 2012-05-16.
Read immediately	Validation of Jacques Losier's employment contract urgent.
Final Report	Market study on the creation of a commercial space in Tracadie in 2020.

Table 2.3. *Examples of e-mail subject matter*

It is important to choose the recipient of the messages carefully so as not to overwhelm those who do not need it. The e-mail writer should limit the number of key recipients, as they will be expected to respond. People who receive a cc copy of an e-mail do not have to respond or take any action. They receive it for information purposes only, so mailing lists should be used sparingly [BIS 13, p. 90].

Attachments add to the storage space for courier services. They should be attached as a priority when sending information externally. By preferring a message with the link to the record, the record is no longer duplicated; the system simply points to it to notify your correspondents. However, these links can only be used if the space where the record is located is accessible and not protected by special access rights. Note that if the record is moved, the link is broken [BIS 13, p. 84].

It is advisable to integrate the e-mail system into the general electronic record management (EDM) system where messages are placed in their appropriate place. If the producer does not have an EDM, all e-mails should be given their archival identifier that links them to other records in the same case and a directory structure synchronized with the archival filing plan should be created. Appendices are often a major management concern because of the variety of s-formats. They should be kept separate from the messages with the metadata indicating the links or converted to a standard format such as XML [KEC 14, p. 178].

In 2005, ISO-19005-1 approved the standard for the electronic archiving of records and the file format of electronic records for long-term preservation. The file format is "based on PDF12, known as PDF/A, which provides a mechanism for representing electronic records that preserves their visual appearance over time, regardless of the tools and systems used to create, store and render the files" [PDF 05, BIS 13, p. 91]. In addition to being a format that guarantees the permanence and integrity of information, it also allows for optical character recognition (OCR) for full-text searching. The Adobe Acrobat 5 tool and subsequent versions can produce PDF/A format. Free virtual printer software can also produce records in PDF/A format. One example is PDFCreator, which is a German open source software. It works in the same way as traditional printers. It allows the addition of metadata and the use of the PDF/A-1b storage format [BIS 13, p. 91].

The PDF/A format should be used to save e-mails for the sake of information integrity and continuity. Since the legal value is increased by preserving the link between the attachment and the message, an e-mail with an attachment can be retained, either:

– by using the Acrobat Pro tool, which allows you to group an e-mail with its attachment into a single record and the attachment remains accessible; by keeping the e-mail in native format during its active life and filing it in the record warehouse. Eventually, a PDF/A migration strategy is applied;

– by migrating from native format to XML. This "open" format makes it possible to use e-mail through various applications;

– by naming the e-mail and the attachment identically when saving as separate PDF/A files, if no tool is available to link them [BIS 13, p. 92].

It is not recommended to keep e-mails in HTML format since it does not preserve the e-mail header identifying the recipient, sender, subject line, date and time of dispatch, nor does it preserve the PST format. PST files are personal folder files associated with Microsoft's e-mail system that allow messages to be stored on the user's computer workstation. They can be easily corrupted if they are close to their maximum size. The MSG format is also discouraged as it does not guarantee the long-term readability and accessibility of e-mail [BIS 13, p. 93].

File names should include the following elements, for example: the sender's name or the name of the person to whom the e-mail was sent; the subject; the date; if the e-mail is external, include "received". There is no need to include this if it is obvious that the record is external, such as in a submission e-mail [BIS 13, p. 94].

The file name of an e-mail attachment should include the name of the sender, an indication of the subject, the date of the correspondence, the attachment itself and an indication of the number of attachments.

Example: Mairie_Tracadie_Centre_Culturel_Soummission_2009_pj2.pdf

In case it is not necessary to keep the e-mail, only the attachment will be kept. If it is necessary to keep both the e-mail and the attachment on the network, the records will have to be saved separately, but the file names will have to provide an element that can link them. It is usually appropriate to organize these elements in the same order as it is likely that the e-mail and its attachment will be identified by the correspondent. Using this form of naming, if records are sorted by name in the browser, the associated records will appear next to each other in the list [BIS 13, pp. 95–96].

Examples: Mairie_Tracadie_Centre_Culturel_Soummission_2009.pdf

Mairie_Tracadie_Centre_Culturel_Soummission_2009_pj.pdf

The Interpares group recommends that in archiving operations, attention be paid to the degree of integrity and authenticity of e-mail messages. Any record sent by e-mail should therefore be integrated into the archiving system as a separate entity (uniqueness). Any message with documentary value must have a unique identifier in the records management system and must be classified and associated with a retention period and disposition. The sender address must correspond to an identifiable person. Where the link between an individual and an address is made by an external tool (database, spreadsheet), this must be maintained and taken into account when developing the archiving strategy. Particular attention should be paid to mailing lists to enable the identification of the persons included in them. Context must be preserved. For example, all header information must be included, along with the date and time stamp with the dates of dispatch, receipt, and possibly the time, which must be integrated into the metadata profile[5] [MIN 13, pp. 43–44].

2.5. Conclusion

Record management standards have greatly contributed to repositioning professionals in the field within a regulatory and administrative framework rather than a historical one, and they are valued by decision-makers.

The ISO standard 15489 of the records management differs from the classical archiving by a difference of viewpoint. The first approach is from the point of view of the producing organization, the proof and the preservation of immediate rights. Its mandate is to take charge of all records produced or received by organizations from their creation to their final preservation or disposal and to optimize information management by facilitating access, consultation, dissemination and archiving of records and the information they contain. The second approach is on the side of history and the preservation of rights over the long term. It focuses on the secondary value of the records that are sought to be identified and preserved among the mass of current archives produced.

The 30300 series of standards, which is a management standard intended for the implementation of records management systems, is complementary to ISO 15489, which it reinforces, because it is at the level of information governance. The ISO 30300 framework now makes it possible to establish a fully consistent and recognized record governance approach in collaboration with teams of legal, quality, audit and internal control specialists, as well as information system managers. Spain is the most advanced in the implementation of ISO 30301.

Discretion must be exercised, however, as there may be a temptation to apply a standard at any cost out of ease or comfort or ignorance or difficulty in judging the value of such an approach. Some operations are the result of a succession of intellectual operations and techniques and methodologies should not be put at the

---

5 In the 1990s there was a lot of archiving of faxes which had legal value. They are rarely used now. The e-mail problem is similar when it comes to the question of form, which is not suitable for preservation.

center of decisions, forgetting the knowledge and skills acquired through individual and collective experience.

However, these standards will support the implementation of record policy to validate the records and preserve the authenticity, integrity, reliability and use of digital records. Without early processing, they will lose their context of creation and they will not have good metadata for proper identification which will make them difficult to archive.

In addition, risk management has become paramount, as there are many threats to information. These include loss of confidentiality, loss of integrity or data, unavailability or inaccessibility of engaging records or simply records lost through misfiling or mismanagement. Added to this is the problem of technological dependency linked to the reversibility of data which can lead to the inability to restore information.

A good example is e-mail, which is now a must in all organizations. Its use can lead to serious problems when the system is poorly managed and archived and can reduce the productivity of the company and engage it in ruinous lawsuits.

3

Appraisal and Classification

The length of time for which records are kept is a sometimes complex subject, but it is a recurring issue in any records policy. It is therefore necessary to be able to assess the relevance of records in order to define the interest in retaining or disposing of them. Appraisal is a prior archival function to determine the administrative utility, historical interest, retention period and ultimate disposition of records. The aim is to determine which records need to be retained for the long term, which implies a longer period of time than the system in which they were created. The aim is to assess the value of the records for future needs. When creating new systems, it is essential to know even before the design and implementation phase whether the records that will be created in the system have archival value in order to target the specific requirements for their retention.

The key to electronic archiving is the mastery of metadata. It requires an intervention from the creation of records, at the time of the deployment of business applications. Recordkeeping metadata can be used to recognize, authenticate and contextualize records and the people, processes and systems that create, manage, maintain and use them. In order to properly archive records, there is a need to identify metadata, including business contextualization metadata, and ensure that it is properly recorded and maintained with the record. "There is a shift from control of records, i.e., the process of collection, to control of metadata, i.e., the process of records creation" [GUY 15c, p. 100].

Good naming of digital files and folders has definite advantages for filing, searching and sharing information, whereas often the recording of records is entrusted to the agents producing the records, who are left free to name the files they create or receive according to their logic. In the event of misnaming, the records may be archived under the wrong versions or misfiled or simply inaccessible for lack of identification.

Also, even if the filing plan is making a strong comeback in professional recommendations, particularly for the ISO 15489 standard, it may be difficult to implement it if the records are difficult to identify. However, the filing plan is the cornerstone of the electronic archiving system. Therefore, the logical and rational organization of records produced and received by an organization is a recommended practice for the smooth running of its activities. Whether these records are printed or digital, the management of archives cannot be left to everyone's whim. Creating and implementing a filing plan is one of the core activities of an organization's records management, along with the record appraisal that precedes it.

3.1. Appraisal

3.1.1. Definition and purpose

According to Carol Couture, appraisal is seen as "the act of judging the values of archival records (primary and secondary values) and deciding on the periods of time over which those values apply to the records in a context that takes into account the essential link between the organization (or person) and the archival records it generates in the course of its business"[1].

The stakes for the appraisal are very high, as computer specialists are generally convinced that exhaustive conservation is not a problem, since the servers have sufficient space. Unfortunately, this view rarely goes beyond 10 years. Keeping everything without appraisal has never been a solution and involves a high cost in the long term. Researchers need intelligent archives, including knowing the sources and what practices and processes produced them, hence the importance of contextualizing records, especially when the records are hosted in the cloud. The notions of provenance, context and respect for holdings are relevant to understanding history and ensuring the origin of data [DUN 15, p. 183].

Appraisal is the noble function, the hard knot of contemporary archiving. As such, it requires a highly scientific preparation and an uncommon quality of judgment on the part of the specialist. The act of judging the values of records is a great challenge. Some people believe that all that is needed to do this is to know the origin and context of the creation. Others rely instead on the use of archives. In fact, it is a matter of encompassing all these elements in the organization of archives: their context of creation and their use by administrations or researchers [COU 97, p. 20].

---

1 Couture, Carol *et al.*, *Les fonctions de l'archivistique contemporaine,* Presses de l'université du Québec, p. 104, 2005.

The notion of archival appraisal was first introduced during the French Revolution with the creation of the *"bureau des triages"* (June 25, 1794). This notion is fundamental insofar as it is almost impossible to preserve the entirety of the archives produced or received by an organization. In this context, appraisal makes it possible to ensure the necessary sorting in order to preserve only those records with secondary or historical and heritage value. However, in the Anglophone and Francophone traditions, there is a discrepancy in the notion of selection. For Francophones, they control all current and intermediate production without any idea of *a priori* selection which will take place at the end of the period of administrative utility in order to conserve records of heritage value. On the other hand, records management focuses exclusively on preserving the quality of a record's evidence, while archiving also focuses on preserving the heritage value with specific constraints for long-term preservation [BAN 09, p. 43].

The first country to take an interest in appraisal was Germany, but with the objective of better conservation. This first approach takes into account the heritage and long-term aspects of conservation by considering archives as evidence. In 1937, after having imposed an inventory of records as early as 1927, the Germans used the content and hierarchical position of the creator organization as a basis for assessing the age of the records. Thereafter, approaches differed depending on whether they were adopted by the West or by Marxist thinking in the East. In 1972, the German archivist Hans Booms questioned the hierarchical importance of the creative organism, refuted the weight of use and demand for preservation, and denied the Marxist scale of values. It is society as a whole to which archives must bear witness. He develops several ideas, including the need for a thorough knowledge of the organization or person who produced the archive; the consideration of the scale of values contemporary to the period of creation of the records. Appraisal should provide as much information as possible in as few records as possible [COU 97, pp. 5–6].

The second approach is led by England, which evaluates to eliminate, because it is a matter of looking after administrative, financial and short-term interests by gaining space. This approach was developed beginning in 1875 and, as early as 1877, the Public Record Office Act confirmed the power to dispose of records no longer of use, but the Act excluded the appraisal of records prior to 1715. It was increased to 1660 from 1898. For Hilary Jenkinson, the archivist is a good servant more than a decision-maker, servant of the records he preserves and servant of the researcher to whom he provides the most relevant records [COU 97, p. 9].

In an effort to dispose of the masses of records quickly, Great Britain, with the Grigg Committee formed in 1952, proposed a two-stage appraisal in which concerns about administrative use and historical research were taken into account. Five years after their creation, it was proposed that only the administrative value of the records be judged. The aim is to rapidly eliminate between 50% and 70% of the records generated by an administration. Twenty-five years after the first appraisal, only the remaining records will be judged for their evidentiary value and only 10–20% will be retained [COU 97, pp. 9–10].

As early as the 1930s, American archivists were seduced by the English approach, which they saw as a means of disposing of records. But in 1940, Philipp Brooks opposed it and put forward two basic ideas: the elimination of duplicates and the importance of defining what permanent value is. It is based on three criteria: the value the records have to the originating institution; the usefulness of the records to the administrative history of the institution; and the historical value of the records [COU 97, p. 10].

In 1946, Philip Bauer proposed to consider the use and costs involved in the acquisition and preservation of archives. He saw four types of uses: by government institutions; for the protection of citizens' rights; for serious research; and to satisfy the curiosity of genealogists or scholars [COU 97, p. 10].

Starting in the 1960s, an American archivist, Theodore Schellenberg, became another master thinker in the field. He defined two essential concepts that are still agreed upon today: primary and secondary value. While he links the first to legal, financial and administrative aspects, he sees two components to the second: evidential value in the historical sense and informational value [COU 97, p. 10].

Records of evidential value are those which inform about the position of the unit in the hierarchy; the function of the unit in the institution; and the activities underlying the function are those records which are essential to the administrative history of the institution. Records of research value are those which provide insight into people, significant events and history. This importance is related to the uniqueness and richness of the information and the number and diversity of users [COU 97, pp. 10–11].

In 1970, the Society of American Archivists (SAA) commissioned a manual on various archival functions, including appraisal. Maynard J. Brichford wrote the manual, which contains basic considerations in archival appraisal:

– characteristics of the records (age, volume, form, function, evidence and information characteristics);

– administrative values (primary value which is legal, financial and administrative);

– research values (uniqueness, credibility, readability, age, physical accessibility; frequency, type and quality of use);

– archival values (how the records relate to each other and considerations of the cost of preservation and storage).

In 1992, Terry Cook developed macro-appraisal. It was created for needs analysis, that is, the study of the institution and the knowledge of the context of creation. In practical terms, it asks why and how records were created rather than their content; how they were used by the original creators rather than their future use; the mandates and functions exercised by the creators; and the testimony of the records rather than an analysis of the internal structures or physical characteristics of the records [COU 97, p. 13].

Carol Couture sees macro-appraisal as a first step in appraisal centered on a thorough knowledge of the creator of the information. This stage must primarily reflect the preferred mechanisms that unite the individual to the society around him. Micro-appraisal is the actual appraisal of the records with the realization of the shelf life schedule. It is a generic concept that encompasses all approaches to evaluating archival records based on the information they contain. At the same time, Hugh Taylor was involved in the development of appraisal in Canada with objectives ranging from the elimination of the ephemeral (England) to the preservation of the permanent (Germany) [COU 97, p. 13].

Thus, Terry Cook focused on the creative institution to prioritize the appraisal process as a first step, bringing an important nuance to the appraisal process. In fact, when he wants to get to know the institution better, it is not to establish *a priori* the value of the records produced according to the relative hierarchical importance of that institution. Rather, the purpose of this institutional knowledge is to enable the archivist to prioritize the institutions in order to propose an appraisal plan. Terry Eastwood questions the utilitarian approach. What is the point of trying in vain to predict future uses of the archives? It is better to study and understand the uses of archives at the time of their creation [COU 97, p. 16].

Finally, macro-appraisal is a comprehensive appraisal strategy developed in the late 1980s at the National Archives of Canada and officially launched government-wide in 1991. It is the social context of records creation and their contemporary use, not their anticipated use, that determines their relative value. It is based on the analysis of the major functions and activities of a government or organization (functional analysis). It focuses on citizens and seeks to document the citizen's relationship with the state, or the client's relationship with a business or organization. This strategy is being challenged and a new approach called the "pan-societal model" is proposed. It aims to record society as a whole and should, according to Daniel Caron, "be based on research, analysis and scientific principles essentially supported by the discourse that informs sociological theory. Macro-appraisal, however, remains a source of reference and some elements of continuity are present in the new recordkeeping methodology" [COU 14, p. 129].

The need for early appraisal is vital in a digital environment, as information about the technological context, much of which is contained in the systems themselves, cannot be found or reconstructed even a short time after the systems have reached the end of their lives. Without this technological context, it is difficult to assess the authenticity of such records, to establish the feasibility of preserving and understanding them in the future [COU 14, p. 134].

It is therefore necessary to identify and then select at a very early stage the records that are essential for the conduct of activities and the preservation of the organization's memory, in order to secure them. The selection focuses on the records consulted and therefore still mastered by the producers. Then, with them, criteria are defined to automatically select useful records. This could be a term used in the naming of a file or the heading of the filing plan. Consequently, the selection criteria are defined with the producer *a priori*, according to his needs and the risks linked to his activity. They are no longer the result of a systematic analysis of the records [MAN 15, p. 298]. It would seem that Catherine Bailey is credited with the first theory on digital records in 1988, in which she reaffirmed the usefulness of the principles of appraisal for digital records with the obligation to intervene as soon as systems are created to ensure their preservation and the need for a description for information retrieval [RAJ 11, p. 71].

Some advocate keeping everything, since technology allows it, both in terms of storage capacity and in terms of search engines and making it available to users on the global network. Others advocate selecting what to keep for reasons of quality, relevance, common sense and the cost of preserving and migrating an ever-growing digital heritage in a society in crisis [CHA 15a, p. 64].

In fact, it is the multiplication of records that makes this work essential, because it is not the information that is huge, but we who are consuming poorly. As consumers of information, we develop bad habits, which leads us to believe that there is "too much information" to process. It is essential to know how to decipher and select information, in much the same way that we must know and choose the foods we put on our plates. Choosing your sources well is essential to better communicate this information and to understand your information environment, but also what happens to the records you produce.

The selection process is reversed. Previously we eliminated, and now we select what is important. In order to overcome the mass of information produced, it is no longer possible to remove unnecessary records from the list of those you want to keep [MAN 15, p. 297]. However, the risk posed by the consequences of disposing of certain records is also a factor that can influence decisions. This estimate is made in relation to the appraisal of processing and retention costs arising from the need to retain. It is an illusion to think of retaining everything. The better the choice of what to keep, and the earlier in the life of the record, the better the long-term preservation can be ensured [HIR 14, p. 28].

Why keep information of little significance under the same conditions of cost, accessibility and security as highly sensitive information? The natural tendency has been to reason as in the paper world, where the conditions of preservation are not all the same, but where overall they do not present as many differences and possibilities as in the digital world. Unquestionably, by the extent of the solutions offered, the digital environment requires us to better specify our needs, at the risk of putting in place an unsuitable, oversized or more serious undersized solution. Thus, electronic archiving must take into account the costs induced by increasingly large volumes to be preserved in a more or less secure manner [ARN 15, p. 212].

If no selection is made, archivists will have to describe the batches of archives collected, a task more erudite than managerial. If selection is made, archivists will work to record the selection choices anyway. However, this is more of a managerial than a scholarly task. The question of the comparative cost of selection and the conservation savings depends on how the selection is organized [CHA 15a, p. 65]. The real problem with increasing volumes of data is not so much the ability to preserve them, but rather their usefulness, which is the basis of good information governance [ARN 15, p. 213].

What will no longer be used runs the risk of being erased one day. It is true that in some U.S. states, it is a long-standing practice to use the rate of use of certain series of records as a criterion for disposal. Below a certain rate, there is no way around it: it is risk-taking. In banks below a certain amount, the evidence of transactions is not kept; it is cheaper to compensate than to keep the evidence. It's cheaper to compensate than to keep the evidence. It's enough to keep enough evidence to respond to current problems and to be able to make hypotheses and research [DEL 15b, p. 143].

Digital archives of private origin may involve more complex issues than those specific to records created by public bodies. A major project began in 2005 called Personal Archives Accessible in Digital Media (Paradigm) and consisted of case studies with the digital records of politicians from Britain's largest political parties. These resulted in a handbook on private digital archives. Among other things, the guide examines the various methods of collecting these archives. The manual recommends using macro-appraisal coupled with functional and technical analysis to identify in advance the creators who could produce a preservation-worthy archive [RAJ 11, p. 86].

With the help of NASA, a team from the University of Illinois conducted a project to establish a methodology and mathematical models for computer-assisted archival appraisal. This tool has made it possible to automatically analyze archives that may include text, images and graphics. It was able to quickly determine the integrity and authenticity of records. It is also possible to determine whether a record is linked to another one and the extreme dates. In particular, the model was tested on a set of records in PDF format. This was a set of natural digital archives that was examined, that is, a series of records in different formats for which there was little control and which were produced by an organization as part of its activities. The analysis made it possible to identify the specifics of these records without consulting them one by one. The relationships between them could also be examined. This work may eventually change the way archival work is done, as many of the functions could be performed largely through the use of a computer. A method where classification and retention periods could be more flexible was discussed [RAJ 11, p. 91].

Similarly, in 2010, the Library of Congress decided to acquire the entire Twitter archive, which produces more than 50 million tweets per day. Two projects carried out in the 2000s are a good illustration of this crazy dream of keeping everything: *MyLifeBits* and *Total Recall*. The first is a system that aims to store on a database everything that can be captured: digitized archive records (articles, books, photos and videos), any record created in digital format (administrative records, e-mails, digital photos), but also web pages, phone calls, private conservations. *Total Recall* goes even further. It is a project that consists of creating an absolute memory to allow each person to record the important or anecdotal moments of his or her own existence [COU 14, pp. 137–138].

Internet culture is a culture that archives everything leading to disinterest in the appropriation of certain information and a lack of decision on what is of value. It is the political deficit that frightens within a digital culture: it is no coincidence that the hierarchization of information, which is the real filter of access to all that is stored, has been left to the search engines that have replaced the archivists.

Previously, the major heritage institutions were responsible for selecting and conserving everything worthy of inclusion in the collective memory according to criteria such as rarity and representativeness. Private archives were relegated to the private sphere. As ephemeral testimonies, they disappeared after a few generations, whereas public memory was systematically inventoried and classified. Digital technology is revolutionizing this state of affairs by allowing individual memory to be preserved without space limitation and, above all, by allowing it to circulate without limits in the public space. The digital person will be able to permanently revive each of their memories in the public space. It is not only the distinction between public and private that disappears, but also the principle of selective memory. Exponential archiving is a double-edged sword: in the past, the value and rarity of a record led to its conservation in a struggle against its inevitable disappearance. Now, technology is driving the need to keep everything regardless of the object concerned. "Once the fruit of an effort, nowadays obvious and almost automatic, conservation no longer comes to frame an established value; at the limit, it even pretends to grant it after the fact by its gesture. We no longer conserve because it is important, but because we conserve that it is important or because we allow it to become important"[2].

The criteria for selecting records to be included in a records management system include "an analysis of the requirements of the regulatory environment, accountability, management needs, and the risks of unavailability of records" [LEP 11, p. 10]. Records of business activities should be organized and linked to the metadata that characterizes the context in which they were created.

A creator's place in the organization's hierarchy and the authority he or she has over the creation of a particular type of record is useful information both for determining the value of a record and for understanding its particularities. For electronic records, identifying the principal creators makes it possible, among other things, to determine the persons authorized to sign the record or the systems put in place to produce the record.

The context of creation determines the main reasons for choosing the form of the record. This choice often imposes itself by custom. For function records produced as part of an organization's particular activities, the context of creation is not always known. It is therefore necessary to identify the context of creation, the particular characteristics of the information recorded in the record, and the purpose for which the record is created.

The study of information content makes it possible to specify the conditions of validity of the records so that the record meets the requirements of its creation. It takes into account the laws and regulations that affect it, the purposes for which it is created, the value it presents at the various stages of its use and its relationship with other records, the general or individual nature of this information, and the density of the information provided. This information indicates the obligations or conditions that a record must meet in order to meet the requirements of what it was created for. These conditions fall within the scope of legislation, custom or obligations imposed by professionals related to these activities such as accountants.

In any organization, the different records produced on a daily basis do not all have the same usefulness, the same value, or the same content. Deciding that a record should be archived and for how long can only be done if there is a clear

---

2 Hoog, Emmanuel, *Mémoire Année Zéro*, Paris, Le Seuil, coll. Essais, 2009, pp. 118–121.

understanding of the context in which it was produced, the activity it records, its potential evidential value and its actual use. Thus, among all the records produced, some are used primarily for their legal value, while others are used for the information, symbol or image they convey. Some information is essential only for a few months; others must be kept for decades. The need to consult records may be regular, episodic or non-existent [ASS 07, p. 61]. At the end of the legal retention period, electronic archives are intended to be destroyed just like paper archives. This good archival practice applied to the computer world corresponds to the last phase of the lifecycle of the electronic record.

In the case of personal data, the obligation relates to the deletion of data whose retention is no longer justified by the rules. Personal data may not be used beyond a certain period of time. Destruction is the best means, but deferral or anonymization may be acceptable alternatives under certain conditions to guarantee the right to oblivion. Let us not forget that the choice of storage period is a matter for multidisciplinary collaboration. It requires legal, archival, computer and managerial skills and, above all, the indispensable collaboration of the professions [CHA 18, p. 74].

The determination of the shelf life is based on legal and administrative criteria:

– probative value of records in case of litigation (records can be used as evidence in legal proceedings, records attest to rights and duties);

– administrative value of the records (the records trace the circumstances that led to a decision). The same record or file may be subject to several different durations, depending on the different uses to which it has been or may be put;

– informational value, which corresponds to business needs and good conduct of business in terms of production, management, operation and conservation of records;

– heritage value, since records are strong contributors to the collective memory and the preservation of history.

Two types of value-added records escape the vigilance of the information systems department in its role of controlling information assets or even business continuity planning. These are records that exist only in physical form or that are created locally in small applications out of concern for efficiency in the face of overly sophisticated software or because their authors are unaware of the value of the information they process [CHA 18, p. 54].

The main objective is to plan their production well and to be able to control retention periods (not to keep unnecessary data and records and, conversely, not to destroy data and records whose retention must be ensured). Indeed, information systems produce data that may have a high legal, strategic and/or heritage value, which are often the only trace of the administration's activity. Their loss would constitute both a legal risk and a major risk for business continuity. These are sensitive data whose irreversible loss and inappropriate dissemination could affect the rights of citizens or sometimes the security of the State [DIS 12, p. 4].

Archiving rules are also made according to the status of the record: record binding or not for the producer, original or copy, master record, single or multiple record. The same record or file may be covered by different durations, depending on the uses to which it has been or may be put, and on its status within the production process. In the case of digital records, it is also necessary to consider the quality of the records: native digital records or digitized records. Under French law, a digitized record is considered a copy [ASS 07, p. 85].

An organization may decide to archive only records that are subject to legal constraints or that ensure the traceability of the company's accounts, and to leave records with information value under the responsibility of the departments. For example, an organization may respond to all complaints, but keep no record of complaints or responses [ASS 05, p. 6].

The relationship in which the record is produced is decisive in assessing its value. Knowing how the business activity (research, operation, care, insurance) or process (accounting, technical control, etc.) that produces a record clarifies the understanding of the record by its user, but does not necessarily indicate the stakes involved in the record and the risk incurred in the event of loss or disclosure. Who imposes this operation? Who is the recipient? Who is affected by the case? Who is likely to hold the company accountable for this action? Thus, validation and dissemination of the record are important [CHA 18, pp. 29–30]. Either the validation must be done by a legal representative in an organization or the person responsible for the processes, in some cases, the general management. Retention periods can sometimes be extended in the event of litigation.

The analysis of the value of the information is compulsorily completed by the expression of the sensitivity of this information. The need to take this sensitivity into account meets the security requirements for the protection of information throughout its lifecycle.

There are several levels of information sensitivity. The first concerns vital information. These are the records and data that are essential to continue operations after a disaster. There are three criteria for this. First, the contractual nature of the data and records relating to cases in progress or in preparation. The second is the use of reference data such as client base, procedures, strategic data, especially confidential data. Secondly, age, because some of the records, even old ones, may be important. A property deed can be old and its unavailability can have serious consequences. Finally, uniqueness: if important information is recorded in only one copy, the risk of loss is increased. Duplication by backup is an action to halve the risk. It is preferable to anticipate the risk of disappearance and to digitize vital contracts [CHA 18, pp. 192–193]. Vital data represents only a small part of the information in the company, about 5%, but it is spread out in various locations. These include major decisions and contracts that require careful backup and long-term management. Databases can be updated on a daily basis. Backup accompanied by a priority restoration process is the most efficient. There is also a whole range of varied writings, internal to the company, the content of which is of strategic interest for decision support. The difficulty with this type of file is that their production is rarely standardized. Without explicit naming rules and coding, it is difficult to control the completeness of the census and to automate backup processing [CHA 18, p. 194].

Then we find the critical information. These are the legally valid records and data that the law requires to be produced, kept or destroyed and the contractual records that engage the company's responsibility according to the legislation in force. Certain records are considered sensitive and are retained for their potentially probative value or for their value in terms of capitalizing on knowledge and know-how or as a means of traceability. The last level or standard concerns all other records and routine and comfort data, the preservation of which is not subject to legal obligations and does not present any particular security requirements [ARN 15, p. 208].

While defining the value and sensitivity of the information makes it possible to qualify the nature of the information more globally, quantitative description is of course essential to meet the needs and requirements and to assist in risk analysis. Identifying volumes in Gigabytes, number of files, formats, average file sizes, etc., is mandatory. Likewise, the levels of usage in terms of consultation will condition future electronic archiving. This type of reference framework also makes it possible to build the essential intellectual archiving tools such as the preservation repository, integrating legal requirements where they exist. It plays an important role in identifying the right levels of electronic archiving services and solutions. Taking into account operational needs, in the technical sense of the term, will also enrich and conclude the analysis [ARN 15, p. 208].

In addition to the specific legal requirements, the decision-making power of those responsible for the activity must also be considered. For example, if the process is framed by a highly formalized procedure, in which the person responsible for the file or the organization as a whole have only a marginal share of appreciation, it is necessary to keep only the initial application and the final decision, accompanied by the rules of procedure established for this activity [ICA 05, p. 29].

Some systems have very low retention functionality, which reduces the quality of their records to a point where their archiving becomes meaningless. Other systems may produce records in a format that cannot be retained, and conversion to a retention format may not be possible. Particular attention must be paid to the relationship between records of archival value and those proposed for disposal. Information systems contain a great deal of linked information and if it is destroyed the authenticity and usability of the records may be diminished [ICA 05, pp. 31–32].

The volume of data to be archived is only a secondary criterion. On the other hand, the cost of intellectual labor and the technical investment required for conversion are important criteria. The cost of electronic archiving is a function of the number of record types and formats that need to be processed, not the total number of such records [ICA 05, p. 32].

Several deadlines must be reconciled to ensure the archiving of the record. The retention period is the time for which a record must be kept. It goes from the creation of the record until the moment it loses interest for its owner. The number of years is defined based on legal constraints, assessment of the risk associated with the retention or destruction of the record and business needs, including historical memory. The administration's recovery period is the period of time during which an administration may require the release of records within the control framework. The time limit for the release of public records is the number of years below which the records are not freely accessible to the public [CHA 18, p. 64].

The limitation period refers to a legal action that the company may initiate or incur. The commercial limitation period is the period during which a supplier may be opposed in court. This concerns, for example, financial obligations to repair environmental damage caused by installations, works or activities, which are subject to a thirty-year statute of limitations in France according to the Environmental Code (article L152-1). The problem is that the limitation periods do not specify which records are useful and can be produced as evidence before a judge: letters, contracts, notes, preferably official records or records exchanged with a third party, but not exclusively. The case of the pay slip is enlightening. Under the Labor Code, the employer keeps a duplicate of employees' pay slips or pay slips given to employees in electronic form for five years (article L3243-4). An action for payment of wages is time-barred after three years from the day on which the person exercising it became aware of the facts enabling him or her to exercise it (article L3245-1). In terms of retention, the longest period is preferred, i.e. five years. However, the actual retention period of the pay slips is often 50 to 60 years in order to assist in the constitution of the employee's retirement file, in particular if the employee does not have the possibility of keeping the digital medium as he is supposed to do for his paper pay slips. In addition, the principle of non-retroactivity must also be taken into account [CHA 18, p. 63].

For certain time limits that are based on legal requirements, there is no retroactive application, so the law at the date of the record must be taken into account. Finally, for electronic records, attention must be paid to interactions: some records are linked to each other, and some records do not really have an end, especially, for example, in the case of e-mail. Many electronic records interact with each other, so if you start destroying some of them, you need to be careful to ensure that it is done in a consistent way, with any links that may exist.

3.1.2. The schedule of conservation periods

It is customary to develop a retention[3] schedule that includes a set of rules that reflect the decisions an organization makes about the life of its records and their final disposition. These rules set out the path that each record produced or received by the organization should follow during its life. It is the instrument that defines the age, the period of time the record is in existence, and what processing it requires in accordance with its age and its disposition when it becomes inactive [MAR 10, p. 57]. It becomes a contractual tool validated by both parties. It promotes dialogue between the parties and provides a common language. It offers a predictive management of the lifecycle of records; it simplifies and rationalizes the management of current, intermediate and definitive archives. Above all, it accompanies the procedures for disposal and deposit defined in an archiving charter. It serves transparency and defines the responsibilities of each department in the selection and preservation of files. To maintain its validity over time, the archive management chart must be regularly evaluated and updated according to the changes that affect the producer in its missions, attributions and procedures [ASS 07, p. 93].

Code	Categories of records	Assets (CUP)	Semi-active	Definitive (disposition)	Observation	Regulatory texts
0100	Administration – General	Cy +1a	0	E		
0125	Development of laws and legislation	Ro	5 years	Sc		
0145	Verification	Fy+1y	5 years	E		

Table 3.1. *Sample shelf life table*

---

3 The term *tableau de gestion* is used in France.

If we consider from the above table that a record for the drafting of a law is closed at the date of 2000 (date of the end of the record), we add five years for the active duration +1 which gives us 2006 for the application of the disposition. The other abbreviations mean "Ro" to replace or obsolete, "Cy" for current year and "Fy" for fiscal year.

The shelf life schedule is usually in the form of a table with four or more columns:

– the code repeats the codification of the classification plan if it exists;

– the category of records contains an inventory of the records produced or received by the producer, classified according to a functional logic, by mission, assignment and procedure, following the classification plan if it exists or reconstituting it if it does not formally exist. Depending on the degree of precision desired, the constituent parts of the files may or may not be listed. Rigor in the formulation of activities is essential: the activity "definition of financial management rules" generates a procedural record used by the activity "monitoring of financial management rules". In one case, this is the master record, in the other a distribution copy. Even if they are both integrated into the records management system, they will not have the same retention rules;

– the "administrative utility period" (AUP) column includes active records and corresponds to the legal or practical period of time during which a record is likely to be used by the producer or its successor. The administration may use information for legal purposes even if it is no longer used on a day-to-day basis. The record may not be disposed of during this date, which constitutes its minimum retention period [ASS 07, p. 95]. This is not to be confused with the current active utility period, which is the period of time during which information will be needed to manage active files, for example, for a personnel file, it covers the time of the staff member's professional activity. From a conceptual point of view, only the AUP is a relevant concept for managing the lifecycle of records. It is in fact event specific to the management of cases which determine the lifecycle of records by making it possible to fix the starting point of the AUP (expiry of a contract, date of issue of a record, date of a decision, end of the accounting period, etc.) and not the frequency of their consultation and the problems of their material management [BUR 11, p. 80].

In summary, for the period known as the current archive period, the records will accumulate in the open files. At the end of the case, the file will be closed, marking the end of the active period to begin the intermediate archival period. The records are kept for the time of administrative utility, after which they are sorted, some are disposed of and some are kept indefinitely.

The destruction of records must be accompanied with or without metadata: in some cases, the record is destroyed and the metadata is retained. It is recommended that records of destruction be kept in a time-stamped journal and that the processes that enable destruction be secure. In some cases, complete erasure of the data may be carried out. Care should also be taken to ensure that transfer procedures are implemented after sorting or unsorted for records that will be kept permanently, for example, for heritage or historical purposes. Finally, if there is hesitation, the retention period may be artificially extended until a further decision is made. This is called a "rendezvous clause".

The administrative utility period (AUP) is calculated from a reference date (date of the most recent record, date of closure of the file or case, date of administrative action such as dates of birth or death of individuals). If not specified, it means that the file is closed. As a general rule, the basic unit of management is the file, but in some cases the rules may relate to parts of the file [LEP 11, p. 15];

– the "semi-active" column is not essential, but it can be added when, for practical reasons, one wishes to indicate after how long the files have to leave the office for the intermediate archive room. This will give one retention period in the office and the other for the duration of the retention period in a secondary storage facility.

However, in the electronic environment it is sometimes necessary to define a current active utility period (CUP) distinct from the administrative utility period (AUP). This is a period during which the data are accessible to all managers in the production tool, in particular personal data to which access is restricted for part of the period of administrative utility for reasons of confidentiality;

– the final disposition column or sometimes the abbreviation final disposition (FD) of inactive records is the destination of a record after the expiration of its administrative utility period. There are several options: destruction (D) or elimination (E), sorting or sampling (S), selective conservation (Sc), and final conservation (C) at the archives. The date of final disposition, that is, disposal or accession, is obtained by adding the date of file closure and the length of time the archives have been in use, to which one year must be added in order to obtain a date in the past year [ASS 07, p. 95].

During the years 1983–1986, in Canada, codes appeared in government shelf life schedules to replace the former nomenclature for "While in Force" (IF) and "Permanent" (P). With the advent of computers and the limitations imposed by the codes used, a way was found to program record management systems so that the machine would be able to interpret and produce reports. In order not to confuse the codes used with years of record retention and to recognize them easily, a three-digit number is adopted far in the numerical sequence 0 to 9. It was Michel Roberge who, at the time, proposed three three-digit codes. The 999 "until replaced by a new version", the 888 "until the end" and the 777 "until after the financial auditor's visit". It is a Quebec codification that was chosen based on the technological possibilities of the time;

– the "observations" column contains useful comments on the records and procedures (references to regulatory texts, progress and development of the procedure, record support, co-instructing departments), explanations of the choice of the duration of administrative utility (deadlines for appeal or prescription, average duration of the procedure) and the final processing of records (explanation of the sorting criteria, identification of the original and duplicates, etc.) [ASS 07, p. 96].

The following columns can also be added:

– the "regulatory text" column, which lists the references of the texts used to identify the duration of administrative utility and the disposition of the record in question (laws, decrees, archive sorting instructions). In the absence of a dedicated column, this information is entered in the "comments" column;

– the "Producer services" column. When the table is common to a set of services, the column of services that contribute to the exercise of the same mission or procedure can be added. This column specifies who is the producer or holder of the records in question. Duplicates can then be identified and specific sorting rules determined for each copy of the file [ASS 07, p. 96].

The shelf life schedule also includes a validation area where the signatures of the parties committing to implement the proposals in the management table must be included. In principle, the archivist, the head of the producer department and their respective superiors are involved.

In addition, it is advisable to include an introduction which recalls the archiving procedures in force, the procedures for managing current and intermediate archives, and the procedures for disposal and payment where appropriate. When the schedule is voluminous, there is also a table of contents that includes the organization of the "category of records" column (missions, attributions, procedures), an index of the files or records described and various appendices that will facilitate reading and application (summary table of files or records to be kept in whole or in part, summary tables of records produced by service, main regulatory texts cited, etc.).

A good management chart should be read, understood and applied by people who were not involved in its development. It must be understood by everyone. In the digital environment, the disposition is still very useful, particularly in determining the processing method to be applied upstream of the lifecycle of records: choice of a more or less perennial format; metadata adapted for short- or long-term research. In the table above, only the disposition is then proposed, but specifying the media considered, the migrations envisaged and the specific points to be taken for the management of certain records.

Code	Duration	Areas and categories	Records in the category	Storage location and tool	Business rule	Points of attention
F		Research, studies, know-how				
F1	99	Intellectual property titles	Patents, research notes	Paper and Scanning		Confidential data
F2	99	Major reports and studies	Technical Studies Series	Paper outsourced until 2001. Digital collection in GED	Ensuring the sustainability of the series (migration every 10 years)	

Table 3.2. *Sample shelf life table according to Arcateg (source: [CHA 18, p. 140])*

3.2. Metadata

The metadata has been much talked about with PRISM cases, or Wikileaks, which showed that NSA services have captured the actions of Internet users and obtained a detailed description of them through their connections, knowing the location, duration and people contacted. The first to use metadata were librarians, when catalogs were computerized in the 1990s, and from an educational point of view, the analogy is often used with bibliographic records, which describe content, and sometimes even context and structure [MAD 15a].

An electronic record consists of both the data containing the encoded message information and the associated metadata. This data on data includes all information that records the production data by specifying source and context [ASS 07, p. 65]. Thus, the Archives de France takes up the definition of the international standard on records management ISO 15489-1 which presents them in the specific perspective of records management as "data describing the context, content and structure of archived records and their management over time. ISO 23081 and ISO 16171 provide complementary elements, where metadata is defined as structured or semi-structured information that informs the creation, recording, classification, access, retention and selection of records over time and across all domains" [MAD 15a].

They make it possible to establish the provenance, facilitate identification and circulation, and specify the entire path of the record, from its birth to its destruction or permanent preservation. This is why organizations and States have felt the need to mark out their use. For example, the government profiles of the *Bibliothèque et Archives nationales du Québec* include a set of metadata to name, identify, describe, classify and manage an information resource throughout its lifecycle, such as the title of a file or record, its creator, its date of creation, and its expected date of destruction [COU 14, p. 123].

The example of the jam jar is often used by Charlotte Mayday to illustrate the importance of metadata. There is a container, the jar and its lid, and its contents are not easily identifiable since the jam may be composed of different ingredients. The label will give the composition of the contents, the type of jam, its origin, if it comes from organic farming. The label is comparable to a bibliographic record of the contents, as the metadata allow the raw data packet to be transformed into understandable and readable information. To extend the culinary metaphor, he will use tools to open the container, accessing the contents using the hand for opening, the knife to lift the lid and the spoon to draw out the necessary amount of jam. In the context of metadata, devices must therefore be provided to access the content, a role that is played by applications or software for reading, encoding, or opening files. Finally, in order to enjoy this jam while preserving all its qualities, optimal storage conditions are needed and the aging of the product must be monitored. In the digital context, in order to avoid data corruption, it is necessary to provide storage and monitoring devices, which can be concretely reflected in the metadata, for example, an electronic fingerprint applied to the packet of data to be archived [MAD 15a].

There is metadata that is used to organize knowledge and to use and exploit the record, that is, internal or external, descriptive, contextual and structural, initial and added throughout the lifecycle, and that keeps the record accessible over time and ensures and controls access. They can be classified according to what they describe (content), how they are created (provenance), when they are created (history), where they are found (location), what they look like (form), and how they are used (purpose) [MAD 15a].

Generally speaking, metadata is divided into three categories:

– descriptive metadata. Describe a resource for discovery and identification purposes. They may include elements such as author, title and description. Elements found in a bibliographic record are examples of descriptive metadata;

– administrative metadata. These provide information to help manage a resource, such as when and how it was created, the type of file and other technical information, and who can access it. This category very often includes rights management metadata and preservation metadata;

– structural metadata. These indicate how compound objects are put together. They identify the data format, media format or type of data representation and file types, the hardware and software needed to render the data, and the compression method and encryption algorithms used, if any [APN 13, p. 16].

Type of metadata	Objectives	Description elements
Descriptive metadata	Identify, describe, classify, prioritize information.	Unique identifiers, physical attributes (media, dimensions, general state, recipients and contract numbers. Bibliographic attributes (title, author or creator, language, key words or subjects, summary of the work).
Administrative metadata	Ensure the management and processing of digital records in the short and long term, identifying the context and provenance and enabling integrity and management of rights.	Provenance, duration of conservation, type and digitizer model, resolution, bit depth, colorimetric space, file format, applications, compression, owner, copyright date, restrictions concerning copying and distribution, management of rights, confidentiality. Conservation activities (refreshment cycles, migration).
Structural metadata	Facilitate navigation and presentation. Describe the way in which the scattered files which constitute the record should logically fit together.	Relationships with other digital objects, vocabulary used in all of the data, examples of resource type, structural plan of pages or internet resources. A logical level defining the links between elements (page number, chapter title) and a physical level defining how digital objects are recorded (repertoire, format, file).

Table 3.3. *Types of metadata*

If one is interested in record management metadata, it should include:

– the point of capture metadata, which should reflect the context in which the records were created and the records were created, the people involved, the content, appearance, structure, and technical characteristics of the record;

– lifecycle metadata, which will document all changes to the record;

– output or destruction metadata, which signals the deletion or removal of the record from the MSR (management system for records). Standard 16171-2 specifies that the deletion process must be approved by an authority, under penalty of nullity [MAD 15a].

For example, the mandatory dossier metadata should contain the physical characteristics, path, classification (domain/object, keyword, process/activity), date of opening and closing of the dossier, dossier identifier, access limit, retention rule (retention period, principal holder, retention rule number), status (archival, registration authority, version), dossier title, administrative unit of the owner.

Metadata contribute to better identification and therefore improved access to information; they support and enhance its evidential value by qualifying it from its creation and documenting its modifications or alterations throughout its life. They contribute to the interoperability of systems when the metadata sets used are standardized. This involves providing for the establishment and use of metadata for each business line or process to reduce the risk of information loss, deletion or omission [MAD 15a].

Metadata serve five main purposes:

– e-business: process steps, location of resources and parties, encryption, digital signatures and business transactions;

– archiving: preservation of information, permanence of support and content, migration, technical metadata for the accessibility of evolving formats, authorization and access control;

– resource description: creator, date, identifier, relationship to other resources; this metadata is as relevant to records management as it is to archiving and must accompany a transfer or accession;

– retrieval: selection using largely the same metadata as the resource description for records management;

– the management of rights of use (creator, publisher, consumer), the content of resources and associated commercial rights [MAD 15a].

Each record or file must have a unique identifier that will enable it to be treated individually throughout its lifecycle. This identifier is the equivalent of an individual's social security number or the classification of an information resource. Its role is twofold. It identifies the individual record if possible so that it does not need to be modified in the future. It makes it possible to identify the precise place the record occupies in the records system by indicating to which documentary aggregates it belongs and what those aggregates are. The individual identifier must fit into a flexible system, capable of admitting in the future records of various types and external identifiers. The unique and fixed identifier preserves the identity and therefore the uniqueness and authenticity of the record especially for portals common to several institutions. Inappropriate and non-unique identifiers could cause confusion when integrating databases and digital collections. Identifiers are treated as metadata and can be integrated with content and format in a single file or even in the file name, but they can also be grouped in a separate table [KEC 14, pp. 113–114].

The description of the context of the record is mandatory because it gives the record its full meaning and value. It consists of assigning metadata describing the producer of the record and the process by which the record was produced, the file to which it belongs, the date and time of the action, and the author of the action. The record's operating context specifies the relationships with other records in the same file, other records outside the file, other files [ASS 05 p. 115]. The context also relates to the history of the producer, its activities, jurisdiction, functions, organizational structure, relationships with other organizations or persons. The technical computer context must also be described when the archive performs an emulation operation [KEC 14, p. 117]. Institutional archival systems must collect and manage business process metadata as an essential addition to understanding the context and correctly interpreting its meaning, as it informs about functions, transactions, security rules, and describes agents or participants. The link between metadata and records must be preserved. When faced with a list of dates, titles and authors, a system can establish an unambiguous link between this list and the electronic objects to which it refers [ICA 05, p. 43].

While context description may become impoverished, content description may, conversely, develop considerably beyond what is feasible for physical records through the exploitation of business information systems, from which many metadata can be automatically extracted to index records. This enrichment of indexing is made possible by the ability of IT to associate multiple values with an electronic file very quickly. This meets the business need to search for a record with very precise metadata: a few dozen metadata per record may be required. This type of query is less necessary for historical research, which favors a general approach to the particular and an understanding of the context, although metadata indexing the record may be useful for certain research needs on the final archives, particularly genealogical research. In the case of serial data, the traditional finding aid, established on a tiered plan, loses its relevance. It is preferable to use an indexing system, which will allow for more efficient research [BUR 13, p. 20]. Indexing the content will assign complementary thematic or descriptor metadata, metadata designating places, organizations, individuals, or a documentary summary and abstract [ASS 05, p. 18].

ISO 15489-1 (point 7.2) emphasizes that metadata is fundamental to ensuring the authenticity, reliability, integrity and usability of an archival record. This implies that:

– the records have a unique identifier, at least in the system;

– metadata provides information related to each particular record (who does what and when);

– the elements required for metadata are created, as far as possible, by automatic procedures;

– records and their metadata are protected from further modification;

– the metadata fully describes everything that has happened to the record since its creation [ICA 05, p. 30].

However, metadata can also be used for different purposes and diverted from their original purpose. For example, the extraction of metadata may not only reveal sensitive information about the past, but also allow an observer to predict future actions. For example, research has shown that a person's location can be predicted by examining patterns in the history of places frequented by friends and acquaintances. One security expert has argued that by listing telephone calls between senior executives of a company and a competitor, a lawyer or a broker, one can get an idea of a possible takeover of the company before it is made public. But there are also telephone crisis lines for victims of spousal violence and rape, suicidal people, veterans, young people dealing with their sexuality, or those suffering from addictions [COM 14, p. 5].

When a web browser is used, this includes the pages visited and dates, user data and possibly the user's login details with the auto-enter function, URLs, IP address, Internet Service Provider, device hardware details, operating system and browser version, cookies and cached data from websites, search queries and search results that are displayed. On a social network site, the name and biographical information provided in the profile, such as date of birth, hometown, employment history and interests are displayed. In addition, there is the username and unique identifier, subscriptions, location, device used, date and time of the activity, time zone, activities, likes, events attended [COM 14, pp. 3–5].

For example, computer scientist Daniel Weitzner says that metadata is more revealing than content because it is easier to correlate events by analyzing constants in a vast universe of metadata than it is to analyze the contents of an individual's e-mail and phone calls. Similarly, terms entered into search engines can be used to identify individuals and reveal sensitive information about them. This information, when aggregated, represents the range of human intentions – a database of people's wants, needs and tastes that can be revealed, archived, tracked and exploited for a variety of purposes and whose production can be ordered by a court of law [COM 14, p. 5].

The Office of the Privacy Commissioner of Canada has determined that when seemingly innocuous information is combined with other accessible information, it can constitute personal information and can sometimes provide a fairly accurate picture of an individual's activities, ideas, opinions and lifestyle. For example, an IP (Internet Protocol) address can be personal information if it is associated with an identifiable individual, and can be fairly revealing of an individual's activities on the Internet. An IP address combined with basic information about a telecommunications subscriber may reveal, among other things, the interests, interests and interests of the subscriber, the people the subscriber associates with, and the trips the subscriber takes. A diagram illustrating the chain of social relationships can show how people in the vicinity of the network are connected to each other. Even the fact that people work at a short distance from an identified suspect can quickly expand the network of relationships to include some people who may not be aware of the suspect's existence [COM 14, pp. 7–8].

3.3. Naming of digital records

Understanding the contents of a folder or file begins with reading its name and therefore the clarity of its statement. But the way of naming them varies from one user to another. Proper naming of files makes it possible to group records together and to differentiate these records by their status (e.g. validated or not). This is why it is crucial to develop and respect common naming rules to facilitate and perpetuate access to information, but also to optimize the sharing and sorting of records.

The use of appropriate record names can help to simplify access to and retrieval of electronic records and to place records in a logical sequence. It helps users identify the records they are looking for and makes it easier to identify the contents of a record from a list. It helps manage record versions and prevents file overwriting. It promotes the migration and preservation of digital records in the medium and long term.

The order of the elements of the file name is preponderant for the classification of the files. It is recommended that the main subject of the record be placed at the beginning of the file name, followed by significant common names to qualify the file, and then specify the type of record, if applicable (e.g. minutes, agreement, specifications). More general concepts are placed before more specific concepts. Common names expressing a subject are placed before those expressing a type of record. The use of verbs, adverbs, adjectives and empty words (articles, prepositions, conjunctions, etc.) should be avoided. Assigning a sentence to name a file is to be avoided and the length of the naming must be controlled. The basic rule must remain that once deployed, it must never exceed the limits of the screen, whatever the level, so as not to impair reading efficiency and not to exceed a record path. In principle, the name of a file should not exceed 31 characters.

The file name must be unique, accurate and meaningful. In principle, it contains the subject, the type of record, the date of creation, the version, the extension if it is classified by subject or one can start with the date if the classification is chronological, but only for board or committee meetings otherwise the dates may scatter the subjects. The name of a file is correct when it is enough to identify its contents without having to open it. (Ex.: conseil_recherche_avis_convocation_2019-06-01.docx). For received files, names are modified as necessary when saving them in the directory structure.

Information	Description	Example
Names/Author/Creator	Optional	DuboisClaire
Subject or title. Avoid vague names (miscellaneous, generalities)	Mandatory Subject, context of creation	Training_Record Management Project_Dematerialization Contract234
Type of record. It is placed at the end of the file before the date. When the extension is .xls or .ods, there is no need to indicate "spreadsheet" or "table"	Optional Nature of the record Understandable abbreviations	board_administration_CR_2007-06-01.doc CR (Report) OJ (Agenda)
Creation date. Standard ISO 8601: 2004 allows the chronological order	Mandatory Creation date	20160506 (YYYYMMDD)
Record or report version. Put the final version of the record in PDF/A format	Mandatory Allows to distinguish between record versions	V01, V02, VF (final), VD (definitive)
Separators	It is forbidden to use spaces	LabAdvice_CR_2014 1217_VD.docx
Administrative Unit	Optional	Management
Extension	Mandatory	docx, xls, pdf

Table 3.4. *File naming elements*

In order to avoid difficulties in the interpretation of a file name by operating systems, the period (".") to replace a space or to separate elements of a file name is never used. The underscore _ to separate the elements of a file name is preferred (e.g. pedagogical_advice_pa_2007-06-01.doc rather than pedagogicaladvicepa2007-06-01.docx). A hyphen (Monthly-meeting) or an underscore (Monthly_meeting) or an uppercase (Monthly_Meeting) separates the components of the word. Accented characters and cedilla, spaces between words and punctuation and special characters, reserved characters in the Windows environment (%, $, !, *, /, etc.) cannot be used. A "0" is placed in front of numbers from 1 to 9 to ensure proper numerical sorting[4].

Bad naming	Good naming
Claire Dubois File	Naming_RulesFiles
File Teacher Education Committee	CommitteeTraining_Record Management
Minutes of the training sub-group meeting May 6, 2016.docx	2016-05-06PVTrainingSubGroup.docx
Specifications archivist of institution 070111.doc	ProfilePost_Archivist_20110101.doc
20100325Interview_evaluation_Dubois.doc	InterviewEvaluation_ DuboisClaire_20100325.doc
Dubois_VF_Application_PermitConstruct_2 0160605.Pdf	PermitConstruct_Application_Dubois_20160 506_VF.Pdf
VF_ManMeeting_CR_20141214.docx	20141214_ManMeeting_CR_VE.docx
VF_ManMeeting_OJ_20141214.docx	20141214_ManMeeting_OJ_VE.docx

Table 3.5. *Examples of file naming*

3.4. Classification

3.4.1. *An intellectual process*

There are many definitions of the "classification" function in archival science. Carol Couture describes classification as "An intellectual process of systematically identifying and grouping similar items according to common characteristics that will subsequently be differentiated if quantity requires. It is therefore a process of grouping record entities into classes based on their common characteristics so that similar entities are grouped together and separated from non-similar entities" [MAS 15].

Classification refers to a mental act that is to be distinguished from the physical operation of storing records. The classification process is often confused with the

---

4 Archivists subcommittee, *Mesures transitoires et bonnes pratiques de gestion des documents numériques*, CREPUQ, pp. 15–16, February 2009.

tool that is the filing plan[5]. The latter is used both to represent the classification of an organization's functions and activities and to classify the records created or received as a result of these activities. This function consists of a set of logically structured conventions, methods and rules of procedure which enable records to be classified by group or category, regardless of their medium and age [MAS 15].

Archival classification has long been concerned with the intellectual and, above all, physical organization of records produced or printed on paper and kept in cabinets, filing cabinets or boxes. The main objective has been administrative efficiency by codifying a uniform and durable framework for classifying and retrieving records. A designated official, usually the administrative secretary, was responsible for the design and maintenance of the filing plan and its updates. It was also responsible for all monitoring and communication up to the archiving or disposal of records in accordance with a retention schedule [MAS 15, p. 179].

According to Fernanda Ribero, the role of archival classification has changed. It is no longer so much a question of organizing and facilitating access to centrally stored paper records as of providing access to information and organic data stored in both shared and personal spaces [RIB 14]. With the advent of digital technology, the dissociation of information content from its medium has led to the dispersion and fragmentation of files, resulting in a blurred record. Agents work in contact with information in scattered formats in systems or applications that may be produced during a dematerialized process. Secretarial services are reduced or no longer have responsibility for record organization. This leads to a multiplicity of personal storage spaces which, however, contain a high added value while being paradoxically inaccessible to others and remain for the most part confidential and out of reach of a record management system [MAS 15, p. 180].

It was then thought that powerful search engines would make it easier to search. But from a record point of view, the search results on Google, for example, deliver many references that are not always relevant and we often stop at the first page of answers. It has been forgotten that at the heart of an organization's activities is access to files and records that are related to each other because they document an activity, a project, relationships with people and companies [ROB 11, p. 0.10].

In connection with classification, the rapid accumulation of records presupposes an analysis of their documentary value; otherwise they may become unmanageable.

---

5 Even if we consider that classification concerns the identification and intellectual ordering of accumulations of documents within funding and that the material operation is classification, we speak in Europe of a classification plan. The physical operation is considered to be storage, not filing, and consists of placing records in an orderly manner in packaging material or storage furniture.

Rational destruction of records in personal spaces that ignore the lifecycle is rare. Destruction takes place at the whim of the supposed owners, especially when they leave or for personal reasons. This problem is compounded by the difficulty in differentiating between digital archival records and other sources of information [MAS 15, p. 180].

While classification refers to an intellectual process, the classification plan is the tool for the structured representation of the current functions and activities of an organization divided into classes, sub-classes and organized hierarchically. The classification plan represents the organization through its activities. It identifies and organizes them hierarchically. The plan may correspond to a hierarchy between processes and sub-processes in the ISO 9001 quality sense. Its degree of finesse may vary according to the activities, and the records management policies decided upon [ASS 05, p. 11].

3.4.2. The hierarchical filing plan

The classification plan is, according to the definition of the *Archives nationales du Québec*, "a hierarchical and logical structure for classifying, filing and retrieving archival records or documentary collections. It is both a collaborative tool and a finding aid that complements content research techniques. The development of a shared classification scheme should be understandable to many people, its logic should be apparent, and its learning curve should be rapid" [GRO 11, p. 4]. It allows an electronic record to be maintained by being attached to the issuing entity with the primary objective of being easily retrievable for reference. The file plan should reflect the business of the line organization. It must correspond more or less to its missions or the organization of business processes.

There is a difference between the notion of a classification plan and that of a classification framework. A classification scheme is a tree structure of concepts (themes, descriptors, organization) at several levels intended to facilitate storage or to guide documentary research. The classification framework is a master plan that organizes the subdivisions of a whole. The classification plan is more oriented towards the needs of the user, while the classification framework aims to rationalize management [CHA 18, p. 124].

It can be said that the classification plans are returning to their fundamental function. They are mainly concerned with intellectual organization and no longer with logistics, as has become a trend. Indeed, for paper, intermediate filing is not only a logical way of de-cluttering offices, but it is also an intellectual operation which makes it possible to prepare the sorting out of what will have to be eliminated in the long term or retained. Moreover, postponing this operation to a later date complicates sorting and searching. From the user's point of view, electronics neutralizes the logistical challenge. The concept of the business file is maintained, because each record is included in one or more groups of records linked by a joint action [HAS 13, p. 34].

The primary function of the classification scheme is to logically and physically group together records relating to the same activity or matter in order to organize information and make it easier to find and retrieve, and to create a classification logic common to the department or organization. The goals are to represent the contexts in which records are produced by recording them in an organized manner to facilitate record retrieval and sharing, information preservation and the reduction of multiple records. It helps to ensure evidential value by maintaining the context of creation and use reflected in the business classification scheme. It also provides a record of processes by organizing the headings within an activity and is a support point for documentation policy while minimizing the impact of staff changes [GRO 11, p. 6].

The objective of classifying and filing records from an administrative perspective is to enable uniform identification of the storage and retrieval of records, eliminate loss of records while ensuring the quality, relevance and security of the records retained. This helps to reduce the time required to access information by accelerating the information retrieval process and to reduce the costs associated with retention and consultation by optimizing the use of space and conservation equipment [MAS 15].

The file plan is also a response to the legal obligations regarding access to information and protection of personal information in the event that a citizen wishes to exercise his or her right of access to information. As well, organizations must be able to quickly identify nominative information in order to protect it or, if necessary, eliminate it according to the right to forget.

ISO 15489[6] specifies that classification is an indispensable management tool for the conduct of an organization's business and as such, each organization must adapt the classification plan according to its needs and operating procedures. It enables producing departments to organize their records by assigning each record, as soon as it is created, to a precisely identified file. Depending on the organization's policy, the scope covered by the filing plan may concern the entire organization, a group of departments in the same sector, a department, a department, a business line, etc. The filing plan may also cover the entire organization, a group of departments in the same sector, a department, a department, a business line, etc. As a result, the

---

6 We use the 2001 and 2016 versions of ISO 15489 indiscriminately to summarize the different requirements.

classification is specific to each organization even though it may include functions and activities common to all organizations [ASS 07, p. 87].

It should be pointed out that in the case of totally paperless production, an electronic record management (ERM) tool is most often used, with the filing plan as the main framework. Every record must be assigned to a heading in the file plan as soon as it is created or entered into the system. For each type of record identified in the classification scheme, the management data (metadata) required for its use and processing will be added: naming rules, access management, retention periods, extraction process to an electronic archiving or destruction module, production and retention formats, etc. [ASS 07, p. 91].

The main properties of a filing plan are:

– simplicity to be understood quickly. Overly general plans imposed on all departments should be avoided. They are often too cumbersome and not all headings are useful in the services. It is often more advantageous to proceed by services which have the same activities; otherwise you will end up with a voluminous and complex work which is difficult to use for research. For this reason, a maximum of three to four levels of description is recommended for ease of navigation and no overly elaborate coding. To be easily understood, the terms used to name the classes must be concise and intelligible. The use of controlled terminology for class names is intended to reduce ambiguity. Titles should be unique and unambiguous so as not to place the same record under different headings. Of course, one always goes from the most general headings to the most specific headings;

– logic in order to cover the scope of activities in a comprehensive and coherent manner. This quality is manifested by the use of a single logical division characteristic at each level of the hierarchy. It facilitates retrieval by allowing a more methodical search within a hierarchical class structure. It should serve as a frame of reference;

– easy to update with an evolving file plan designed to reflect the ongoing development of the organization's activities while remaining stable. Its flexibility ensures that all records can be integrated without making major changes to the logical structure. In an organizational context, this quality is manifested by the use of administrative and operational functions and activities as the first criterion for logical division. It should be remembered that the filing plan should reflect as accurately as possible the mandates, functions and activities of the records creator. It should be based on the existing and not the virtual. Above all, the structure of the file plan must be sustainable and be usable by several people, simultaneously or successively. In some cases, at the lower levels of the filing plan, it is preferable to use serial filing: chronological and/or alphabetical (personnel files, school files, scholarship files, accounting records) [ASS 07, p. 89];

– the authority with a classification plan built on consensus. This quality ensures the level of accessibility of the classification plan by all users. It is a question of ensuring that a person responsible for the classification plan is appointed who is the only one authorized to delete or add headings so that everyone has the same reference system. This is even more relevant for shared folders, so that users do not modify headings as they produce records and have a formalized naming of their files with version numbers;

– universality so that it can be used by any application or environment. This quality can be manifested by the use of a single filing plan for the organization of all digital or paper records. It promotes uniformity in the classification of records held under several different applications [MAS 15].

Several organizational logics can underlie the structuring of the filing plan:

– the record filing plan defined for a process or activity. The process logic implies a more global and collective vision of activities: activities common to several departments are grouped under a single entry, the activities of a department can be split up, with the insertion of entries corresponding to the activities of other participants in the process. This more rational organization is also more difficult to set up, as it is more difficult to understand by the users who need to be trained [GRO 11, p. 9];

– the filing plan by type of record. A plan by type of record or record typology (mail, circular, contract) does not in any way imply either its function or its purpose (recommendation, study, complaint). It creates areas where it becomes difficult to retrieve information and make the link between several records of different nature that have contributed to the same operation [GRO 11, p. 8];

– the thematic classification plan. It organizes the different fields of knowledge in which the subjects contained in the records fit. Records are classified on the basis of the similarity of their subject or the knowledge conveyed. A thematic classification plan organizes the records by highlighting their information content, independently of any work process. Its structuring proves more complex to conceive than a simple enumeration of a sequence of activities because of the technical language that generates more ambiguity in the expression of a theme. Thus, for a laboratory classification, it is organized according to the observations and work of the laboratory, whereas a documentation center is organized according to academic logic [GRO 11, p. 7];

– the classification plan by functions and activities which, since the 2000s, has been the model that seems to be favored almost everywhere in the world. The hierarchical model is the most widespread and the only model authorized by MoReq2. Its effectiveness is linked to an intuitive mode of use. The user will consider the list of the highest level classes in the plan and locate among them, to the exclusion of the others, the one that covers the record he is looking for and so on until he finds the record itself [GRO 11, p. 11]. The hierarchical file plan categorizes all the series of records that document the functions and activities of an organization, enables their use, and makes it possible to establish a retention schedule for lifecycle management. It provides the ability to identify essential records or document sets, those containing sensitive or confidential information, or personal information to manage access rights [ROB 11, pp. 0.09–0.10.].

According to the Records Management Standard, it is suggested that an activity-based classification scheme be used which presents "the hierarchical relationships between functions, activities or actions and operations within the organization". Functional classification systems will be more effective and sustainable because they are based on analysis of the actual activities and processes of the organization rather than on the subject matter of the records, frequently changing organizational structures or other conventional characteristics used to classify records. This organization, at least for the first few levels of the classification scheme, facilitates the understanding of the creative context, particularly for the interpretation of the information being confirmed, but also for its administrative or legal value [GRO 11, p. 7].

The functional and hierarchical classification plan has gradually replaced the one based on organizational structure, which was considered too unstable, especially in a context of permanent reorganization of services involving a redistribution of activities and classification by theme or subject. A structure based on the organization's administrative units, record media, types of records and chronology should therefore be avoided. Similarly, a plan by type of record or documentary typology (mail, circular, contract) in no way implies either its function or its purpose (recommendation, study, complaint). It creates areas where it becomes difficult to retrieve information and make the link between several records of different types that have contributed to the same operation [GRO 11, pp. 7–8].

The norms and standards agree in recommending that the classification plan be organized according to the missions and activities of the organization. The choice can be made to break down the activities either by entity of the organization or by process. The logic by entity aims at setting up classification plans adapted to each service, which facilitates their appropriation by users. In the process logic, activities common to several departments are grouped under a single entry. The documentary production of a service is therefore split between several processes. This organization can be more difficult to set up, as it is more complicated for users to understand and it is essential to train and support them [ASS 07, p. 88].

The hierarchical classification plan is based on an organization's typical current functions and activities. A distinction is made between the management functions common to each organization and traditionally placed at the top of the main classification list. This is followed by operating functions specific to an organization's mission: research and development, marketing, customer management. It proceeds from the general to the specific and lists all activities and business processes generating records related to each of the functions [MAS 15].

The filing plan is an intellectual structuring of records and files in relation to each other, usually in the form of a multi-layered tree structure. The most difficult part is to prioritize the classes. The subdivision criteria are imperatively the criteria for access to records prioritized according to search habits. It is important to clearly delineate the boundaries between activities even if they contribute to the same objective in order to limit the depth of the classification plan. Beyond four levels, the plan is less operational because of the many manipulations in the search strategy [GRO 11, pp. 22–23].

The identification of the classes of the plan requires the analysis of the business processes which are declined in:

1) missions, activities (e.g. Human Resources Administration);

2) management objects to which the activities relate (e.g. personnel files or buildings under construction, experiments planned in a research program, employees receiving training, etc.);

3) operations that break down activities. The difficulty is to know how much finesse it is useful to go down to:

- at the level of the operation such as investigating a case, leading a working group (for example, Staff Compensation);

- at the task level, such as filling out a form, writing a report, validating a note (e.g. Payroll Management) [GRO 11, p. 19].

An organization must respond to the missions entrusted to it, for which it carries out a certain number of activities. The generic classes are constant and unique, and represent the missions and activities, most of the time appearing at the highest levels of the tree structure. They are defined when the classification plan is created. The subclasses or classes are used to designate by name the particular objects to which the activities apply, and correspond to the notion of folder (business folder, customer folder, geographical folder, etc.). They are added to each other as the organization's activities progress [GRO 11, p. 14].

It is also possible to associate repeatable classes for operations and tasks. These are classes that reproduce identically from one generic class to another or from one instance class to another. They refer to operations performed in a work process [GRO 11, p. 15].

It is necessary to define the perimeter to be covered by the filing plan and to decide whether existing records will be taken over and integrated into it, either totally or partially. The documentation policy must also allow for the selection and prioritization of the categories of records to be included in the classification plan:

– core business records resulting from business activity (for a buyer: business consultation files, market files; for a teacher: course materials, grading, publications). Files relating to processes or activities: hiring staff, equipment and material purchases, vehicle maintenance, administrative records management, quality control and administrative planning;

– supporting records related to the activities and functions facilitating the operation of the structure (employment contract, internal regulations, application form for authorization, plans of the premises, purchase requests);

– records relating to individuals that generally contain personal information that should be protected as required by existing legislation (records of employees, shareholders, interns, students, professors);

– records relating to organizations. These records are generally more informative than operational in nature and do not relate directly to any business or internal management activities (records of suppliers, sponsors, funded organizations, partners);

– records relating to business objects such as buildings or land, projects to be carried out, publications to be produced, grievances filed by unionized staff (records of buildings, vehicles, advertising campaigns) [ROB 11, p. 3.13];

– informative records that enrich and feed the business activity (working documentation, reference system, for a buyer: the commercial code, the public procurement code, internal circulars on purchasing policy. For a professor, publications by colleagues or websites) [GRO 11, p. 10].

Sabine Mas, in her thesis on record classification, showed that a small number of first-level classes and a logic based partly on a division by activity classes significantly affect the speed of retrieval of targeted records. This suggests that a slight extension of the first levels is preferable to increasing the number of sub-divisions. Beyond four levels, the filing plan will be less operational due to an increase in the number of manipulations in the search strategy. In order to locate a class, it is necessary that the class is quickly visible, and therefore the number of directory openings in an MS Windows environment must be limited. Concretely, when we notice that the classification plan is too deep, we must make sure that we do not treat several activities in one, by carrying out a complementary analysis of the represented process, and try to rebalance it by "raising" the level of certain activities, or by inserting activities allowing groupings [GRO 11, p. 23].

Choosing an open increment is essential at least on the lower levels to be able to make the plan evolve. This coding is useful even in the case of the deployment of a specialized computer system in which class scheduling is not imposed, as it facilitates the application of automatic business rules for the archiving system or clearances [GRO 11, p. 27]. The computer operating systems used in organizations lend themselves well to the implementation of the institutional file plan as a tool for organizing digital records. The file tree structure of the file management system allows for relatively easy migration of the logical and hierarchical structure of the records classification scheme [MAS 15, p. 188].

> **Restructuring of the *Commission de services régionaux de la Péninsule acadienne* shared file (New Brunswick, Canada)[7]**
>
> A research and development partnership in record management has been established between the Université de Moncton, Shippagan campus, and the *Commission de services régionaux de la Péninsule acadienne*[8] (CSRPA) (2017–2019).
>
> This involved studying the adaptation of the classification plan to the needs of the services, the definition of description and preservation metadata and the procedures to be put in place to improve information governance.
>
> The organization's shared folder contained 48,000 folders comprising 72,000 files, which meant selecting representative folders to implement a naming and classification method with a consideration of the number of levels (missions, activities, actions).
>
> To fully understand the documentary typology, we conducted an initial test using the files in the "work tools" folder, which includes 111 files and whose records are more of a documentation nature and do not offer any confidentiality issues.
>
> The main problem arose very quickly, as the filing plan had up to eight levels making direct access to the files difficult. For example, in a first selection we counted 783 files for only 494 files when it should have been the other way around. Approximately 40% of files were eliminated and the levels were reduced to a maximum of two or three levels.

---

7 Study conducted by Florence Ott, professor of records management and Vincent Dugas, research assistant and graduate of the Bachelor's degree in Information Management at the University of Moncton, Shippagan campus.
8 We would like to thank the CSRPA and especially the Director of Planning of the Urban Planning Department, Mr. Benjamin Kocyla, for making this study possible.

Approximately 400 test files were selected for renaming with the finding of many empty folders of which 136 were eliminated. We then used the titles to see the naming and try to target a coherent organization and create themes. We identified 62 relevant themes that are divided into 439 documentation files. This brings us to an average of seven files per theme.

However, 124 documentation files failed to justify the creation of a theme and were grouped together to discuss with the Director whether some should not be eliminated or should be placed in other files.

After some discussion, it turned out that two levels were sufficient: either the theme folder and then the files concerning the theme with a standardized naming.

Example: Theme_Object_Location_Date Career_Permit_Caraquet_2019.Pdf

The study was extended to other files with the grouping of certain files and their classification in alphabetical order, which did not pose any difficulties of comprehension. It was the same for the naming of the files since the titles were very explicit; it was just important to standardize the metadata by specifying the order of the titles, removing the spaces between terms and putting a capital letter in their place or a low hyphen and to reduce the number of levels.

It was decided to reproduce the themes of the town planning classification plan in the archive file to enable the records to be integrated as and when they are archived, while keeping the same classification structure. When a file has reached archiving age, it will simply be moved to the folder of the same name.

In each by-law locality file, we have included a "WorkingRecord" file. This makes it possible to put all working versions. When the last version is validated, we add VDef for final version, but all versions remain in word in this folder to be eventually annotated or reused. The final version is also converted into Pdf/A format for filing.

For the classification and naming levels of the Arrested folder:

– first level: localities (Caraquet, Tracadie, etc.);

– second level: folder archives by locality and Stop files.

There are five description fields:

– locality: location of the zoning interpretation;

– zoning: type of by-law;

– order no.: the number of the order as modified by the interpretation;

– article no.: number of the amended article;

– object: briefly explains what the amendment is about. This field is optional;

– year: year of interpretation.

For example: [locality]-[typeOfRegulation]-[stopNumber]-[StopType]-[date]

Caraquet_Zoning_211_Order_Modif_2017

By-law types include as a field: Map, Construction, Subdivision, Municipal Plan, Zoning. For Caraquet we add Heritage.

Order types include naming: DocOriginal, Amended, Redrafted.

Another problem has arisen for the retention of e-mails with high administrative or legal value in ".MSG" format of Outlook or in "HTML" format. Compatibility was not possible with Macintosh computers and storage in the cloud. Therefore, 4000 e-mails had to be converted to "Pdf/A" format.

Two training sessions were given to the agents with practical work to launch the method and make them apply the naming procedures by asking them to rename files and integrate them in the right folders. Good e-mail management practices and guidelines were recalled and the requirement to convert binding e-mails to Pdf/A format was reiterated.

In conclusion, the Director of Planning confirmed an interesting gain in the organization of information and an increased awareness of his staff in the naming of files, which facilitates the management and exchange of records. For the shared folder, 72,000 files have been processed and it is on the way to becoming the institutional and documentary base of the service with guaranteed backup and archiving. It should be noted that the deletion of empty folders created a priori without taking into account the existing one has made it possible to reduce the number of files to 26,700. Subsequently, by deleting unnecessary levels of headings, the final retention of 14,800 files was reached, a 70% gain in loans, still containing 72,000 files for which the retention periods still have to be defined.

A Naming Charter has been set up and respected and a classification tree of the files of the "town planning department" has been drawn up. A manager has been appointed. Another interesting point is that the right of access to the shared institutional folder is now well defined under the responsibility of a person specifically assigned to validate the files and is the only person authorized, along with the director, to modify the folders. Naming guidelines have been compiled in a record distributed to officers. The digital records to be archived have been organized in an architecture similar to the active file plan. Metadata for each type of record such as by-laws, contracts and agreements, policies, meetings and commissions and committees were finalized in a procedures document. Best practices in the management of e-mail are evident. Officials wish to continue the study on the legal aspects for digitized or digital native records with a validation procedure and the development of a retention period schedule.

The development and implementation of the classification plan involves different actors and different levels of responsibility depending on the actions to be carried out: design, validation, monitoring, evolution, classification of existing records, classification of new records, definition of access rights to classes, administration [GRO 11, p. 19].

Communication and training are an integral part of the project. It is important to involve users from the design stage of the filing plan to encourage its subsequent adoption, and to provide training on a one-to-one basis or in small groups. A file plan that is well designed from a theoretical point of view will be ineffective if employees are not trained in its use. Regular updates of the tools are inevitable to ensure that the classification tool meets the user's needs.

The end user must remain at the beginning of the analysis in order not to lose sight of his or her classification needs and practices, since it is now up to him or her to classify and, indirectly, to evaluate the records in a digital space that is closely linked to it. Dissatisfaction with methods or systems deemed inadequate will be a source of resistance and may lead to the adoption of circumvention strategies.

Consequently, methods for identifying and retrieving records of business or archival value must be described to help employees distinguish between records of archival value and those that have simply accumulated over time in personal information spaces [MAS 15, p. 192].

It is fundamental to make users aware of the issues and the approach and to get them to adhere to the project. It is necessary to document and above all explain the classification system to users. A simple paper copy of the filing system with explanations is disconcerting for users of an electronic system, and is largely insufficient. The terminology may be too generic and not correspond to the employees' own semantics in their field of expertise. Examples can be put online, workshops organized with the service's referent to show users the potential gains in terms of searching and securing information, of which the filing plan is a pivotal element [GRO 11, p. 31].

It is important to recognize that the cognitive effort involved in the act of classification, increased information overload, lack of time, and the way things are done in the organization can lead individuals to use more personal classification schemes to organize their digital records in a work environment. They no longer have to negotiate or adhere to the naming conventions, classification rules, changes and exceptions they use. Therefore, to limit the risk of failure or rejection, users must quickly understand the logic of the classification scheme or they will quickly get into the habit, in order not to waste time, of classifying records by default in inappropriate classes, leading to the failure of the project.

The method of hierarchical file organization has been criticized. Tree structures of files with a single classification are designed contrary to the minds of individuals who may associate an item of information with different categories. Often, it is more laborious to find them, as folders hide the longest files, as one has to navigate through the hierarchy. The individual has to decide which category the information best fits into making the process cognitively cumbersome. This unique classification must also anticipate future usage needs, which is difficult because of changes in usage over time [MAS 15, p. 182].

In principle, officers seem to understand the usefulness of this system for harmonizing filing and documentation practices, for sharing information within units and in the event of a change of position. The main problem seems to lie more in how to help users implement it, because a majority of them cite lack of time as the main obstacle to implementing or using the institutional filing plan [MAS 15, p. 189].

However, the filing plan, which is based on the functions and activities of the organization, is criticized for being too static and rigid. It is more responsive to the needs of records managers than to the needs of employees. It does not take into account the search methods preferred by officers who must manage and file their records at their workstations. However, traditional classification has undeniable advantages for organizations in terms of standardizing and contextualizing information and does not seem to be on the verge of disappearing [COU 14, p. 152].

Despite these disadvantages associated with the hierarchical model, this navigational structure is still appreciated and even preferred to the use of faceted classification in personal digital information spaces [MAS 15, p. 191].

Example of improved management of a shared file at the Université de Moncton Library on the Shippagan Campus in Canada.

Sharing information is an important issue because, regardless of the medium used, the information must be reliable and available. The emergence of collaborative tools, particularly shared files, requires standardization of practices. This is why the library's shared folder, created in 2006, has proven difficult to use because of an obsolete filing plan and the absence of precise rules making it difficult to access essential records and producing a multitude of versions and duplicates.

There are many drawbacks, such as the absence of a person responsible for file management, a lack of sharing of records useful to staff, a lack of security of the content which can lead to the deletion or modification of records and does not guarantee their authenticity, the absence of common rules for the identification or naming of files and for the length of time they are kept. In addition, some files lack metadata and it is sometimes difficult to trace the producer and provenance of the record. Most serious of all, however, is an outdated filing plan that is not always suitable for digital records. Many files are found in several folders of the plan and it is difficult to find the final version. The decimal classification of the records blocks out nine headings, which prevents new headings from being added if necessary.

To achieve this, the dysfunctional and overly complicated filing plan was completely redesigned. Then, a specific "Training" element of the shared folder was chosen to capture a representative sample of the various problems that could be encountered in setting up the shared folder. The records proved to be easy to identify. As most of the producers were no longer in post, this made it possible to assess the current utility of the records. The file consisting of 416 files and 69 folders was sufficiently representative. A reflection was carried out on the organization of the file by considering how to organize the sub-headings within the source file itself. Starting with 69 files, this was reduced to six. It seemed more relevant not to create a sub-folder, as the naming was sufficient to find the information in the file.

Improvements have been made to the file naming rules to facilitate searching and eliminate unnecessary versions. Information sharing is increased and accessibility to all authorized staff is facilitated. Documentation and circulars from the central library are no longer duplicated, reducing filing and retrieval time and retention costs. The project has increased staff confidence in the widespread use of digital information, and the Library Director has decided to follow up on the shared file and assume responsibility for the filing plan.

3.4.3. The faceted classification plan

Shiyali Ramamrita Ranganathan, an Indian mathematician and librarian of the first half of the 20th Century, was the first to introduce the concept of faceted classification in the field of records management and for classifying books in libraries. His theory provides a syntax for expressing and representing "manually" the subject of a record. He proposes a first level of division between the major fields of knowledge under the name of "main facets". There are five of these facets: personality refers to the object referenced in the record; matter refers to substance, property or quality; energy refers to the main operation or action described in relation to the object; space refers to geographical location; and time refers to time [MAS 12, p. 81].

The faceted model makes it possible to highlight components or characteristics of an activity without putting them in the hierarchical logic of the plan. A facet can be assigned to several types of records. It is effective when the organization wishes to provide records governance for processes that involve multiple departments when the hierarchical model creates duplicates to represent activities and records that are shared by multiple departments [GRO 11, p. 12].

Basic facets of faceted classification
Personality: category of persons or organization or the theme or purpose of the record or file. E.g.: Human Resources.
Energy: action in relation to the object at the origin of the record or file. E.g.: Hiring.
Material: the substance, ownership or quality of the record or record. E.g.: E-mail.
eSpace: the location in space of the action on the object of the record or file. E.g.: Human Resources Department.
Time: the place in time of the action on the object of the record or file. E.g.: Fiscal year 2010.

Table 3.6. *Presentation of the five basic facets (PEMST) of records and the faceted classification file (source: [ROB 11, p. 1.20])*

Faceted classification is based on an analysis of the characteristics of a representative part of the objects to be indexed. The five main facets make it possible to represent both the subject matter as well as the content of production and use of the records and by extension of the files. These basic facets need to be supplemented by secondary facets. Once the facets have been identified, a finite set of terms (controlled vocabulary) can be defined and validated for each of them: lists of choices of objects, actions, record types, responsibility centers, years, dates or chronological periods. The facets selected can constitute as many indexing metadata in a section of an integrated record management software solution. It is used to describe and index the identified objects to be accessed and managed [ROB 11, p. 1.20].

Facet theory provides a syntax for representing the subject of a record. Facets are categories corresponding to different perspectives on the subject of a record or file (action, location, target audience). Values are "tags" associated with these facets. These values can be thought of as metadata that describes the information element by means of a keyword or term. Unlike records, facets and their corresponding values are not hierarchical, and individuals can assign as many values to a data element as they wish [MAS 15, p. 183].

The effectiveness of faceted classifications lies in their ability to integrate the analysis of the different dimensions of an information object, facilitating the characterization and access to this information through multiple perspectives. Rather than having a single organization of digital records, users can create different virtual views of records that have been classified according to the faceted classification scheme. When saving a digital record, the user of the faceted classification scheme can choose by indexing or labeling between one or more preset values in one or more facets using a drop-down menu. This labeling allows the record to be associated with one or more classes within the faceted classification scheme [MAS 15, p. 184].

Description	
PowerPoint presentation during a GEIN1000 course session given in winter 2019.	
Facets and values	
Activity	Course management
Type of record: PowerPoint course	Course PowerPoint
Academic session:	Fall 2019
Record recipient	Students
Course acronym	GEIN1000
Session	Course 3

Table 3.7. *Example of a record labelled using faceted classification in a university context (source: [MAS 12, p. 91])*

The flexibility and expressiveness of a faceted classification that relates the content of the record (closer to individual needs) to the context in which it is created (documentary needs) would overcome the difficulties encountered in attempts to implement classification schemes, improve search accuracy and better manage institutional information throughout its lifecycle [MAS 12, p. 82].

Records created as part of business processes should be considered as "business objects" that provide a record of actions taken and decisions made. A business process is defined as a sequence of several actions at the same level that shows the order in which actions occur and where different actions can be performed by different people. It can be operational focused on the mandate of the organization or administrative supporting the business process (human resources, financial). Process mapping is an essential component of the methodology to identify the facets that would be used to both classify information from a perspective while meeting the specific requirements of the user's tasks [MAS 12, p. 85].

If we take the example of the activities of professors, they relate to teaching, service to the community, administrative tasks and research. They are not only responsible for managing a course and planning and evaluating student work. They are also administrators, lecturers, researchers and authors. There are seven main divisional criteria: activity (exam appraisal), type of record (course outline), sender of the record (students), recipient of the record (director), version of the record (final), academic term (fall 2010) and course acronym (SCI6114). The list of concepts identified by the business process and the analysis of the names of the numerical directories, recurring values or keywords and terms used in the directories (course outline, director) are extracted and they have been grouped in a limited number of classes (e.g. type of record) or in new classes (record recipient). The facets and values related to these facets were derived from these classes [MAS 12, p. 86].

Generic facets	Specific facets
Actor (last name employee, first name)	Record version
Position (teacher)	University term (Fall 2019)
Role (teacher-researcher)	Winter 2020
Department (Science)	Course acronym (GEIN1010)
Activity/Task (course development, appraisal, etc.)	Recipient of the record (student, principal)
Type of record (course notes, lesson plan, etc.)	Sender of the record (student, principal)

Table 3.8. *Generic and specific facets of course design and delivery (source: [MAS 12, p. 87])*

Some comments emphasized that faceted classification could find its full potential in the context of shared records that are created and used by team members and stored on a common server. There is also the important link between the selection of records to be classified using faceted classification and the archival value of the records. There is a need to establish both the business and archival value of administrative records while attempting to balance these perspectives in the choice of facets and values to be made available to users [MAS 12, p. 101].

The individualism that characterizes the classification of organizational records should motivate records managers and archivists to rethink their methods in order to provide solutions that would not only standardize the personal organization of digital records, but also prevent problems related to the retrieval of these records. According to Sabine Mas, "a more egalitarian approach should be achieved where the user becomes a partner with the records manager in the construction and maintenance of classification schemes. Given the pressure of working under pressure, it is essential to offer users the simplest, most specific and most comprehensive model possible from the outset in order to reduce the cognitive and emotional effort associated with any classification act while demonstrating the usefulness of this model for classification and retrieval" [MAS 12, p. 106].

3.5. Conclusion

The noblest, but at the same time most difficult work is that of record appraisal, as it requires a great deal of reflection since it will decide the disposition of the records. Retention schedules are a privileged tool that offers producers and managers a reasoned, planned and organized way of analyzing the relevance of the records to be preserved. Resulting from the cross-examination of the producer and the professional, they enable the standardization of procedures for the management and conservation of archive records. For the archivist, it is an indispensable reference system that encompasses irreversible decisions that must be taken if good information governance is not to be prevented and the collective heritage is not to be jeopardized.

Another important element of record management is metadata, which is data that provides information about other data. It is the information that is generated when technology is used to put activities in context. The generalization of the use of metadata facilitates intelligibility, exchanges and subsequent research and becomes a major issue that ensures better information sharing, better reuse and readability as well as traceability of information. Metadata can be used for various purposes, such as the recovery, reuse, authenticity, reliability, maintenance, conservation and selection of records. Metadata is particularly important because it establishes the relationship between a record and its functional and administrative context. In other words, electronic records are dependent on the proper documentation of their business context, but more importantly, they are dependent on metadata that describes how the information is recorded. There are three types of metadata: descriptive, administrative and structural. They can range from the creation of a record to a phone call or a chat. In the context of communications, metadata provides some detail about the creation, transmission and delivery of a message. In this regard, metadata may, for example, indicate the date and time a telephone call was made or the location from which an e-mail was accessed. Metadata is generally described as information about an electronic or digital record, but the concept of metadata is undeniably broader.

Furthermore, the proper naming of a digital file or folder is the corollary of the filing plan and meets the criteria of traceability and identification. The interest of naming is to associate to the file, as soon as it is created, a certain amount of metadata. In addition to file naming, it is possible to create record models (reports, notes, standard letters) to be used by the organization concerned.

The file plan should be seen as a tool and not as an abstract constraint. It provides a logical and hierarchical structure for classifying all records, in all media, that organizations produce or receive in the course of their activities. As classification is often perceived as a constraint, this function is relegated to the background without any real accountability and relies on the memory of a few elders. It is, however, essential within any company, as its proper use will determine the quality of the services rendered. Postponing the classification until later is not a sustainable solution. Moreover, experience shows that every employee spends a significant part of his or her working time finding records that are badly filed or incomplete, which will inevitably lead to a deterioration of the working environment that can lead to poor decision-making. A record is not only filed when a file is closed, but also in order to retrieve it later and thus make it accessible. This cannot be improvised. Filing must be methodical and rigorous. It is a guarantee of good information management and, above all, of information sharing, which reinforces collaborative work.

4

Sustainability of Information

The sustainability of the information lies in the system's guarantee that an electronic record will be returned in an intelligible manner throughout its retention period. Part of the documentary memory of our society created and preserved on digital media is already compromised, and the costs of restoring electronic records are very high. In addition, the fragility of the media and technological obsolescence must be addressed.

It is often thought that digitization is the most efficient way to preserve information while reducing storage problems. However, validation operations are neglected during dematerialization and the fate of the original records is not always well understood. Expeditiously, digitization is replacing microfilming as an alternative access and storage medium to the original records. Digitization can be an illusion of cost-effective, permanent preservation. The process is time-consuming and expensive, both in the production and maintenance stages, and long-term preservation is not guaranteed. In fact, digitization has maintained the illusion of "non-archiving" since everything is directly accessible.

Furthermore, there is a tendency to confuse back-up and archiving as well as electronic record management (ERM) with the electronic archiving system, which is the only guarantee of good preservation. The latter is a technical process that consists of maintaining a complete record over time. This involves maintaining the completeness and integrity of the data, its validation and usage metadata for a period of time and in a manner described in the records management metadata, which includes retention period, location, responsibility and method of destruction. It is a whole process that must be thought out, controlled, validated and brought into compliance with the rules on access and protection of personal data.

This is why it is necessary to put in place strategies for the sustainability of information, in particular through the migration of formats and systems and a reflection on the storage capacities of digital records by guaranteeing the reversibility of systems. From this point of view, cloud computing is far from convincing because of the difficulty of precisely locating data or using a cloud computing service limited to a particular territory. The question of the location of archives has to be addressed from two aspects: the geographical origin of the data to be archived, as regulations are not harmonized across the world, and the transfer of personal data.

4.1. The problem of conservation

4.1.1. *Sustainability of information*

UNESCO adopted a Charter on the Preservation of Digital Heritage on October 17, 2003. In its Article 5, it states that the preservation of the digital heritage is fundamental. To preserve it, measures must be taken throughout the life of the information. This starts with the design of reliable procedures and systems to produce authentic and stable archives. Article 8 states that the content, file functionality and documentation should be retained to the extent necessary to ensure the authenticity of the records [COU 14, p. 168].

One of the characteristics of sustainability is certainly to be able to access information over time, but especially in an intelligible way so that it can be interpreted. Given the particularly rapid evolution of technology, long-term conservation represents a real challenge whose answer is as much technological as it is organizational. This requires, on the one hand, a system-independent encoding of data either by very simple, open and therefore relatively durable encoding formats; by standardized formats adapted to preservation, such as PDF/A; or by XML-type data structuring that makes it possible to do away with a proprietary format while facilitating navigation within the records and its use [CAP 07, p. 28].

Keeping the memory of actions and facts is becoming increasingly important for management because of the increase in the number of long-term actions, whether it be the adoption of projects, more complex equipment or the construction and maintenance of nuclear power plants, not to mention food control or industrial accidents that can affect generations. Some of our actions and their consequences may go beyond the scale of our lives. Archives are becoming a tool for managing societies across generations. The fixed and precise memory of archives is indispensable to ensure this continuity, which is now vital for mankind [DEL 12b, p. 195].

A policy for the long-term preservation of digital records or data can be summarized as a policy that will technically and organizationally ensure regular and remote backups at different sites, the use of durable media, procedures for disaster recovery, replacement of media at the end of their life, and migration of data to new media as their use becomes more widespread with periodic verification of data readability and format conversion of data at the end of their life [SOY 12, p. 113].

In terms of preservation, the data is preserved during its lifecycle by detecting degradation of formats and media and, if necessary, migration is carried out. It is imperative to trace all elements that affect the life of the archive such as consultations and metadata changes, for example. The scheduling of the destruction of outdated data should not be forgotten, for reasons of cost and risk of unnecessary storage, legal obligation in the case of personal data, and the reliability of the archive's holdings where all the information stored must be relevant [RIE 06, p. 33].

Storage	Conservation
Default storage.	Conservation motivated by the value of the records, legal obligations and the interest of the owner.
Ignorance of the value of the records, often a mass that is not easily exploited and difficult to access.	Continuous monitoring to maintain the value of evidence and documentary content.
No tracking of the lifecycle of records.	Limitation of the duration to the information asset value followed by transfer to a dedicated service.
Unscheduled elimination due to lack of space.	For records that no longer have value, controlled destruction according to pre-defined procedures.

Table 4.1. *Differences between storage and preservation (source: [CHA 18, p. 45])*

To achieve good conservation, several elements must be taken into account. The metadata indicates the name and version of the data format of each record and the identification of the software with which it was last created and modified, as well as any format changes. A regular technology watch is carried out on them to prepare controlled conversion procedures for those that cease to be compatible with new software. It must be possible to export records data automatically or semi-automatically into open retention formats without loss of essential aspects of the content, structure and context of the records. The records and their context are understandable without the need for external information by maintaining detailed system documentation [ICA 05, p. 31].

It is advisable to keep electronic records in multiple copies. The solution is to keep the original in optimal conditions, to keep a backup copy in a remote location and to have a copy for use. The three copies can be on different media, such as the original on DVD, the backup copy on tape, and the usage copy on hard disk [KEC 14, p. 189]. For long-term preservation, the received version and the last two migration versions are retained as recommended in the ISO 27001 information security standard.

4.1.2. Digitization

According to the Provincial Archives of New Brunswick, digitization, also known as imaging or scanning, is defined as "the process of converting any paper or non-digital record, including text, photographs, maps, microfilm and other works, into digital form" [APN 13, p. 4]. Electronic conversion is accomplished by scanning a record, which produces an electronic representation of the original in the form of a bitmap image, also known as pixels.

Digitization not only provides better conditions for consultation, but also the creation of an information medium whose quality will be maintained over time. The color of the original records can be preserved and the different generations of copies are of identical quality, which is not the case with microfilm. This major change is taking place with the first online releases on the Internet networks, which were an immediate success: in 2003, three services put their civil status online, 17 in 2006, 38 in 2008; 45 million pages were available online on September 1, 2007, and already more than 90 million by the end of 2008. The archive services first put online the collections related to civil status, eagerly awaited by genealogists, the cadastre and iconographic collections [BAN 10, p. 74].

The impact of the digitization of heritage funds, particularly those related to genealogy, is significant in terms of the number of visitors to the site thus opened. As soon as an archive service puts its collections of parish registers, civil status and population census online, the site is immediately visited by several tens of thousands of connections per week and by several hundred Internet users connected simultaneously, thus creating a virtual reading room. This undeniable success is accompanied by the development of new practices, with the increasingly active participation of Internet user communities. If the diffusion has made genealogists disappear from reading rooms, on the other hand, new audiences, sometimes far away from the territories concerned, are appearing. These new communities come into contact with each other, thanks to the new user-friendly tools offered by the web, through blogs, forums and other discussion lists. Very quickly, the archive services realize that attentive readers are behind their screens who immediately report any errors in the distribution (missing pages, truncated images, dating errors in the finding aid, etc.) and thus contribute, through this active participation, to improving the quality of this distribution and of the finding aids associated with the sources [BAN 10, p. 80].

But digitization does not only affect archives, it also affects all organizations. They see many benefits. They see a solution to reduce the mass of paper records and physical space. With digitization comes the introduction of electronic record management, which should improve work efficiency through improved access to and sharing of information. It can also reduce the handling of fragile and valuable records that must be preserved because of their intrinsic value. In the event of a disaster, this provides a duplicate archive that allows for the recovery of at least the digital copy of the records. Access rights can also be used to control who can see the records [APN 13, p. 6].

Success depends on extensive preliminary operations, including reconstituting the backbone of the funds, classifying and inventorying them, pruning and putting the files in order. In 1996, Guy Braibant noted that, being more space efficient than their predecessors on paper, new archives are at least as expensive or even more expensive in terms of personnel and operating resources [SER 15, p. 397]. Records handling requirements may impose the need for additional resources in terms of hardware and software, staff, and storage space. Legal requirements for the preservation of authentic and reliable records may limit the ability to handle digitized records and possibly the requirement to retain the paper version of the records even after they have been digitized [APN 13, p. 7].

There are three different ways to scan records for access:

– page images. The scanned record is static and cannot be changed or manipulated. The record cannot be searched unless appropriate metadata is added to allow online browsing or navigation;

– full text with Optical Character Recognition (OCR). This method translates the scanned record into machine-readable text, allowing it to be edited or manipulated. OCR does not work well with handwritten original records where the error rate may be high. The OCR software must distinguish between black and white areas of text. A problem that frequently occurs is caused by text that has variable or low contrast. OCR software can often have difficulty properly scanning text with typographical variations, rare or foreign characters, or old lettering forms. As a result, OCR accuracy is only 95% to 98%. This means that between 2% and 5% of the conversion of images of words in a text is inaccurate;

– coded text or full text with markup. This option requires the organization to provide the same choices and options as for full text, but must add a "search" function by placing selected text between tags, using either Standard Generalized Markup Language (XML) or Hypertext Markup Language (HTML) [APN 13, p. 7].

Before you start scanning, it is important to define a method and ask the right questions. It is a question of determining whether the dematerialization of a work process is indispensable, specifying the stakes of the digitization project and the expectations of the users, presenting in a detailed manner the cost/benefit ratio (hardware, software, human). The objectives may relate to the safeguarding of originals threatened by physical deterioration, the distribution of printed records in high definition (book publishing), the online distribution of an otherwise correctly preserved record or the destruction of paper records with no archival or graphic value, to reduce the volume of physical archives.

In general, the most advantageous records to digitize are those that support costly transactions; are frequently requested, handled, accessed and reproduced; must be kept for a long period of time; must be communicated in different locations; are homogeneous in form and content; and are voluminous and take up a lot of space. It is preferable that these records be already filed and have a filing plan to facilitate intellectual processing and indexing. On the other hand, digitization is not always the best solution; dissemination is the main objective.

Legal constraints on the reproduction and dissemination of archives may hinder digitization. The obtaining of material and intellectual property rights as well as authorizations for reproduction, including the identification of the creator, must be documented. It must be ensured that if the objective involves wider dissemination, it is achievable within the framework of the Copyright Act as well as privacy and personal information protection laws and contracts for the acquisition of records. The question of the legal value of the records to be digitized must be studied in the knowledge that the digital version of a record or file may be used either as a use copy, to facilitate processing, or as a substitute copy, with a view to the eventual total electronic management of a process with evidentiary value. This digital copy is *prima facie* evidence in writing. It should be possible to consider that it emanates from the author of the original. This reasoning is valid only if the faithfulness of the copy in relation to the original cannot reasonably be questioned. Elements such as the metadata of the record, the procedure for scanning and electronic archiving, and the person under whose control the scanning took place cannot be emphasized as crucial to convincing the judge that the process was not tainted by fraud [DEM 12, pp. 36–37].

Another question that often arises is whether paper records should be retained after they have been scanned. This depends on the level of risk identified and the cost of double archiving. In any case, archiving of originals that is limited to disordered storage making the records unusable, at least at an acceptable cost, is an aberration. If it is a simple use copy, the paper version of the record or file remains the only one with evidential value. The paper original cannot be destroyed. If it is a substitute copy, the electronic version of the record must have the same evidential value as its paper equivalent. Copyright, privacy and the use of electronic signatures must also be taken into account. The filing time of the paper record must then be taken into account in calculating the time needed for the scanning operation. If the digital record has all the attributes of authenticity. It can be substituted for the paper record and can be disposed of after a certain amount of time [SOY 12, p. 111].

If a record is to be selectively retained or preserved in archives and if there are plans to destroy the original records after scanning and declare the scanned record as the official record of business activity, the record should be scanned as master image files due to the risk of technological obsolescence. If the digital format is to be preserved over the long term, there must be a technological watch and significant investment to ensure the permanence of the information. Digitization formats must be adapted to the needs of users and the potential of the computer system (recommended formats). If the resources are not available, it will probably be necessary to change the objective. Impediments to long-term preservation lie in the initial decisions, which tend to focus on selection and conversion.

Conservation challenges can be grouped into two categories:

– technical weaknesses: mishandling, improper storage and obsolescence of formats and storage media, unsupported compression, file integrity including content backup, context, fixity, unsecured reference and provenance, limited compatibility of access interfaces;

– organizational and administrative challenges: insufficient institutional commitment to long-term preservation, lack of preservation policies and procedures, insufficient human and financial resources, inadequate administrative metadata, changing copyright laws.

When digital data is stored on optical discs, the memory device consists of a burner, optical discs, disc storage equipment (CD tower or jukebox) and the necessary software and computer applications. The general criteria to be considered for storage technology are speed (read/write, data transfer), capacity, reliability, standardization, and suitability for the tasks required and cost[1].

The most complicated thing is to clearly assess the duration of a project, which must have a beginning and an end. Between these two ends, the manager must

---

1 Cornell University Library, *De la théorie à la pratique, didacticiel d'imagerie numérique*, Department of Research, Cornell, 2002–2003, online, http://preservationtutorial.library. cornell.edu/tutorial-french/tutorial-french.pdf.

marshal resources to create deliverables on time and within budget. Project milestones and the pace of work must be defined. To ensure a realistic schedule, a pilot phase can be undertaken in which the time and associated resources can be quantified. This will avoid overestimating production capacity, especially in the early stages of the project.

If a service provider is used, certain types of records can lead to particular technical constraints and therefore additional costs. These may be fragile, bound records, very large records, records requiring special unfolding operations, heterogeneous formats within the same type of record, or very small records requiring heavy handling.

When choosing scanners, it is important to take care to define their quality, their speed and to pay attention to the quality-to-weight ratio of the output files. It is necessary to define the needs of the users and to guarantee the fidelity to the original record while taking into account the constraints of volumetry. The ability to choose the input mode, number of bits, resolution, original media, etc. is an important factor to consider when purchasing compatible software. It may not always be possible to create an image derived from a lower quality image of a high-quality image, but under no circumstances will digital technology be able to render detail that has never been captured. In some cases, when a high-quality scanner is purchased, software is provided [APN 13, p. 9].

The usefulness of an automatic character recognition tool can also be assessed. A public body should use a metadata quality control register to record the quality assurance process. It can decide how it records these results internally to allow for greater functionality and accessibility with its workflow. Image quality control records should be maintained for the life of the images [APN 13, p. 34].

There are several types of devices:

– large format scanner. It is used to scan maps, plans, architectural drawings, site plans and posters. It is similar to the flatbed scanner, but larger;

– flatbed scanners are used to scan paper records, photographs, negatives and films, slides and printed materials;

– scanner with an automatic feeding device, similar to a flatbed scanner, but with an automatic feeding device. It should only be used for scanning a large number of sharp, high-contrast records with printed characters. It may crumple or tear fragile records;

– vertical scanner for scanning books or other records of different sizes that cannot be laid flat. It allows copying from a raised position, which reduces the damage to books when trying to lay them flat. The top of the line includes software that adjusts and compensates for distortion caused by the page curve;

– film/side scanner for scanning slides and films. It produces a higher quality image;

– digital camera. A camera with a non-interchangeable lens is not recommended for scanning projects. Ideally, a digital single-lens reflex camera should be used. This type of camera can produce high quality images, with appropriate image resolution, suitable for archiving and publishing [APN 13, p. 8].

The important factor to remember about continuous-tone records is that the reproduction of tones and colors is as important, if not more important, than resolution in defining image quality.

Resolution is the precision and fineness of detail of a digital image. It is expressed in number of dots per unit length, usually in dots per inch (dpi) or pixel per inch (PXPP). The higher the resolution, the more information is recorded and the greater the file size and the storage and transmission bandwidth requirements. The resolution will need to be adjusted according to the size, quality, condition of the record and the use of the digital object. In general, it is recommended to use:

– 600 dpi for images;

– 300 dpi for retention files. The conservation file is a reproduction of the record that is as faithful as possible to the original, created for the purposes of long-term conservation and high-quality printing. It does not dispense with the need to preserve the original record;

– 150 dpi for broadcast files. The broadcast file is the one that is intended to be broadcast to the public for quality consultation and current quality printing;

– 72 dpi for viewing files. The viewer file is intended for general viewing on the screen and is not suitable for printing[2].

Compression is related to algorithms designed to reduce the size of an image and is expressed primarily in terms of lossy or lossless compression. Lossy compression removes some of the stored information. It is not recommended when the paper record is replaced by the scanned record as an official business record, as the accuracy of the image may be questioned. However, lossy compression images, such as JPEG images, occupy a smaller file size and take less time to load. Lossless compression keeps images identical to the originals. This is the case with the TIFF format, but images require more memory and take longer to load [APN 13, p. 23].

---

2 Direction des Archives de France, *Écrire un cahier des charges de numérisation*, Ministère de la Culture et de la communication Comité de pilotage numérisation, February 2008.

The master image is the image of the highest possible quality (archive image). It must be able to support a wide range of user needs, including the creation of derived images for printing, display and image processing. This means that the digital image can be reproduced as a readable facsimile when the result is the same size as the original paper record. It is also about preserving legibility and the ability to access data without loss of information, interoperability between systems, and the ability to retrieve and easily access information stored on optical discs.

Characteristics of the original	Recommended settings for master files	Recommended file format
Sharp, high-contrast records and printed matter (e.g. laser-printed or compound text)	1-bit bitonal mode or 8-bit grayscale – adjust the scan resolution to achieve a quality index of 8 for the smallest significant character; or 1-bit bitonal mode – 600 dpi for records with the smallest significant character measuring at least 1 mm; or 8-bit grayscale – 400 dpi for records with the smallest significant character measuring at least 1 mm.	PDF/A or TIFF
Records with poor legibility or diffuse characters (e.g. carbon copies), handwritten notes or other marks, low inherent contrast, smudges, color fading, halftone illustrations or photographs	8-bit grayscale – adjust the scan resolution to achieve a quality index of 8 for the smallest significant character; or 8-bit grayscale – 400 dpi for records with the smallest significant character measuring at least 1 mm.	PDF/A or TIFF
Records in grayscale where color is important for interpreting information or content, or for obtaining the most accurate representation possible.	24-bit RGB mode – adjust the scan resolution to achieve a quality index of 8 for the smallest significant character; or 24-bit RGB mode – 400 dpi for records with the smallest significant character measuring at least 1 mm.	PDF/A or TIFF

Table 4.2. *Recommended scanning standards for master files (source: [APN 13 p. 23])*

Quality assurance procedures must be established before the start of a digitization project. They provide the means to measure, monitor and analyze the project and to improve the process if necessary. They ensure the integrity, reliability and accessibility of the digitized records. Specific controls must be established and maintained to assess the quality of the digitization equipment; the business process of creating the digitized image; and the metadata. These include an indication of when testing and calibration of equipment will take place; procedures for verifying results such as the proportion of digital reproductions that will be visually inspected and how long original records should be retained after scanning to ensure that quality verification procedures can be performed; procedures for reimaging if quality standards are not met; and roles and responsibilities for verification and approval of results [APN 13, p. 12].

All quality assurance procedures must be documented and approved by senior management. All quality control data (such as records, reports, decisions) must also be maintained. This supports the authenticity of the records and can contribute to future long-term retention decisions. Internal procedures adopted by the organization should also be reviewed annually, or as required to reflect changes in process or new technology [APN 13, p. 29].

Date	Decommissioning	Quality control	Results (Ok/Fail)	Identifica-tion	Problems	Comments
2019-01-30		Jean Bats	Failure	00044	Poor color and contrast	Image rejected and rescan requested

Table 4.3. *Quality control register of the scanned image (source: [APN 13, p. 34])*

Many problems can appear such as interrupted or illegible characters, poor contrast or color, missing images or portions, or incorrect image size [APN 13, p. 33].

There are four rules to be followed to achieve good quality: the calibration and adjustment of equipment; the scanning density chosen according to image quality and storage capacity; the scanner spectrum must be able to render all the colors of the original record; the use of a greyscale to capture the photograph.

Particular attention should be paid to metadata that should enable lifecycle preservation and communication, especially in the case of digital archives. Metadata is an essential element of the digitization process as it is designed to help classify and index records to enable faster and more efficient retrieval of information. It provides consistent identification of records, preserving their authenticity and implementing retention and disposal requirements. They also play a role in the long-term preservation of digital records by helping to identify key information for the conversion and migration of records and placing it in context by providing information about the creator, organization and subject [APN 13, p. 16].

Date	Decommissioning	Quality control	Results (Ok/Fail)	Identifica-tion	Element	Comments
2019-01-30		Jean Bats	Failure	00044	History of the event	Date of the event not included in the metadata

Table 4.4. *Metadata quality control registry for the metadata of the digitized record (source: [APN 13, p. 34])*

4.1.3. The challenges of archiving

According to the International Council on Archives, "the archival function is the group of interrelated activities necessary to enable the protection and preservation of archival records and to ensure that these records are accessible and understandable" [ICA 05, p. 10].

Electronic archiving is still a term that is generally more widely used than digital archiving, as evidenced by more than 8,200 records published on the French-language Web on the subject in 2015 (4,850 in 2014) compared to a few hundred in 2004. The expression "digital archiving" has evolved from about 100 publications to more than 2,500 in 2014 and then more than 3,500 in 2015. A strong increase in the expression information governance can thus be observed, which seems to be becoming rather fashionable with 4,470 publications in 2014 (and 5,970 for 2015) against 339 in 2004 without, however, its combination with that of electronic archiving being very marked (165 results in cross-criteria in 2014, 135 in 2015) [GUY 15b, pp. 105–106].

Archiving projects are multiplying because of the risks attached to the quality, security, sustainability and usability of information over time. Many of these projects are victims of their complexity, the lack of visibility of priorities, the frequent inadequacy of proposed solutions and the complexity of standards.

When it comes to electronic archiving, it would be an illusion to believe that a single solution could be found because each organization has its own specificity. This is contrary to the fundamental principle of archiving, which is to always analyze the production context. Any electronic archiving policy must be based on a relevant analysis of the context, of the documentary typologies produced in the context of an organization's activities which, by definition, are unique. An approach that says that it is sufficient to follow a standard to the letter or to purchase software is not intellectually satisfactory [HAS 13, p. 34].

How can we ensure the sustainability of digital information in the face of obsolete formats and media, and guarantee access to electronic records and their legibility over time, when they are extremely fragile and the technological environment is constantly changing? Archiving today is necessarily a matter of anticipation and digital archives, in order to be managed, exploited, preserved and consulted properly, require strong collaboration between producers, computer specialists and archivists [ASS 07, p. 61].

The majority of written material is produced or exchanged using office automation tools and electronic messaging. However, they are mostly records that facilitate day-to-day work and are generally not designed to be kept in this digital form. These tools are generally used by agents individually, often outside any organized information system. The production of volumes of information in digital form is considerable and they clutter servers, disks and e-mail software, although the majority of this information has a very short life expectancy and use [BAN 09, p. 29].

The minimum requirements for reliable electronic archiving concern constraints on the identification and authentication of the origin of records, the integrity of archives and information packages, their intelligibility and readability. It also includes the retention period of the archival object, the traceability of operations, and the availability and accessibility of the archive [BAN 09, p. 40].

We understand the whole issue of digital archiving. First of all, to have a clear idea of how to transform data content into information content. Thus, we have all the descriptive, identification, structural, management, administrative, legal and technical elements at our disposal to restore this content in all its intelligibility to the community of users beyond those who produced it. Next, we need to be familiar with the organizational environment of the electronic archiving service to be implemented. It concerns the functions of collection, control, storage, management of descriptive data, access, administration and planning for sustainability. It is also about establishing a broad dialogue and cooperation between information managers, that is, archivists and computer specialists. Long-term preservation must also be ensured through the choice of open s-formats, media monitoring, format and media migration campaigns, and a policy of duplicating archives at two remote sites. The integrity of the archives will be ensured by cryptographically based technologies (fingerprinting, logging to ensure traceability of operations) [BAN 10, p. 75].

The introduction of electronic archiving systems as soon as records are created means that the confidentiality rules applicable to the field of activity concerned must be taken into account. Beyond the management of communication deadlines that archivists are accustomed to managing, it goes without saying that very recent archives can be particularly sensitive and must therefore be strictly protected against unauthorized access. It is imperative that this requirement be met in order to gain the confidence of the producing departments. The challenge is to prevent the disclosure of legally protected secrets [BUR 11, p. 81].

It appears that a relevant angle of attack is first and foremost to determine the priority or majority need. Is it the rapid availability of information, its integrity, its confidentiality or, above all, its sustainability? Thus, the basis of the solution can be based on the major objective sought: a patrimonial archiving, an archiving with evidential value, the preservation of know-how, or a better risk management. Archiving becomes a form of service to be declined according to objectives such as proof or the reuse of information.

Principles	Requirements
1 – Accountability	Policies and procedures approved by management, led by a senior manager and adopted by all agents.
2 – Integrity	Application of procedures to maintain authenticity and reliability of records.
3 – Protection of information	Access authorizations, security and confidentiality of management tasks.
4 – Conformity	Possibility to demonstrate that activities are conducted in compliance with laws and that the archiving system is audited.
5 – Accessibility	Quick retrieval of well-archived records.
6 – Conservation	Retention periods in compliance with regulatory and legal constraints.
7 – Destruction	Time-limited eliminations or transfer to historical archives.
8 – Transparency	Description of the archiving process and traceability of management actions.

Table 4.5. *The eight generally accepted recordkeeping principles (GARPs) defined by the Association of American Record Managers (source: [CHA 12, p. 21])*

For electronic archiving, there are five issues that apply perfectly to information assets:

– legal: the main risk is that the data required by an audit or judge may not be produced in the required form, as they must have characteristics of authenticity, integrity and non-repudiation;

– logistics: the data has been well archived technically, but it is difficult to access, it is unusable, or the data exists but the means to decode and interpret it has been lost;

– secure: confidential, strategic and personal data may be disclosed because they are insufficiently protected or should have been destroyed;

– technical: problems of interoperability between systems and the challenge of long-term data sustainability, given the recurrent obsolescence of formats, media and restitution tools;

– financial: the cost of a fine or court conviction, time wasted searching for information, or investment in tools not maintained over time [CAP 07, p. 29].

Archiving actually meets three distinct needs:

– the company must prove what it has or has not done and must also be able to produce, in the event of litigation, the records necessary to defend its rights and interests;

– it must be possible to reuse data in the conduct of business, such as studies that have already been done and can be reused in a new project, rather than recreating the information, which can be costly and time-consuming;

– it is in the company's interest to preserve its memory, both to build a corporate culture and to communicate with its customers, partners and employees [CAP 07, p. 29].

The success of implementing archiving in an organization depends as much on a real change in management habits as it does on technology. Organizational behaviors must change. To be successful, it is necessary to involve all relevant people in the organization in the process from the outset, provide good information on the objectives and benefits of good records management and archiving to all those involved, prioritize practical aspects such as user satisfaction and focus on training needs [ICA 05, p. 34].

There is a need to develop a global mapping of data to be archived, that is, data to be identified and captured in an archiving system, in order of priority:

– in addition to the current data that is regularly backed up, other, older data that is vital to the business is also stored, which is essential for the company to restart its activity in the aftermath of a disaster;

– data of a legal and regulatory nature in order to meet the requirements of the tax authorities, social organizations and to ensure the protection of personal data;

– the data supporting the interests of the company in case of litigation;

– information for future activity and historical memory.

Each type of data or record has several characteristics that make it possible to organize its archiving, in particular the sensitivity of confidential information, which is unique and difficult to reconstitute, or on the contrary, routine or comfort information; the frequency and urgency of consultation according to the type of record or data; this criterion makes it possible to optimize storage [RIE 06, p. 9].

Archiving processes for identification and capture require more detailed procedures:

– identify the data and records to be archived among the mass produced;

– avoid multiple copies by designating a person responsible for archiving;

– facilitate automatic data capture through naming and ranking rules;

– verify the quality of the archived data (complete, consistent and reusable information);

– define the necessary and sufficient metadata to manage each category of data: source (activity, author, recipient, context), keywords, file attachment, linked records, format, original application, medium, security index, access rights;

– ensure the integrity and therefore the traceability, as soon as the record is validated, that is, from the moment it acquires its value as evidence and testimony [RIE 06, p. 32].

If the saved information is not archived, the archived information must be backed up in order to be secure.

Backup system	Archiving system
Concerns data that can be modified.	Fixed addresses, validated data.
Allows restoration of lost data as part of a disaster recovery plan.	Concerns the conservation of data to comply with legal and regulatory obligations and possibly historical and heritage needs.
Usually organized offline and on another site.	Allows online consultation and can also provide for offline concept.
Must allow fast restoration and efficient access, but at a very unpredictable frequency.	Provides access with a relatively regular frequency, but generally decreasing over time.

Table 4.6. *Differences between the backup and archiving system (source: [RIE 10, p. 17])*

Archiving is not computer backup. The latter is a security copy of a set of electronic information in order to protect against incidents, loss or theft. It has a limited lifespan and its support is unusable outside its technical environment.

Backing up means guaranteeing the security of records and software so that they can continue to be used. The entire work environment or anything that has changed since the last backup is copied to a hard drive. No distinction is made between draft records and final records between work in progress and work completed, between successive versions of the same records. We work on the short term to restore everything in case of breakdown or disaster. Archiving means precisely identifying the records to be preserved and putting in place practices and operations to guarantee, in the long term, the preservation and legibility of these records. Sustainable storage aims to preserve bit sequences. In both cases, one is led to make copies on storage media external to the computer, but this is not sufficient for archiving. Backup and archiving can be complementary operations: daily backup, or weekly backup because it concerns records that are used and modified frequently, archiving every six months or annually, but allowing permanent access to certain records regardless of their age [HUC 10, p. 36].

Functional standards for electronic archiving that focus on the issue of maintaining the integrity of digital information are among the most numerous. Unlike preservation standards, they are at the heart of issues that go beyond the archival community [MES 15, p. 139].

The French standards NF Z 42 013 and NF Z 42 020, which are widely used by French electronic archiving professionals, place the burden of proof of the integrity of electronic data on the operation of the electronic archive containing it. It is based on a system or WORM2 media or by creating, throughout the operation of the system and the lifecycle of the archives kept there, a body of evidence to demonstrate their integrity [MES 15, p. 139].

The logging recommended by the NF Z 42 013 standard, which consists of the automatic recording by the system of all events occurring within it, is practiced within the framework of an information systems security policy. It is distinguished by the keeping of two logs: the archive lifecycle log, which lists all events occurring in the archive, and the event log, more common in information systems, which keeps track of technical logs, access logs, errors, etc. Each line of the log identifies by a fingerprint the archived object affected by the recorded action. The logs are then time-stamped at least once a day [MES 15, p. 139].

Another possibility is to electronically sign or at least time stamp each status of the archived object to attest to its integrity, whether or not the archived object was electronically signed at the time of its validation. As the entire burden of proof is on this device and not on a bundle of evidence, it becomes essential to regularly renew signatures and timestamps as soon as the encryption or hash algorithm that created them becomes obsolete. Finally, it is recommended that the electronic signatures to be retained over the long term be supplemented by the addition of metadata that may prove to be quite cumbersome, such as the Certificate Revocation List of the certification authority. While the security gain provided by such a solution is real, the need for an electronic signature system to use a key management infrastructure raises questions as to its cost and sustainability over time [MES 15, p. 139].

The falsely virtual nature of digital information means that the issue of storage is forgotten. Its management is left to technicians who are not responsible for the contents and ignore their value. The retention period of files is left aside. Digital technology has shifted the storage problem, but has not solved it. The multiplication of servers increases costs and makes the recovered data unreliable, with the risk of leakage of outdated data [CHA 18, p. 15].

Unlike paper archives, frozen in time, immobile, with slow degradation, digital archives are like plants. They must live. If they are not regularly maintained, they perish [HUC 10, p. 231].

We no longer keep what is memorable, but simply everything that is memorable. It must be seen how one accesses the archived content and which new rules organize and manage this content. But search engines make already popular content more visible and information that deviates from the norm less and less visible. It is necessary to return to the humanistic skills of content specialists in order to retain information for the memory of the future and remove irrelevant information [FRE 13, p. 14].

Nevertheless, security issues are still manageable and controllable if they are well understood. On the other hand, little attention is paid to electronic archiving. The challenge is to find a cure for what could be called "corporate Alzheimer's". Because if we are not careful, it is indeed the memory of organizations that is likely to disappear partially or even totally and how can we then function without memory? [RIE 10, p. XV].

According to a 1999 survey, 44% of the pages from the previous year are no longer displayed or are significantly altered; other research estimates the average page life to be between 44 and 100 days [KEC 14, p. 183]. In online scientific publications, one third of references and citations are out of control after 10 years [KEC 14, p. 184].

Web archiving involves taking into account composite, interactive and scalable records. The web forms one of the main vectors of the culture of societies and the memory of its different communities. Web records are an integral part of its digital heritage [COU 14, p. 141].

There are several forms of techniques:

– web content management that focuses on capturing the content of the site at the expense of its form;

– snapshots. As of June 2013, the *WaybackMachine Archive* website reports that it has archived 346 billion web pages. The project also serves as a digital library. Although it aims to collect all publicly accessible web pages, it does not capture the deep web, that is, databases and other records and software related to websites;

– maintaining websites online, a method that attempts to combine the dissemination of active and archival materials on the same website [COU 14, p. 144].

Library and Archives Canada (LAC) is a founding member of the International Internet Preservation Consortium. The institution began collecting Government of Canada websites in December 2005, in the form of snapshots that contain all the content of a website. The collection takes place twice a year using the Heritrix robot. LAC's indexing robot is programmed to exclude any content from a department's Intranet or Extranet. It does not collect databases that require the user to enter search terms or online forms. Searches are performed by keyword, department name, URL or type of record format [COU 14, p. 146].

As we can see, the stakes of electronic archiving are important for digital records produced or received by organizations, but also for all dynamic records and databases that transit through intranets and the web with all the problems of restoring links between records, knowing the authors and ensuring updates and the sustainability of the information.

4.2. The differences between electronic record management and electronic archiving systems

There is sometimes confusion between electronic record management (ERM) and electronic archiving (EAS). Electronic management is the dematerialization of paper and its transmission into the business processes of the company, which has little effect on the organization of work. It must manage record repositories, complex records such as contracts or technical records. It ensures the daily management of records and allows the modification of records as well as the production of several versions. It includes the integration of office applications and search tools to access records. It sometimes includes the management of retention periods, but the storage is under the control of the users who decide on the disposal of the records.

Electronic archiving is a distinct field that deals with the medium- or long-term preservation of the integrity of a record by reliably identifying its author and date of production. It is a system that consists of receiving, preserving, processing, and restoring archives, packets of information, and archival objects and which is based on a computer platform [RIE 10, p. 108]. The archived data requires an adapted, reliable, time-resistant and sufficiently secure medium, which is not backup. The requirements must guarantee the safety, security, integrity, sustainability and traceability of records and facilitate the search, use and communication of information.

Electronic Record Management System (ERM)	Electronic Archiving System (EAS)
Authorized modification and production of multiple versions.	Modification prohibited.
Destruction of records by their producer possible.	Prohibition of destruction of records outside of strict control.
No tracking of the lifecycle of records.	Limitation of the duration to the information asset value and then transfer to a dedicated service.
May involve the management of shelf life.	Mandatory and rigorous control of shelf life.
May include an organized storage structure under user control.	Requirement for a rigorous filing structure managed and controlled by the administrator.
Mainly concerns the daily management of records for the conduct of business.	Can facilitate day-to-day tasks, but is also intended to build a secure repository of the organization's evidentiary records.

Table 4.7. *Comparison of characteristics between an electronic record management system (ERM) and an electronic archiving system (EAS) (source: [RIE 10, p. 19])*

The Electronic Records Management System (ERM) should help to define and manage the types of records or data as soon as they are captured and define the appropriate retention period to ensure a secure collection of evidentiary records.

It prevents records from being altered and provides a strict filing structure for preservation and storage. The destruction of records is subject to strict validation and control of retention periods. Management is carried out by the system administrator and not by the users. It involves the definition of documentation rules (classification scheme, naming rules, metadata, record indexes), lifecycle management rules, access (clearances) and security rules. Finally, it also imposes technical rules (formats of records, storage media, sealing or signature, time and date stamping).

Electronic records management or integrated records management systems are seen as complementary rather than competing with EAS. These management systems allow a record to be created, even before it is frozen, and rules, such as communicability and versioning, to be applied to it during a pre-archiving period, and then to begin routine archiving before it is transferred to the electronic records management system. The main function of the latter is to ensure that the evidential value of the data continues until the end of a period of administrative usefulness of up to one hundred years, or even eternity for data to be kept as an asset [BEL 16, p. 49].

For files that are active over a long period of time, it is possible to put them on shared access in an electronic archiving system (EAS) common to the producing and archival departments, whereas in the paper world these files are generally placed in chronological sections in the archives, which creates an unjustified break from the point of view of administrative and documentary use. While it is possible to consider duplicating these files in a business ERM and in an archives' manual electronic records management system, the functional and documentary value is not obvious, and budgetary constraints may prevent this solution [BUR 13, p. 18].

In the field of electronic archiving, a French standard is used, NF Z 42-013, which dates from 2009 and which was transposed at the international level into ISO 14641 in 2012 and revised in 2018. It has been reviewed in depth, structurally and conceptually. Among the new elements are an adaptation to the OAIS conceptual standard and the addition of content on reversibility. The functional, organizational, or infrastructure requirements of an EAS have also been separated. It is silent on the necessary retention periods for records and organization. The main objective is the permanence, integrity, non-modification, security and traceability of the management of records that are archived. In addition, operations are logged to keep track of them. At the archival level, in the archives' lifecycle log, traces of operations, deposits or destruction are kept, for example.

Characteristics of an EAS	Comments
Reliable	Continuous and regular operation protecting the record from any modification.
Integrates	Access control that prohibits any abusive actions in the system.
Compliant	Operation in compliance with applicable regulations, e.g. record shredding.
Extended	Consideration of all records in the relevant perimeter.
Systematic	All relevant records are produced, stored and managed in a systematic manner.

Table 4.8. *Characteristics of an electronic archiving system (EAS) according to ISO 14641:2018 (source: [RIE 10, p. 21])*

The standard is an ideal, whereas the EAS is a technical and functional reality. What counts is the ergonomics of the tool, its adequacy with the needs of the organization, its sustainability and reversibility. The electronic archiving system is a specific computer system designed for the long-term preservation of digital content. This means durations that are significantly longer than the normal lifespan of the components of a usual computer system, which will require precautions. This computer system must guarantee accessibility, always in the long term, the continuity of preservation and the security of the entire system. The operation of an electronic storage and retrieval system is based on three pillars: specialized software, computer hardware, including for permanent or durable storage, and the security of the contents and management procedures for this system.

From a legal point of view, the ISO 14641:2018 standard on electronic archiving specifies the characteristics of the system that must guarantee the fidelity, integrity, sustainability and security of the records kept so that they can have evidential value and be admissible in a procedure [APR 14, p. 43].

The main functions of an electronic archive system are primarily concerned with the business classification plan, which consists of a system identifier, a classification code and a title. The system must also allow for the classification of records into as many hierarchical levels as necessary and also contain a system identifier, code and short description. It must also manage the concept of record type and retention rules, as well as the conditions of access and communicability. For certain sensitive applications, a classification level (confidential, secret, top secret), user authentication and access rights must be assigned [LEP 11, pp. 29–30].

The standard specifies the key elements of an archiving system:

– recording of record operations with logging of all record operations and their associated metadata;

– storage medium adapted to conservation needs and with protections in accordance with requirements;

– shared management allowing several copies of records on different sites to be managed in order to protect them;

– conversion and migration while preserving the qualities of the records;

– easy access, retrieval and use of records;

– reliable management of retention periods and the disposition of each record;

– when the archiving system is shut down or in the event of a malfunction, it is impossible to add new records;

– audits for the improvement of the permanence and implementation of a training plan.

Functions	Definitions and additions
Capture-Connection	Secure capture of records and data with evidential or documentation value.
Ranking	Structured and hierarchical filing plan, metadata, full text indexing.
Business rules	Confidentiality management. Access rights (consultation), entitlements (right to do), formats, retention periods, triggering of archiving.
Compliance, probative value	Electronic signature controls, time stamping, integrity, accountability, traceability, suspension of retention periods.
Conservation	Adapted support, traced migrations, file format conversion.
Interrogation-Return	Query by unique identifier or metadata, rights-based retrieval, on-screen consultation, printing, unit or mass retrieval.
Deletion	Deletion with or without a confirmation request, secure deletion, immediate complete deletion and elimination of backup copies.

Table 4.9. *Functions of an electronic archiving system (EAS) (source: [RIE 10, p. 21])*

The implementation of an EAS is based on the prior definition of the organizational perimeter that will be affected and the documentary perimeter concerned. Indeed, not all digital records are necessarily managed and stored in the same way: databases and computer applications may thus present characteristics that justify the choice of specific solutions. There is therefore no universal EAS. The system needs to be adaptable to the environment and business needs, so it is important to analyze the context and processes of record production within the organization that will be using the system [ASS 07, p. 72].

Even more than for paper, the intervention of the archive service must be articulated with the needs and constraints of the producing service. It is desirable to set up a shared responsibility for the EAS, distinguishing between the responsibility of a business administrator, assumed by the producer service, and the responsibility of an archive administrator, assumed by the archive service. Ideally, the archives should take the lead in designing the EAS, because of the predominantly documentary component of such a system [BUR 11, p. 81].

The deployment of an electronic record management system has two fundamental components: the implementation of a record management policy or archiving policy and the use of technical tools specific to the digital environment and intended to facilitate the perpetuation of information, in particular programs to automate the migration of formats.

The EAS is responsible for collecting, managing and retaining information for future reference. It provides assurances of integrity (protection against intentional and unintentional alteration), sustainability (ensuring the long-term legibility and usability of records), security (duplication and retention of data at two or more remote sites), confidentiality (controlling access to records), and traceability [ASS 07, p. 71].

The special feature of an EAS is that it ensures the retention of data even before questions of availability arise. Data is secured, beyond the "classic" redundancy of systems and facilities, by doubling copies (duplication, synchronous or asynchronous replication) at remote sites, by choosing different types of storage media, and possibly by having a back-up application server [DIS 12, p. 16].

Be careful not to confuse EAS with the offer of electronic safes. The latter are designed to secure data and records with evidential value. An electronic safe is a "component of an information system consisting of software or a software/hardware combination that preserves the integrity of digital objects over time" [DIS 12, p. 16]. CASs can thus control such a component. The perpetuation of digital information is specific to electronic archiving and concerns both technological monitoring, particularly with regard to formats and media, and the implementation of migration plans for formats or media.

4.3. Sustainability strategies

4.3.1. Emulation

It consists of keeping the original digital file intact and in bringing preservation techniques to its environment by recreating its original software context.

Emulation can be a solution to hardware obsolescence. Emulation software allows older software to run on newer technical platforms. However, there is a risk in doing so, because technical platforms are constantly evolving and the emulator will have to be adapted to keep pace with each of these changes; moreover, the use of old computer applications requires knowledge that is all the more likely to disappear as the existence of these applications is prolonged [ICA 05, p. 36]. For example, one can imagine emulating a Macintosh of a certain version on a PC with Windows NT, so as to be able to use a CD-ROM originally published for Macintosh only. Emulation has become a museum conservation practice and is mainly applied to the preservation of game software or digital objects of all kinds.

4.3.2. Migration

In the 1980s, the *Centre national d'études spatiales* (CNES) used one of the first pieces of office automation equipment available on the market. Ten years later, with the development of microcomputing, the proprietary systems developed earlier disappeared from the market, although the records have been preserved. Unable to migrate the records to the Microsoft Word software that was later retained, the records had to be re-entered. Eight years later the records saved in 1990 with Microsoft Word version 2.0 for PC were no longer fully compatible with Word 97 for Windows. For all the records to be retained, the text could be retrieved, but the layout of thousands of complex tables was completely reworked. At the time, it was thought that this was a youthful error in computing, but today we realize that not all migration problems have been solved [HUC 10, p. 12].

Changes can also affect the logical structure used to record the information, which is usually referred to as the file format. Sometimes these changes are the direct result of changes to the software. In any case, even if the most recent version of the software is capable of reading old format files, errors can occur when switching from one version to another, and it can be difficult to be certain that all files will be transformed without error unless one is familiar with both the file format and the software used to create and read them [ICA 05, p. 42].

One of the most commonly accepted conclusions of all those involved in the preservation of electronic records is that some form of migration is necessary to ensure their long-term survival. Migration applies both to the periodic copying of records to new media, of the same or different types, and to the transfer of information from one file format to another [ICA 05, p. 42].

The migration is then done when the old format is obsolete, or the old media is no longer maintained, or its technology is obsolete, or the media has simply reached the end of its life. Care must be taken to ensure that the integrity of the records involved in the migration is respected and that all records have been transferred from the old media to the new ones [RIE 10, p. 242]. Migration is the only answer today to the rapid obsolescence of technologies and the need for sustainability. Insofar as no medium is sufficiently durable, one must anticipate migrations intended to change media on a regular basis. For each of these migrations, it will be necessary to evaluate as precisely as possible the ins and outs of the migration in terms of costs, time required and the risks of temporary unavailability of access to information. It is also essential to record and keep track of all these migrations [RIE 10, p. 82].

There is also migration, which concerns the logical format of the retained data, we will then talk about format conversion. The technical integrity of the record, based solely on the sequence of bits and bytes retained, will obviously be lost. Consequently, every precaution must be taken with regard to the description and validation of the process used in order to always be able to guarantee the integrity of the information content. It is essential to keep a record of the details of the operations carried out, which allows proof to be provided, if necessary, that the data have not been modified in their content [RIE 10, p. 83].

Ultimately, migration consists of refreshing the file by transposing the data into a new envelope that is in line with technological developments. According to Interpares: "Keeping an electronic record is strictly speaking impossible; only the ability to reproduce it can be preserved. Therefore, the long-term preservation of digital archival records is achieved through migration, with its various techniques, from simple bit-by-bit copying to the respectful transformation of the record through metadata and the traceability of repeated changes in formats and storage media in accordance with ISO 14721, known as OAIS (Open Archival Information System)" [CHA 15a, p. 66].

4.3.3. The choice of formats

The format is an essential component of the digital record, as it expresses both the vector for its exchange between information systems and a guarantee of access over time. Throughout the lifecycle of the record, concern for the format in which the records are represented must be constant. To do this, tools adapted to the various processes of creation, display, conversion and control must be available [APR 06, p. 20].

There are different types of formats and their choice can be fundamental in order to guarantee the sustainability of a digital record. Claude Huc defines them as follows:

– proprietary format: it is defined by a company or a private owner who has the corresponding intellectual property rights or copyright (PDF, GIF). It is to be avoided for records to be archived, because the owners consider these formats as a trade secret and only the software they distribute can create and open records in this format. Users are captive even if the format is made public by its owner. The use of the format is subject to fees, royalties and restrictions. A software publisher can file for bankruptcy and disappear overnight [HUC 10, p. 113];

– open format: it is published and free of rights, with no restrictions on use or implementation. The data format is interoperable and the technical specifications are public [HUC 10, p. 114];

– closed format: the proprietary format is not published. Its structure is unknown to users, except those who defined it. In practice, it is a format that has been defined by a software publisher who has decided to keep the specifications of this format secret [HUC 10, p. 114];

– published format: the specifications are published and accessible to all without restriction. This does not mean that this format can be used without restriction. It is not necessarily an open format. The format can be published because its owner has specified the uses that were allowed. An example of an open proprietary format is the PDF format developed by Adobe [HUC 10, p. 115];

– standardized or standardized format: it is said to be standardized when it conforms to a standard issued by a standardization body (ISO, AFNOR). A standardized format is in conformity with a standard which is vaguer and has been proposed by a smaller committee of experts.

One reassuring thing is that the distribution of formats is very uneven and the first few dozen formats already represent more than 95% of the records on the Internet [HUC 10, p. 116].

Until 2000, the s-formats of the Microsoft Office suite were closed, while public administrations, especially European ones, created a huge amount of office records in these formats. As the preservation of these records was a strategic issue, Microsoft, under pressure from governments, resolved in 2003 to publish the formats of its files. However, in 2008, it succeeded in defeating the opposition to obtain international standardization of the file format of the next Microsoft Office suite. This file format is called Open Office XML or OOXML ISO 29500 standard. However, this OOXML specification is problematic, as it contains 7,000 pages and numerous technical additions of great complexity. The development of software capable of reading and creating files in the OOXML format involves very significant investments that are almost prohibitive. One could say that it is a false opening [HUC 10, p. 118].

In order to select suitable archiving formats, it is recommended to ensure that the format is widely used or has been the subject of a European or international standard, or at least to have public and easily accessible specifications. It is desirable to have a certain stability with a not too rapid renewal of versions, two to three years being a reasonable periodicity.

It must also be ensured that there are at least two software packages, developed by different publishers, available on the market that uses this format, or there must be an *Open Source* software, that is, whose source code is distributed under a license that allows anyone to read, modify or redistribute the software that supports this format. Such software is capable of interpreting the records and making the information contained therein understandable to the intended user community.

The long-term retention strategy requires limiting the formats to be maintained and must have validation functions (check for compliance with the expected format) and conversion functions. When the record is captured, the system must record its retention metadata, including file format and version, for future batch conversions. It is recommended that the record be saved in a durable format such as PDF/A and checked by the author at the end of the production phase before any archiving operation.

The criteria used for sustainable formats are:

– the diffusion of the format is important. It is used by a lot of software and the converters are better;

– the format is independent of any software and hardware;

– the format specifications are published and well documented in order to develop better applications;

– the format is transparent (compression, encapsulation, encryption may prevent automatic identification and control of format attributes);

– the metadata of the format are numerous and facilitate its exploitation.

	Opening	Independence	Diffusion	Particularities
Doc	Proprietary format.	Low.	Low because it was replaced by docx in 2007.	Volume dependent on functionalities used.
Docx	Open standard.	Good.	Very good.	Average volume. Dependent on functionalities used.
PDF	Published proprietary format.	Average. Dependent on functionalities used.	Very good.	Average volume.
PDF/A	Open standard.	Good.	Average.	Average volume. Used for ERM and long-term archiving.
ODF	Open standard. ISO 26300 standard.	Very good. Microsoft Office 2007 authorizes the recording of data.	Low.	Low volume. Used by OpenOffice.
TIFF	Open standard.	Good. Supports quality-controlled and lossless compression types.	Very good.	High volume. Used as a digital format.
JPEG	Open standard. ISO/IEC IS 10918-1 standard.	Lossless compression with controlled quality	Average. Adopted by browsers. Widely used in photography.	Low volume. More than 16 million color tones available.
JPEG2000	Open standard. ISO/IEC IS 15444-1 standard.	Good. Choice of compression, without or without lossless.	Low. Not recognized by cameras and hardly recognized by browsers.	Low volume. Used especially by professionals but not by the public.
WAVE	Published format.	Good.	Average.	High volume.
GIF	Proprietary format but the patent falls within the public domain.	Good. Lossless compression.	Good display but limited to 256 colors.	Low volume. Format used a lot at the start of the Internet, but does not perform well.
PNG	Open standard. ISO/IEC 15948: 2003 standard.	Lossless compression. Independence regarding display devices.	Recognized by all current browsers.	Accepts images in grayscale or color. Aims to replace GIF.

Table 4.10. *Selection criteria applied to some formats*

Furthermore, the format must be simple, present the content well and be error-resistant, and have the ability to automatically detect and report possible conversion problems or errors. It must be compatible from the bottom up, if it is part of a development cycle and if possible no intellectual property should prevent free use [KEC 14, p. 146].

The chosen format must be able to represent all the information and its links contained in the record and considered significant. It provides flexibility in the way in which information is retained and in the choice of what is retained. For a textual record, the words and the order in which they appear are meaningful and, generally, aspects such as pagination and section numbering are also important, especially if there are internal or external references to sections or pages of the record. On the other hand, the font or font size used does not matter as much, although formatting choices such as the use of bold, italics, or underlining are a material element of the meaning of the text [ICA 05, pp. 47–48].

In general, a preservation format for records and their metadata should be chosen that is independent of any software or hardware that has proven its longevity and is widely used and distributed. Ideally, the format chosen will be defined by an international or national standard. Otherwise, it should be defined by a published standard and not subject to patent or license. This guarantees a sustainable access to the records in front of hardware or software suppliers. Even if there comes a time when there is no longer any software on the market capable of processing the files stored in this way, the very existence of a standard means that it is still possible to recreate software to read, restore, process and reformat the files. If the standard comes from a recognized standards body, one can be sure that copies will be available in legal deposit libraries, or other similar institutions, in perpetuity. If it is from a less established organization, it may be prudent to keep a copy with the records [ICA 05, p. 47].

Once created, the record will undergo new versions, until the final version, which will be validated and will remain frozen in time. This is the capture stage, which can be done in a records management system or in an electronic archiving system. At the time of capture, it will be possible to keep the record over time, converting it into a format that can be opened or standardized, such as PDF/A, which is a sustainable format.

The ISO 19005-1: 2005 standard defines the conditions of use of the PDF format for long-term preservation. The PDF/A-1a level (advanced) imposes the guarantee of the respect of the visual representation of the record, the management of Unicode and the logical structuring of the contents of the record (tags, language, etc.). The less restrictive PDF/A-1b level (b for basic) only requires the respect of the visual representation of the record [LEP 11, p. 18].

Object types	Production format	Preservation format
Textual record	DOC, ODF, RTF, TXT	XML, ODF, OOXML, TXT, PDF/A
Presentation record	PPT, ODP	ODP, PDF/A
Spreadsheet	XLS, ODS, CSV	XML, ODS, CSV, PDF/A
Image	TIFF, PNG, JPEG, GIF	TIFF, JEPG2000

Table 4.11. *Recommended data formats for sustainability (Haché, M.-A., Pérenniser l'éphémère numérique: un défi paradoxal à relever [bachelor's degree thesis], University of Moncton, Shippagan campus, 2018, p. 69)*

The aim of PDF/A is to guarantee the legibility over time and the integrity of digital records. These rules essentially include full access to all elements of the record. In other words, fonts must be embedded in the file, no transparency is allowed, images in JPEG2000 format are not allowed, etc. Each file must be accompanied by XMP metadata for harmonization. Each file must be structured according to a specific formalism, better known as "tags". This standard format has a number of restrictions compared to PDF, but it incorporates within the format all the elements necessary to render the record and the fonts it requires. The result is an increase in the size of the files, but at the same time it makes them independent of the platforms on which they are used. One of the technical difficulties has been the question of the valid PDF/A format. Some programs are suitable for transforming office records into PDF/A, but are not very effective for transforming PDF into PDF/A. Some applications create PDF/A but do not pass validation tests. It is therefore essential to use PDF/A validators to judge the quality of the records produced.

Since no format is designed to be permanent, it is important to check the format of the files frequently and, if necessary, consider converting them to new readable formats. If this technology watch is not maintained and format conversion is not done in a timely manner, there is a risk of losing the information.

Conversion between formats is a major function to be mastered. This conversion must be carried out when the files are entered into the archiving system, in the event that the input format is not a target format, and the test and conversion procedures must be logged. Input formats must be free of license fees for their use. There must be at least one software package available to convert from this format to those selected as the archival format.

This method therefore consists of specifying a limited number of target formats. We are talking about three or four s-formats for each domain (images, text, e-mail, etc.). The number of input formats should not be multiplied even if they are intended to cover the needs of the administration. Input formats will be tested using tester software to ensure that they meet their specifications.

Files can be converted with each new software version to keep all formats up to date. However, this type of multiple migration may result in the loss of some file characteristics if the conversion processes are not properly verified [ICA 05, p. 35].

The conversion and migration of records of archival value to an open preservation format can also be undertaken. This is the most promising option for long-term preservation. In order for these records to remain available, accessible and enduring, they must be integrated into an archival system. If a third party is used to maintain the archive, this requires well-designed control and regular inspection of the records [ICA 05, p. 35].

The conversion of data into storage formats must be done with care, as the data is so dependent on each other in a system. If these links between them are broken, they may lose their authenticity and integrity before they are archived [ICA 05, p. 36]. In 2002, UNESCO estimates that the Internet contains one billion pages with an extremely short lifespan, ranging from 44 days to two years. The White House site was completely erased when George Bush became president. All the speeches and official communications of the Clinton administration disappeared overnight. Most of this content had been backed up by the National Archives and Records Administration (NARA), which archived several versions of the site throughout the years of the Clinton presidency, but a very large number of Internet links to this content hosted on other sites were broken.

The aim should be to be able to make an automated conversion from the original format to the preservation format, with automatic detection and reporting of possible conversion problems or errors. Thus, the minimum manual effort is required and the system is reliable through the detection of anomalies indicating problems that require human intervention. Having an automated system, or at least a well-defined process for handling flows, promotes the auditability of the preservation process and helps to demonstrate the integrity of the end result [ICA 05, p. 48].

In the digital environment, the record should be kept in a format supported by the contemporary technical environment of the person who wants to access it. The record must remain legible. The digital record is transferred to a more reliable medium, in a format adapted to the technical requirements of the moment. Access to the information is indirect since it requires an information system (storage media, reading device, software, etc.). Packaging takes into account the compression rate, the control of a conversion, encryption and formatting. These choices must be sustainable and allow the best legibility for users, by complying with standards or adapted reference frames. The choice of a broadcasting format may be different from the preservation format. It must allow for the readability of the record by the recipient, which leads to the elimination or restriction of the use of proprietary formats [APR 06, p. 15].

Finally, four procedures will facilitate the fight against the aging of formats:

– save records in a standard format, such as PDF/A;

– regularly convert files to a newer format to extend their readability;

– at each file conversion, verify that the newly created files are consistent with the original files to ensure their integrity, and recalculate their fingerprint to record the conversion operation performed. All conversion and migration operations must be logged;

– make sure that playback is guaranteed when you play it back [AGE 16, p. 3].

4.3.4. The obsolescence of formats

There is a tendency to confuse the notions of storage or backup and long-term archiving, whereas the progress of hard drives and the fall in prices allow information to be retained easily. Archiving, on the other hand, poses a broader problem because of the limited lifespan of digital media at 5 or 10 years. Attention was initially focused on the fragility of the medium, which was then essentially magnetic. In the early 1990s, archivists implemented a refresh of the information carrier by periodically recopying data from one carrier to another. This technique remains effective as long as the information is encoded in a format that is independent of the hardware and software platform used to produce and use it, and as long as the software used to interpret the encoding format is maintained or replaced by a new version that ensures backward compatibility with at least the previous version [LUP 00, p. 44].

Thus, for the preservation of a large amount of information, removable media such as magnetic tape were first used before switching to digital optical disks, most often WORM (Write Once Read Many) or recordable Compact Disc (CD) type disks. These technologies have become obsolete due to their unreliability and costly maintenance due to duplication and migration. Magnetic disks are once again considered to be a preferred archiving medium because of their increasing capacity, which doubles every eighteen months or so and now reaches terabyte (TB) capacities at a constant cost [LEP 11, p. 19].

After several decades of thinking that information was linked to its medium, organizations realized that these media were not sustainable. They changed their approach and began to design electronic archiving systems with software as the overriding element [AGE 16, p. 2].

The main challenge of the digital age is the sustainability of electronic archives. The obsolescence of digital carriers and, even more so, of information encoding formats is bringing the lifespan of digital information objects to an end in five or ten years. This is also the case for engaging records [SER 15, p. 65]. Eric Ketelaar noted that, based on a format obsolescence every three years, an individual's record to be retained 75 years should be migrated 25 times over its lifecycle [CHA 15a, p. 66].

It is estimated that the average lifespan of a file in .doc or .xls format is five years. Beyond that, in order to avoid problems with layout, fonts and incompatibilities of all kinds, the file must be converted. And this lifespan is even shorter for certain specific formats, especially those resulting from modeling software used by architectural firms, for example, which evolve even more regularly. In addition to the format, the storage infrastructure also plays a major role in this sustainability. Because all media (optical disks, hard disks, SSDs, magnetic tapes and others) also have very short replacement cycles. And even if in an ideal electronic archiving system the hardware should be replaced by the software, the storage infrastructure must be sufficiently robust, redundant and scalable to guarantee this sustainability. Hence the importance of regularly migrating archives to a new storage system. Ultimately, this dual technological obsolescence creates a temporal paradox between the lifespan of the written word (often several decades) and that of information technologies, which renew themselves much faster [AGE 16, p. 4].

Ensuring the sustainability of records means keeping them over time. It means being able to access the contents of a record that you have created today with the means available, using a computer, an operating system and a software application that do not yet exist and whose characteristics are unknown. Ensuring the portability of a record means ensuring that this record, created with a given computer, operating system and application, can be read today, elsewhere on any other operating system with other tools. Sustainability and portability are close. The first term refers to time, the second to space, but both suggest that these goals can only be achieved if the characteristics of the records are not intrinsically dependent on the system that enabled their creation. Portability is a necessary condition for sustainability [HUC 10, p. 14].

For storage media with large volumes and medium and long-term conservation, that is at least 10 years, preference should be given to fixed media such as servers or magnetic tapes. The trend to store data on large servers, or on removable hard disks, facilitates the migration of data from one site to another. However, if storage is limited in time and volume, removable media such as optical disks (CDs, DVDs,

Blu-Ray) can be used, ensuring that quality, non-rewritable material is used. It is advisable to avoid removable disks as the only option, as they require frequent and therefore expensive migration and to store other data on the same media as those related to the digitization project. Regardless of which option you choose, it is essential to keep all master files and metadata on two types of media stored in separate locations, because no media is forever [SOY 12, pp. 111–112].

The pressed CD is used for sound recordings and multimedia applications, but there is also the recordable CD as an archival medium for the digitization of heritage records by archives, libraries and museums. Accelerated aging tests show that burned recordable CDs are more fragile than pressed CDs. Studies of "natural" aging of the first disks stored in good conditions show that the protective varnish on the metal layer ages and can lead to oxidation. Also, the average life expectancies reported by test laboratories such as the National Media Lab for recordable CDs are in the order of five years, and for pressed CDs the figures commonly reported range from 10 to 25 years [LUP 00, p. 45].

In the field of digital information, it soon became clear that not only did the carrier have a very limited lifespan, even under good preservation conditions, but that, in addition, peripherals, computer programs and information processing methods were disappearing in favor of new techniques with a validity cycle of two to five years [LUP 00, p. 45].

Three types of conservation media can be used:

– the physical WORM (Write Once Read Many). This is a non-rewritable medium. The writing of the data is made by an irreversible notification of the support, which guarantees the sustainability and the integrity;

– the logical WORM. It is a support which is technically rewritable, but which is going to be locked against modifications of the archives, by an internal software device imagined by the manufacturer thus "owner", which is not standardized;

– rewritable media with imprint. This time common media are used, nowadays magnetic disks, and modifications are still possible. However, when the archives are recorded, an imprint of the archived records will be taken, and this will make it possible to check that, later on, these repositories have not been modified. The fingerprint is stored in the system.

4.3.5. The open archival information system (OAIS)

The reference model in terms of assistance to the project owner in the management of an archiving project is the open archival information system (OAIS). Elaborated within the space framework and developed by the Consultative

Committee for Space Data Systems (CSSDS) created in 1982, it became the ISO 14721 standard in 2003. The French version was published in 2009. This standard is generalist, but it is fundamental, as it describes the conceptual framework on which the majority of electronic archiving systems implemented today are based. It is recognized in the scientific, industrial and heritage fields. Due to the rapid obsolescence of technologies, we tend to look for technical solutions to solve the problem. The archiving of digital information is too complex and requires too many different skills to be solved in a single package. It requires an adequate organization, competent people, a set of procedures and applicable standards, appropriate technical means, and standardized archive certification mechanisms [HUC 04, p. 88].

It is an abstract model that does not give any technical specifications, but offers a vocabulary and a theoretical framework for thinking about different archiving scenarios. This model focuses on the data and therefore the content rather than the process that generates the records and how they are used. Very theoretical, it defines the functions, responsibilities and organization of an electronic archiving system for archiving both digital and physical information.

The OAIS model defines electronic archiving as "a set of people and systems whose responsibility it is to preserve [digital] information and make it accessible to a target user community". It is transferable to all organizations. The focus on methods and people is as important as the focus on IT tools or systems. This model is particularly applicable to organizations responsible for making information available over the long term, and the technologies used may vary depending on the means or choices of the organizations.

It has the advantage of providing a reliable and unique terminology to handle all concepts related to the preservation of digital data. It covers all the issues that need to be addressed to set up a preservation system. It describes the components of such a system at the internal and external organizational level. However, it does not give any s-formats, rules or techniques for preserving digital materials. It does not describe the computer applications and techniques to be implemented, neither software nor hardware. It does not give any specifications for implementing such a system.

The OAIS defines four types of digital migration from a long-term archiving perspective: refreshing or copying to an identical medium, duplication or copying to a new type of medium, repackaging, which in addition implies a change in the logical organization of storage, and transformation. The first three types of migration relate to the management of storage media and the fourth to the content of the digital object and its format. It is well suited to long-term preservation needs, but is criticized for not imposing a specific method of implementation although it does guide it and does not recommend software or technical systems [RAJ 11, p. 79].

The OAIS model identifies four main stakeholders in an archiving system:

– the Archive[3], that is the operator of the archiving system, understood as archive service. More precisely, it is the organization responsible for perpetuating the information it receives and therefore for preserving it and making it accessible and understandable in the long term to a target user community. The Archive negotiates with information producers to ensure the quality of information content and preservation information to meet the needs of the target user community. It acquires sufficient mastery of the information provided and obtains descriptive information for the target user community to find the information content of interest to them. It has a documented strategy and procedures to ensure the retention of information in the event of unforeseen events and to provide an authenticated or traceable copy of the original [ROU 12, p. 62].

The idea of accountability is very strong in the model; at all times, the archive must be able to prove that it has done its job well. This responsibility includes relations with producers: it involves negotiating agreements on payments, especially technical clauses. It also includes obtaining from the producer all the rights necessary to handle the records, in particular intellectual property rights. The Archive also guarantees that it will provide its user community with understandable, available records, and that it will do everything in its power to preserve the records over time: this is a kind of contract between the Archive and its user community;

– the management represents the decision-makers, who determine the mandate, priorities and orientations of the Archive, in coherence with the general policy of the company. It has the task of supporting the system politically, financially and over the very long term. It can also provide instructions for the use of resources, negotiate conflicts between the players and evaluate the performance of the Archive in the form of an audit;

– producers are the persons or organizations that provide the information to be retained. The producer delivers the information to the Archive in an agreement called a "payment protocol" which defines the terms of payment, the data model to be used and so on. The producer may be a researcher in a laboratory developing scientific data, a private individual, etc. The producer may be a researcher in a

---

3 The standard establishes a number of concepts designated by a vocabulary, the definition and explanation of which occupy an important part of the text. Some terms are to be understood in an acceptance different from their usual meanings, so they are marked with a capital letter as in the case of the Archive as the archive to avoid any confusion.

laboratory developing scientific data, a private individual, etc. The producer may be a researcher in a laboratory developing scientific data;

– users are the organizations and individuals who have access to archived objects. They are people or systems connected to the Archive's services to search for archived information that is useful for its activities, and to retrieve that information. It is a target user community to which sustainable access to information must be guaranteed.

In summary, upstream of the Archive is the Producer who provides the information to be kept and downstream the Consumer who requests access to it. The Archive is placed under the supervision of the Management which defines its field of action and directs its work according to its expectations [ROU 12, p. 63].

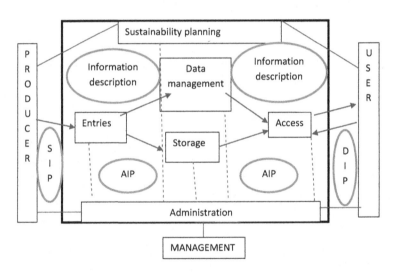

Figure 4.1. *OAIS functional entities according to the Consultative Committee for Space Data Systems (CCSDS) scheme*

The OAIS model is based on the idea of different information packets (Information Package – IP) depending on whether they are produced, stored or communicated. The Information Package (IP) is a conceptual container in which the information content and the prescription description information (PDI), that is, the metadata of this content are gathered.

This information packet is also associated with packaging information that enables the components of an information packet to be linked and identified. An information package is a collection of information containing both the basic object, the record to be archived and the associated additional data or metadata. The content of a package may be a single file, a composite set of plans, maps, images, etc.

The standard defines three types of packages that correspond to three stages in the life of the information:

– the Submission Information Package (SIP) that Producers work on before archiving. This SIP package is delivered by the Producer or Submission Service to the archiving system;

– the Archival Information Package (AIP) stored in the archiving system and consisting of information content and associated persistence information (PDI). The AIP is the information format suitable for preservation over time;

– the Dissemination Information Package (DIP) received by the user in response to his request to the archiving system. It corresponds to the communication of information. This packet comes from one or more Archived Information Packets (AIP) [RIE 10, p. 87].

Thus, the Archive receives Submission Information Packages (SIPs) which it transforms into Archive Information Packages (AIPs) and restores on demand into Distribution Information Packages (DIPs). Each package has three main types of metadata associated with it:

– metadata for searching metadata records;

– metadata indicating the copyrights related to the records and the conditions of their distribution;

– technical metadata needed to control the integrity, preservation and tracking of records over time [RIE 10, p. 240].

Finally, the Descriptive Information is a set of information extracted from the representation information and the perpetuation information. This set consists mainly of package descriptions and allows users to search, order and retrieve information from the archiving system thus functioning as an index [RIE 10, p. 87].

An archival object can be thought of as the original record with two sets of metadata associated with it. The first is intended to complement the information contained in the record itself: index, format, origin. The second set of metadata allows the record to be managed over time: retention period, level of confidentiality, trace of possible migration. If the information in the first set is fixed, the information in the second set follows the evolution of the record throughout its archiving period and is therefore modified accordingly [RIE 10, p. 88].

For each packet and at each stage there are computer files corresponding to the object or record that we want to keep and metadata about that record. An information packet (SIP, AIP, DIP) is thus a conceptual container of two types of information: Information Content and Perpetuation Information [ROU 12, p. 64].

Content information is the Data Object, which can be physical (such as a book or record) or digital (a sequence of bits written on a digital medium) and its Representation Information, that is its format, its structure (character encoding), its meaning (language, abbreviation) to enable the target community to understand the object. The information content and the PDI are identified and encapsulated by the Packaging Information. It is composed of a content data object which corresponds to a digital object consisting of a sequence of bits in the form of an electronic file generated in a given format and its information representation. The latter is information that translates a content data object into more explicit concepts.

The package can be retrieved using a Package Description. It is essential to ensure the perpetuation of an Information to preserve at the same time the Information Content, the perpetuation Information, the Packaging Information and the Package Description Information of the package and for each one the data object and its Representation Information [ROU 12, pp. 64–65].

In order for the information content to be correctly preserved, it must be accompanied by Prescription Description Information (PDI), which breaks down as follows:

– provenance information that records the history of the information content. It provides information on the origin or source of the information content, on any changes that have occurred since its creation, and on who has been responsible (responsible for recording the data, information on data storage, handling and migration);

– context information that describes the links between information content and its environment (reasons for creation, relationship with other data content objects);

– reference information that identifies and describes the mechanisms for assigning identifiers to information content. It includes identifiers that allow an external system to unambiguously refer to a particular information content (ISBN);

– fixity information which describes the mechanisms to ensure that the content of information has not been altered without being traced [RIE 10, p. 86].

The system distinguishes six functions: input management, storage, data management, system administration, sustainability planning and access management. All the functions identified in this model must of course be covered by the organization. The four essential operational functions of the OAIS model are input, archive storage, data management and access.

Operational functions can be organized into three distinct services. These comprise a set of people, technical means and financial or other resources, in charge of a clearly identified mandate:

– the ingest entity receives the SIPs, checks their quality and generates the AIPs in accordance with the Archive's standards and transmits them to the storage entity. It also extracts the descriptive information that is transmitted to the Data Management Entity [LUP 00, p. 52]. This entity collects and prepares the data and takes care of all the tasks related to the deposit; the purpose of the entry is to validate the SIPs, to indicate to the depositor that the information has been properly taken into account by the system. This unit also has the role of converting SIPs into AIPs. It is no longer just a question of identifying the records that need to be archived, but also of specifying the formats in which they are to be delivered, the means by which these digital objects will be sent to the Archive [HUC 04, p. 91];

– the Storage Entity receives AIP, manages storage, renews media, provides disaster backup, and forwards PII to the Access Entity to fulfil orders [LUP 00, p. 52]. It manages the media pool, including monitoring aging, replacing media, managing available space, correcting writing errors, writing files to be archived at remote sites, and backup procedures. Technologies to ensure the integrity of the files kept (digital seals) are included in the functions [ROU 12, p. 66];

– the access entity communicates with data consumers by receiving requests, filtering access to data that has special protection, and transmitting responses to consumers [LUP 00, p. 52].

To these operating entities, the standard adds other complementary entities:

– the Data Management Entity is responsible for managing the database that collects all the descriptions of the AIPs held by the Archive and ensures their updating in collaboration with the Input (description update) and Administration (system update) entities [ROU 12, p. 67];

– the entity responsible for administration is responsible for the day-to-day operation and management of the archiving system. It ensures the constant monitoring of activities. It requests reports from each functional entity documenting the steps in the archiving process. Traceability is guaranteed by the keeping of event logs that are permanently stored. It has a communication role with the outside and provides activity reports. It negotiates the payment procedures (periodicity, file format, type of information, media used) and assesses the needs [ROU 12, p. 66];

– the entity responsible for preservation planning provides some monitoring of obsolescence and the emergence of technologies to anticipate the decisions needed for preservation. It also ensures that communication services are consistent over time with the needs and expectations of users [HUC 04, p. 90].

The OAIS is therefore a complete system that takes into account the record from its deposit in the archives through the management of archiving and metadata to the conservation and communication of records, specifying the mandate and responsibilities of each entity.

4.4. Cloud computing

The idea of relocating information around the world or virtualizing it through popular concepts such as cloud computing is increasingly being discussed. It is at the heart of the project to pool the technical and human resources of IT departments. This mode of organization consists of providing access, via a network, to physical and/or virtual IT resources, remote from the offices where the agents physically work and adaptable to the customer's needs. IT specialists no longer talk about resources, but about services. It is therefore a set of processes for using the computing and/or storage power of remote computer servers through a network, generally the Internet. The resources are shared and the computing power is configurable according to needs. The cloud computing thus allows for a fully modular and adaptable architecture where the user only pays for what he uses. Adjustment is dynamic and does not require human intervention. Additional capacity can be easily and quickly allocated, sometimes automatically. For the user, the capacities can appear without limits and increase simply by paying more [APR 12, p. 8].

Caution should be exercised in outsourcing archives and in knowing the country of location of the archives and the server clusters containing the systems, data and records. Archives may be stored at a third party whose headquarters are located in the same country as the client organization but whose servers or those of subcontractors are located in other countries. The service provider may also decide to change storage locations without informing the organization. Secondly, technological obsolescence may pose a risk to the readability and usability of digital information content. Both the organization and the provider must plan for the migration of systems, data and records to the new software and hardware media. The organization's IT equipment must remain compatible with that used by the service provider. Open formats should also be favored to support the legibility of information over time.

Compatibility of software and hardware media is also an issue when employees and business units adopt outsourced collaborative platforms without any institutional control. It is important to identify them.

Metadata in digital archives should be maintained in an appropriate manner to preserve the authenticity, accuracy and completeness of the information, thus facilitating its retrieval and use, while clearly defining access rights, especially in the case of outsourced digital archives [HIR 14, p. 201].

If the service provider is mandated to carry out destruction or removal of archives according to the retention periods set out in the retention schedule, it must be ensured that all copies are destroyed or removed. Clear measures must be established with the service provider in the event of cessation of activity or takeover by a competitor. A business continuity plan should provide for these options to avoid temporary unavailability [HIR 14, p. 202].

There are several cloud computing services, but the solutions adopted by companies are mainly of the order of financial optimization, whereas they will keep in-house control of certain components deemed critical or risky [APR 14, p. 14].

First of all, IaaS (Infrastructure as a Service) is a model where the provider is responsible for providing a technical infrastructure with an operating system and file access. It is the lowest level service that consists of offering the deportation of servers that are entirely managed by the client. In cloud mode, flexibility and granularity are achieved through operating system virtualization. The platform, wherever it is located, is run by virtual machines and resources can be allocated and released on demand, without interruption [APR 12, p. 9].

This type of infrastructure is able to meet the deployment needs of large companies or organizations, but with multiple small entities where the establishment of an IT infrastructure is not possible or not desired [APR 12, p. 15].

The user company therefore acquires the licenses for the electronic archiving system and takes over the implementation of this software. It rents a cloud infrastructure from the service provider comprising servers, storage and network with a pay-per-use model. It accesses this infrastructure on the Internet to implement and manage its electronic archiving system. In the majority of cases, to access the servers in IaaS mode, a VPN (Virtual Private Network) is used to connect the user company with the service provider. Guaranteeing quality of service and network security is the responsibility of telecommunications service providers. The service provider must guarantee the availability of technical access so that the customer can retrieve his content himself by emptying the storage space allocated to him [APR 14, p. 12].

The PaaS Service (Platform as a Service) is a configuration in which the provider makes available, in addition to the infrastructure, a number of software services such as the operating system, databases (database as a service), an execution environment, programming languages and specific tools. By providing access to infrastructures and their operating tools, in particular for development platforms, it may also serve as a development or computing environment. In this configuration, the user does not have to worry about the management of operating systems, storage space and associated backups, and the bandwidth needed to access resources. The customer then has a turnkey environment ready to host SaaS applications, but not only SaaS applications [APR 12, p. 9].

By abuse of language, SaaS (Software as a Service) is often referred to as "cloud computing", whereas SaaS is just an application of cloud computing. In SaaS mode, applications are hosted on the provider's platforms, available online and generally accessible via a web browser allowing accessibility without prior deployment on client workstations [APR 12 p. 9]. This service is found in directly usable applications such as Gmail or Office 365.

The service provider provides both the infrastructure and the archiving solution (servers, virtualization layers, storage, networks, server operating system, application software, including that of the electronic archiving system). The service provider shall be responsible for the security of the electronic archiving system, the application security being ensured by authentication services set up by the service provider. The service provider must be able to conduct complete and secure reversion operations [APR 14, p. 13].

The user company rents a service from the service provider, in particular on the basis of licenses for the electronic archiving system, on the basis of a monthly rent including software maintenance and cloud infrastructure. The user company then consumes the electronic archiving solution on demand, according to its real needs [APR 14, p. 13].

The management of record storage on the cloud is growing rapidly due to the emergence of new file storage services called Storage as Service. Several players offer more or less secure storage space with almost unlimited capacity expansion possibilities (Cloud Files from Rackspace, Amazon Cloud Drive and Amazon Cloudfront, Windows Azure Storage and Drive) [APR 12, p. 9].

A number of services related to record management are offered free of charge in cloud mode to users such as DropBox. However, it is up to the users of these services to study the general terms and conditions of use in order to ensure that the intellectual property rights of the files registered and the regulations in force in the country where the service is hosted are respected [APR 12, p. 9].

The implementation of a record service in SaaS mode makes it possible to transfer to the service provider all the problems of managing the record processing chain and to focus solely on the use of the service with the immediate availability of the service. It is not possible to modify a standard infrastructure in order to adapt it to some specific needs. It is up to the user to adapt to the service offered by the provider. In the context of record management, the volume of flows requires significant storage space (particularly for multimedia flows). We should not limit ourselves to studying the cost of the proposed application service, but also take into account the volumetric constraints and check that the SaaS offer includes support for these volumes [APR 12, p. 15].

In the current state, record solutions in SaaS mode do not allow you to set up a particular requirement. They are often much more restricted functionally than those that can be offered outside SaaS mode. Software publishers who offer record management systems are very often obliged to restrict the services of their solution to a minimum and to close the possibilities of opening up to allow integrators to enrich the basic solution [APR 12, p. 15].

The "public" cloud is a deployment model in which cloud services are potentially available to any customer, public or private person. The boundaries of a public cloud are imprecise, and the customer has virtually no restrictions on accessing all the services in a public cloud, regardless of whether the data is relevant to them or not. The "private" cloud offers services to only one customer, who controls the resources. A private cloud is designed to precisely limit its boundaries and restrict access to its services to a single organization.

Hybrid Cloud refers to the fact that different types of clouds coexist together, mixing both private and public cloud offerings depending on the needs and types of data, especially to meet peak load requirements. The issue mainly concerns interoperability between different environments (communication protocols, security, etc.). The question of mutualization is therefore a twofold issue:

– that of the supplier: the mutualization can concern all or part of the layers, from the computing and storage infrastructure to the archiving software that delivers according to the attributes expected for quality archiving. The question arises in particular of the mutualization of the archives of the various customers. However, credibility is established over time and is lost very quickly in the event of a problem;

– that of the client (the legal entity): data pooling is generally perceived as a risk. Verification of the level of service rendered is more difficult and it is a favorable price that will make the perception of risk acceptable. Reversibility is also a criterion, as is the location of the archives. In practice, little attention is paid to the sharing of a file storage service open to all in the cloud. On the other hand, more attention will be paid to archiving that ensures the company's compliance in all its regulatory aspects, including the location of its archives [APR 14, p. 16].

To these notions should be added that of the "community" cloud, which is a public cloud, but which is exclusively reserved for customers with similar needs, and that of the "sovereign" cloud. The data is stored and processed entirely on the territory of the country concerned and whose location is known precisely by the customer.

The outsourcing of record management in a cloud environment seems, at first glance, likely to bring economic benefits. Indeed, the pooling of services and resources allows small organizations to have technical resources that would be impossible to envisage in a traditional environment. In a context where there is an exponential increase in unstructured content managed and preserved by any organization, whatever its size, this may appear to be a real opportunity, allowing small organizations to have high-performance solutions without having to worry heavily about the storage, processing and security capacities required for record management. In the same way, large organizations find in the cloud environment a flexibility, speed of implementation and responsiveness that bring economic benefits. These computer clouds are enriched by added archiving values that make them massive data managers for professionals (Big Data), including the largest, IBM, which manages the data of 33,000 subscribers with its supercomputers, making it the largest archive institution in history [DEL 15b, p. 134].

Cloud computing solutions offer new avenues that organizations and individual organizational stakeholders have quickly grasped. The latter find it useful to host their records in the cloud for easy remote access and sharing. They choose the solutions they find most user-friendly and advantageous without necessarily contacting the information technology unit, and without always taking the time to properly evaluate the terms and conditions of the service agreement.

Arguably the most attractive factor for consumers interested in the cloud is the potential cost savings resulting from reduced data management costs. The cost of the hardware and software is absorbed by the cloud provider, so the consumer does not have to worry about managing his or her infrastructure. The elasticity of the cloud allows the consumer ease of use if they wish to increase or decrease the level of service or resources they receive from the provider. However, this can also mean relinquishing control. Also, if the consumer wishes to exercise a higher level of control over certain characteristics of the cloud, data security, data availability, or the ability to manipulate and customize the infrastructure, he or she must assume the consequences or the price [MAK 14, p. 18].

	Out of the cloud	Cloud mode
Content creation	Use of software installed on client workstations or on the company's servers and accessible for workstations connected to the company network. Creation of content in the company environment.	Need to be logged in to synchronize the records created. Possible interaction and interoperability between internal and external resources.
Capture of analog and digital records (paper, sound, video, etc.)	Requires an individual, pooled, or outsourced digitization infrastructure for the company.	Requires access to a capture infrastructure or a connectable device to send captured records to its hosted space. Verify that the infrastructure provides adequate security as required.
Post-capture retention of non-digital source materials	Difficult to implement. Refer to the entity's Archiving Policy.	Difficult to implement. Refer to the entity's Archiving Policy.
Storage	Sizing of infrastructures and forecasting of developments. Control of the location of information and volumes. More questioning for the evolution of capacities.	Ease and speed to increase storage space, but beware of the associated cost and the uncontrolled explosion of volumes. Contractually specify the location of the information. Increase and contraction of processing capacity as required.
Operations	Direct responsibility of the company on the IS. Direct management of recovery plans, service continuity and availability, at the company's financial expense.	Outsourcing of services and related responsibilities. Mandatory contractualization of recovery, service continuity and availability plans based on service objectives.
Access to records	Technically check the deadlines and conditions for making records available. Ensure control of access to records and associated rights.	Contractually ensure the deadlines and conditions for making records available. Ensure that access to records and associated rights are controlled.
Reversibility	Ensure that backups are usable and sufficient. Audit the backups to verify that they are usable under the required conditions: Maximum allowable interruption time, maximum allowable data loss.	Ensure contractually and technically that it is possible to recover records stored in the cloud (usable backups, maximum allowable downtime, maximum allowable data loss).

Table 4.12. *Evolution of practices in the cloud environment (source: [APR 12, p. 16])*

Cloud computing can provide a satisfactory solution to backup problems, but it is not clear that there is a reasonable path for long-term archiving. It is not universal and cannot meet all needs. Yet the companies providing these services call on more powerful companies by renting storage space to them or by duplicating their own data, which lessens the impact of a sudden accident in the stadiums of the device although the Internet itself does not store anything, as it can only put a user in contact with distant preservation reservoirs. This stored information is stored on a tape or hard disk which does not have an infinite lifespan. The preservation system is quite opaque and is more effective for short-term preservation, because in the long term one can fear the disappearance of society and wonder who will care about returning the information to the user. In addition, privacy issues can be crucial when the data is sensitive [HOU 10, pp. 27–28].

Encryption of archived data may, at first glance, appear to be the most secure solution for protecting data. This may be true in the short term, but is a very strong constraint in the archiving field. In fact, key management and the lifespan of the algorithms used for encryption are major obstacles when the data must be preserved identically in the long term. There are areas where content encryption is mandatory, such as for health data. In these cases, the provider offers additional services for key management, but there will always be a "master key" whose sustainability and security will be the exclusive responsibility of the customer [APR 14, p. 34]. In case of certification, the auditor verifies the existence of at least two archiving sites and visits each site to verify the application of the methods described in the "System Technical Description File".

Contracts with cloud providers, which themselves employ a chain of subcontractors, are often highly stereotypical and do not incorporate specific constraints based on the sensitivity of the data or the legislative and regulatory environment. There is a divide between European and North American cloud providers. European participants are more inclined to show the security measures developed within their organizations to meet customer needs and industry standards, while North American providers are much stingier in their explanations [MAK 14, p. 15]. The US approach to regulating the protection of personal data is a far cry from the European approach, which is based on comprehensive standards of protection and the existence of an independent data protection authority. US cloud providers are subject to the Freedom Act, a law authorizing the US administration, in the context of the fight against terrorism, to access all the data they host, regardless of the nationality of their customer and the location of the infrastructure, without prior authorization and without informing their customer. Furthermore, the United States does not have an independent data protection authority and does not have a general framework for data protection in the private sector, but rather sector-specific laws. Market regulation is favored over state intervention. Such regulation is either voluntary, through the development of internal codes of conduct, or contractual, through agreements between economic operators and consumers. Some countries have very strict legislation with anti-terrorist laws, industrial espionage laws or, more generally, public order rules that allow national public authorities to compel cloud providers to communicate customer information that they hold on the territory of these countries [APR 14, p. 19].

The cloud archiving contract must include a clause organizing an audit by an independent company or authorizing the customer to organize this audit himself. The audits will verify in particular that the provider takes measures to safeguard or delete the archives, to prevent illegal transmissions, to prevent transfer to an unauthorized country and that the security and confidentiality measures put in place cannot be circumvented [APR 14, p. 36].

The latter must be able to certify the implementation of archival lifecycle logs and EAS event logs. A clause must be included to provide for the ability of the service provider to restore the content, but also the traceability elements associated with the content (archive lifecycle logs). The logs generated by the service provider should only contain information related to the content archived for its client [APR 14 p. 36].

Traceability is thus one of the conditions that must be ensured by a digital archiving activity. It must be of a systematic nature and help to record all events that may have affected the operation of the system or the records. This traceability is itself expressed through logging and therefore produces the event log, which is itself a record with evidential purposes. The latter must be able to certify the implementation of the archive lifecycle logs as well as the EAS event logs [APR 14, p. 36].

Proof of disposals must be traced in the logs and disposal certificates themselves archived. Similarly, in the case of data return, whether in the event of a change of storage provider or a transfer of activities, it is important to have a guarantee that the data returned are properly disposed of and can no longer be accessed in any way [APR 14, p. 38].

The SLA (Service Level Agreement) guarantees a customer of a cloud archiving solution the availability of archived data and related services (payments, consultations, refunds). The service provider must ensure:

– the level of availability of the network: the provider must prevent network disruption or saturation following the failure of one of the elements of the network infrastructure;

– the level of availability of consultation services: in general, this corresponds to an unavailability of approximately 45 minutes per month or 9 hours per year.

The service provider must also propose a two-tier security plan: the business recovery plan (BRP), which allows a cold restart of the activity after a disaster, with restoration of the archiving system; the business continuity plan (BCP), which allows a hot restart by redundancy of the infrastructure on one or two remote sites with real-time data replication. These plans are designed to minimize data loss and increase responsiveness in the event of a major disaster. The BCP must be virtually transparent to users and must ensure data integrity without loss of information [APR 14, p. 31].

One of the identified risks of archiving in the cloud is the technological dependence on the provider, that is, the impossibility to switch to another provider or to return to an in-house solution without loss of data. This risk can be controlled by the contractual requirement of a reversibility and/or interoperability clause. The reversibility clause should be accompanied by a detailed reversibility plan [APR 14 p. 32].

In the event of the bankruptcy of the cloud archiving provider, the customer who owns the archived data may retrieve the data provided that the data is separable from all other data at the time the bankruptcy proceedings are opened [APR 14, p. 32].

It is also necessary to analyze all the costs according to the typologies of use of the records throughout their lifecycle:

– costs related to the deposit and storage of records;

– the cost of access to records by users (frequent access to records can have a significant financial impact, depending on the invoicing method used);

– costs related to the return of records to the producing entities, as certain invoicing methods may minimize costs when making payments, but impose heavy charges when returning all or part of the records, thus limiting the real economic interest. The same is true for reversibility, where the technical dimension of the operation can induce significant costs in the overall economy of the model [APR 12, p. 13].

4.5. Conclusion

For civilization to progress, successive generations must be able to accumulate new knowledge. However, continuity in the development of many disciplines is by no means assured. It is often forgotten that the weak point of informatics is its short-term view of documentary production. The possibilities of acquiring large masses of data and archives are counterbalanced by the fragility of the media and technological obsolescence which, without procedures and methodology, will lead to the irretrievable loss of an entire information heritage.

Sustainability is linked to all the choices concerning the digital record: structure of the information content, organization of the information, data codification, access and restitution procedures, and recording medium. On the one hand, it is necessary to choose durable solutions such as guarantees on the integrity of the record, the record format, and the recording media. On the other hand, provisions must be implemented to guarantee continuity, that is, back-up copies, migrations with the change of media and the change of software version, recodification with the change of presentation and structuring format, and reconfiguration of the message which may have an impact on the information content, which implies special provisions relating to the integrity of the message [APR 06, p. 21].

High demand may justify digitization for preventive conservation purposes since it will limit the handling of records. It is generally not useful to digitize records that are rarely consulted. It is therefore necessary to identify the records to be digitized and describe their history, medium, size, importance in terms of volume and interest, and verify their confidential or non-confidential nature. It is also questionable whether putting records online stimulates interest and increases the organization's notoriety. However, it should not be lost sight of that the primary objective of digitization is to ensure better dissemination of archives.

It is important to develop an archiving strategy from the outset and to define the roles and responsibilities of the various stakeholders much more precisely and explicitly. There is a need for a legal authority responsible for the content of information as a guarantor of authenticity, and a preservation authority responsible for maintaining the integrity and permanence of records.

Electronic record management is not reliable enough to ensure proper archiving of essential records, as the disposal and sharing of information is based on producers and not on a validation body and harmonization of procedures. ERM manages records that can evolve or be modified.

This is why the electronic archiving system, which as opposed to ERM manages fixed, fixed and unchangeable records to which retention periods are attached, remains the only guarantee of permanent archiving. One can rely on the OAIS model of electronic archiving which is transposable for all organizations and more specifically for those who have to process information to be preserved over the long term. This model provides an organizational structure composed of people who accept responsibility for preserving information and making it available to a designated group and a set of procedures.

Indeed, the mandatory migration of formats and data carriers must be taken into account in order to preserve the integrity of the digital object, while allowing the user to continue to use it, to carry out information searches and to be able to re-read the data in an identical manner. Finally, if mass data storage seems to be solved by cloud computing, one must remain cautious because it concerns only current and non-confidential information, but not important records to be preserved in the long term. Perhaps it is necessary, beyond technology, to put the human being back at the center of the system and offer him/her all the resources and means necessary to guarantee the proper management and preservation of record production.

Conclusion

The way we look at archives has changed, but so has the way we manage and preserve them. In the past, the rarity of records required strict conservation geared towards research and scholarship. From the middle of the last century onwards, the abundance of records led to a selection and evaluation of their relevance to encourage elimination. Today, the overabundance of data imposes new procedures. Evidence, administrative management, scientific and technical use of records have amplified the importance of archives in a society of knowledge and therefore of memory. The need for authenticity is fundamental to constitute reliable sources. Integrity must be demonstrable in order to ensure that the record can be consulted for as long as it is needed.

The development of information technology and the widespread use of electronics in the production, distribution and storage of records have made the problem of archiving more acute, since these new information media have different characteristics from those of paper. "The whole of society is now being transformed by the reign of data. The power to inform, to train, to organize is in the hands of those who hold and manage massive data" [DEL 15b, p. 134]. Even if data represents a great wealth for the companies that possess it, it requires long and arduous work to achieve this supposed valorization. It is necessary to identify them, to know how to access them and who is the holder. We must then study the content of the data to understand its meaning and potential, and finally ensure its quality in order to be able to use it.

Yet there remains the huge mass of public paper archives that cannot be digitized and vital digital records whose authentic value must be preserved. And let's not forget that a paper record in a repository seems harder to find and hack than data on any secure server. The development of cybercrime and state intelligence poses a real threat to privacy and individual freedoms. Several logics clash. We wish to protect the inalienable and imprescriptible moral rights of authors and personal data, but we must face up to the need to share and transmit knowledge. How can confidentiality, secrets and privacy be protected when the imperative of transparency reinforces and increases the injunction that all records must be accessible and the conviction that all records constitute evidence?

Even if digitization promotes dissemination, it should not be an end in itself. It is not just about creating a digital image transformed into pixels or reducing the mass of paper archives. It is to implement all available processing to best satisfy the user's need or wish. New uses are emerging and societal demand will continue to evolve.

The management of information and records is of considerable importance and even economic value. The mandate of records management becomes crucial because by focusing on the lifecycle of records from their creation to their final retention or disposal, it optimizes access, consultation, dissemination and archiving of records. While information technology allows for a certain number of automatic entries, it does not eliminate the necessary intervention by producers. Records management places the needs, uses and habits of individuals at the center of its system. The user is an actor who plays a major role in the description of archives. Systems must adapt to his or her needs and practices. The archivist is no longer alone, for he or she recognizes in the producer an important player with whom collaboration is essential. This reversal is due to the impossibility of making downstream inventories of huge documentary sources, and the professions must collaborate by contributing their analyses, techniques and knowledge.

Also, in the digital world, a record management system includes objects to be manipulated according to certain actions represented as parameters provided to a computer application as well as the specification of the roles necessary to perform these actions. Basically, a record management solution will include the management of digital objects, a classification scheme to put them in context, a metadata profile defining them as records and the definition of accesses with the specification of roles and possible actions on the objects in the system.

Standardization and the importance of rules in the processes of recording and sharing digital records promote the interoperability of systems while providing recourse in the event of litigation. Standards exist to provide a methodology, meet archival requirements, enable the evaluation of existing systems, and present strategies for controls and recordkeeping. They include the definition of record retention periods and the management of the integration of these records within the archival system. Emphasis is placed on the importance of capturing and recording records in the records management system. Capturing is the process of recording a record, linking it to a classification scheme, adding metadata and storing it in the records system. Metadata is the set of descriptive records of a digital record. The metadata model that will be selected is important because it allows the major characteristics of the digitized sources to be defined and their main attributes and descriptors to be identified. It is recommended to use existing models that are preferably structured, standardized and widely used. Recording consists of assigning minimum identification metadata and then classifying the records which must first be properly named in order to facilitate information retrieval and sharing. However, the standards need to be adapted to the needs of each organization so as not to make the procedures more cumbersome and less effective.

With the explosion of shared folders and cloud computing, the filing plan is back in full force. As the ISO 15489 standard reminds us, it is both a collaborative tool and a search tool that complements content search techniques. Its implementation presupposes that it is comprehensible to all and simple to use. It requires a common logic based on the missions and activities of the organization. Its headings will serve as a basis for the organization of record retention schedules, another indispensable tool for controlling and monitoring the mass of records.

The fragility of the digital medium does not facilitate the archiving of heritage, which is the perpetuation of information. In this context, preservation becomes a proactive gesture that requires, at each technological cycle, to migrate information content to other formats and also to choose the right preservation media. In addition to these measures, technology watch is essential with the monitoring of the aging of media, the conservation of several copies on different storage media and the regular control of the integrity of records. The regulatory framework also encourages, in the interests of security, the retention of at least four copies of the same record in different locations and on different storage media in order to[1] be able to generate authentic copies of archived records. However, we should not forget that technology does not guarantee long-term conservation without procedures and migration and that industries promise 30-year conservation periods, which seems difficult to achieve in our daily practices and seems very optimistic.

Indeed, the risks of non-production of digital records are numerous. A record can be poorly produced or badly preserved, it can lose its authenticity and integrity before the judge. The risks of deleting or modifying records voluntarily or by mistake are possible. There is a technical risk due to poor storage or backup. The consequences can be the loss of a lawsuit, the loss of vital business information such as a manufacturing process or costs in searching and reconstructing a record.

Another danger is the non-reversibility of information systems that store records. This will prevent a company from continuing its activities and defending its rights.

---

1 Afnor standard NF Z42-013: March 2009: Specifications relating to the design and operation of computer systems for the purpose of ensuring the retention and integrity of the records stored in these systems.

The concept of reversibility encompasses transparency in the evaluation of solutions and throughout the entire lifecycle of the system, traceability during migration, the opening up of description formats and logs, and the identification of the responsibility of the company owning the records [DEM 15, p. 144].

The documentary space has expanded globally. It gives everyone new responsibilities to preserve good information literacy practices. Archivists are part of this globalization. They must rely on a multidisciplinary approach as they are faced with the creation of prodigious masses of digital records. The profession is based on theoretical knowledge and a constantly evolving body of field experience. Records managers hold a large share of the content discussed and used by staff and aim to capture the content they produce. Through their cross-functional vision of activities, they will help organizations to become more efficient, save money and present a better image while meeting regulatory obligations through good record management.

References

[AGE 16] AGENCE DIGITALE BY SERDALAB AND ARCHIMAG, Le logiciel d'archivage électronique, le pilier de la confiance, White book, 2016.

[APN 13] ARCHIVES PROVINCIALES DU NOUVEAU-BRUNSWICK, Normes de numérisation, Gouvernement du Nouveau-Brunswick, 2013.

[APR 12] APROGED, Documents et cloud computing: Guide de bonnes pratiques à l'intention des organisations françaises ou européennes, Association des professionnels du numérique, Paris, 2012.

[APR 14a] APROGED, Archivage sur le cloud: pratiques et perspectives de la gouvernance de l'information numérique, White book, Association des professionnels du numérique, Paris, 2014.

[APR 14b] APROGED, Chantier de la gouvernance de l'information, Paris, 2014.

[APR 06] APROGED, La maîtrise du cycle de vie du document numérique: présentation des concepts, Report established by the DGME/SDAE – APROGED working group, Association des professionnels du numérique, Paris, 2006.

[ARN 15] ARNAUD J., RIETSCH J.-M., "L'archivage électronique : mettre en place les niveaux de services et solutions adaptés aux différents besoins", La Gazette des archives, no. 240, pp. 205–215, 2015.

[ARN 12a] ARNAUD J., "Gestion des documents d'activité: définition, principes et concepts", La Gazette des archives, no. 228, pp. 104–119, 2012.

[ARN 12b] ARNAUD J., "Une politique de gestion des documents d'activité pour une gouvernance documentaire stratégique", La Gazette des archives, no. 228, pp. 154–173, 2012.

[ASS 17] ASSOCIATION DES ARCHIVISTES FRANÇAIS, "Meta/morphoses. Les archives bouillons de culture numérique, Forum des archivistes", La Gazette des archives, no. 245, 2017.

[ASS 07] ASSOCIATION DES ARCHIVISTES FRANÇAIS, *Abrégé d'archivistique: principes et pratiques du métier d'archiviste*, 2nd reviewed and enlarged edition, Gal'Art Editions, Paris, 2007.

[ASS 05] ASSOCIATION DES ARCHIVISTES FRANÇAIS, ASSOCIATION DES PROFESSIONNELS DE L'INFORMATION ET DE LA DOCUMENTATION, "Comprendre et pratiquer le Records Management: Analyse de la norme ISO 15489 au regard des pratiques archivistiques françaises", Documentaliste-Sciences de l'Information, vol. 42, pp. 106–116, 2005/2.

[ASS 70] ASSOCIATION DES ARCHIVISTES FRANÇAIS, *Manuel d'archivistique*, SEVPEN, Paris, 1970.

[AUF 05] AUFFRET M., *L'archivage pérenne des documents numériques*, Centre Informatique National de l'Enseignement Supérieur (CINES), available at: http://2005.jres.org/paper/47.pdf, 2005.

[BAK 10] BAK G., *Les effets du Web 2.0 sur les modèles d'information: Cycle de vie et continuums*, Bibliothèque et Archives Canada, Initiatives numériques de BAC, available at: http://www.collectionscanada.gc.ca/digital-initiatives/012018-3403-f.html, 2010.

[BAI 15] BAILLARGEON, D., *De quelle sorte d'archivistes aurons-nous besoin en 2030?*, in SERVAIS, P., *Archivistes de 2030: réflexions prospectives*, Academia/L'Harmattan, Louvain-la-Neuve, Publications des archives de l'Université catholique de Louvain, pp. 19–32, 2015.

[BAI 16] BAILLOUX A.-M., "Une approche de la normalisation par la définition des processus d'archivage dans le domaine hospitalier", *La Gazette des archives*, no. 242, pp. 139–147, 2016.

[BAN 15] BANAT-BERGER F., *Les transformations du métier de l'archiviste face aux nouveaux modes de production dans les administrations en France*, in SERVAIS, P., *Archivistes de 2030 : réflexions prospectives*, Academia/L'Harmattan, Louvain-la-Neuve, Publications des archives de l'Université catholique de Louvain, pp. 33–45, 2015.

[BAN 14] BANAT-BERGER F., NOUGARET C., "Faut-il garder le terme archives? Des archives aux données", *La Gazette des archives*, no. 233, pp. 7–18, 2014–1.

[BAN 12a] BANAT-BERGER F., "Un métier à part entière, l'archiviste un généraliste de l'information : qu'en est-il en 2012 dans le nouvel environnement numérique?", *La Gazette des archives*, vol. 226, no. 2, pp. 117–126, 2012.

[BAN 12b] BANAT-BERGER, F., *Les fonctions de l'archivistique à l'ère du numérique*, in DELPIERRE, N., HIRAUX F. AND MIRGUET F. (eds), *Les chantiers du numérique: dématérialisation des archives et métiers de l'archiviste*, Actes des 11ᵉ journées des Archives, Académia/L'Harmattan, Louvain-la-Neuve, pp. 39–59, 2012.

[BAN 10] BANAT-BERGER F., "Les archives et la révolution numérique", *Le Débat*, Gallimard, no. 158, pp. 70–82, 2010-1.

[BAN 09a] BANAT-BERGER F., "La prise en charge des archives électroniques en France dans le secteur public", *Archives*, vol. 40, no. 1, pp. 27–69, 2008–2009.

[BAN 09b] BANAT-BERGER F., DUPLOUY L., HUC C., *L'archivage numérique à long terme: les débuts de la maturité*, La Documentation française, Paris, 2009.

[BEC 14] BECHARD L., FUENTES HASHIMOTO L., VASSEUR E., *Les archives électroniques*, Association des Archivistes Français, Paris, 2014.

[BEL 16] BELIN A., RIETSCH, J.-M., "Archivage électronique et analyse de risque: les nouveaux défis de l'archiviste", *Archives*, 46(1), pp. 47–60, 2016.

[BER 13] BERGMAN O., GRADOVITCH N., BAR-ILAN J. *et al.*, "Folder versus tag preference in personal information management", *Journal of the American Society for Information Science and Technology*, vol. 64, no. 10, pp. 1995–2012, 2013.

[BIS 13] BISSONNETTE N., "Gestion des courriels : stratégies, technologies et bonnes pratiques, note et bilan d'expérience", *Archives*, vol. 44, no. 1, 3, pp. 77–113, 2012–2013.

[BOR 09] BORGHESI A., CAPRIOLI E., COLIN P., "Les critères d'authenticité d'une archive électronique", *Archimag*, Fédération des Tiers de Confiance du Numérique, April 2009.

[BOU 14] BOUTIN M., Gouvernance du numérique; création de valeur, maîtrise des risques et allocation des ressources, Paris, 2014.

[BUR 13] BURNEL A., "Vers une nouvelle pratique archivistique", in *Actes du colloque international de la Courneuve*, "Quand l'archivage devient électronique", organized by Archives diplomatiques et les Archives nationales de France, pp. 15–24, February 5 and 6, 2013.

[BUR 11] BURNEL A., SERVANT H., "Vers une nouvelle pratique archivistique", *La Gazette des archives*, vol. 223, no. 3, pp. 71–84, 2011.

[CAL 09] CALENGE B., *Mettre en œuvre un plan de classement*, La boîte à outils, Presses de l'ENSSIB, Villeurbanne, 2009.

[CAP 07] CAPRIOLI E., DE KERVASDOUE P., PEPIN J.-F. *et al.*, *Protection du patrimoine informationnel*, Cigref-Fedisa, Paris, 2007.

[CAR 15] CARDIN, M., *Ni tout à fait la même, ni tout à fait une autre : la formation archivistique en 2030*, in SERVAIS, P., *Archivistes de 2030: réflexions prospectives*, Academia/L'Harmattan, Louvain-la-Neuve, Publications des archives de l'Université catholique de Louvain, pp. 47–60, 2015.

[CAR 12] CARON D. J., *Du contenu au contexte et du contexte au contenu, notes d'allocution aux Archives nationales des Pays-Bas, Réflexion sur l'évolution de l'évaluation*, Bibliothèque et Archives Canada, available at: http://www.bac-lac.gc.ca/fra/nouvelles/allocutions/Pages/reflexions-evolution-evaluation-bac.aspx, 2012.

[CHA 18] CHABIN M.-A., *Des documents d'archives aux traces numériques: identifier et conserver ce qui engage l'entreprise, la méthode Arcateg*, Klog Éditions, Bois-Guillaume, 2018.

[CHA 15a] CHABIN M.-A., *L'archiviste de 2030 entre archives numériques et utilisateurs connectés*, in SERVAIS, P., *Archivistes de 2030: réflexions prospectives*, Academia/ L'Harmattan, Louvain-la-Neuve, Publications des archives de l'Université catholique de Louvain, pp. 61–72, 2015.

[CHA 15b] CHARBONNEAU N., DAVEAU F., DAVID F. *et al.*, *L'archiviste de référence, de savant à médiateur*, in SERVAIS, P., *Archivistes de 2030: réflexions prospectives*, Academia/L'Harmattan, Louvain-la-Neuve, Publications des archives de l'Université catholique de Louvain, pp. 89–108, 2015.

[CHA 15c] CHARAUDEAU M.-O., FRITEL A., HUOT C. *et al.*, "Et demain ? Archivage et big data", *La Gazette des archives*, no. 240, pp. 373–384, 2015.

[CHA 12] CHABIN M.-A., Le records management : concepts et usages, available at: http://www.arcateg.fr/wp-content/uploads/2017/03/MAC-Le-Records-management.-Concept-et-usages-2012.pdf, 2012.

[CHE 12] CHEBBI A., Archivage du Web organisationnel dans une perspective archivistique, Information Sciences PhD thesis, Université de Montréal, Faculty of Arts et Sciences, Montreal, available at: https://core.ac.uk/download/pdf/55651641.pdf, 2012.

[CLA 10] CLAERR T. (ed.), *Numériser et mettre en ligne*, Presses de l'ENSSIB, Villeurbanne, 2010.

[CLI 19] CLINET S., FUENTES HASHIMOTO L. (eds), "La gouvernance des données", *Archivistes!, Bulletin de l'Association des Archivistes Français*, no. 128, 1st semester, pp. 22–31, 2019.

[COE 19] COEURE S., DUCLERT V., *Les archives*, La Découverte, Paris, 2019.

[COM 05] COMITE CONSULTATIF POUR LES SYSTEMES DE DONNEES SPATIALES, Modèle de référence pour un Système ouvert d'archivage d'information (OAIS), CCSDS 650.0B-1(F), Blue book, 2005.

[COM 11a] COMMISSION DE NORMALISATION 11 DE LA CG 46, Introduction à la série des normes ISO 30300, Systèmes de gestion des documents d'activité et intégration du records management et perspectives d'évolution de l'ISO 15489, White book 1, March 2011.

[COM 11b] COMMISSION DE NORMALISATION 11 DE LA CG 46, Introduction à la série des normes ISO 30300, Systèmes de gestion des documents d'activité et intégration du records management et perspectives d'évolution de l'ISO 15489, White book 2, October 2011.

[COM 12] COMMISSION DE NORMALISATION 11 DE LA CG 46, *ISO 30300-30301*, Systèmes de gestion des documents d'activité, Définition, modélisation, intégration aux autres normes de système de management, White book 3, May 2012.

[COM 14] COMMISSARIAT A LA PROTECTION DE LA VIE PRIVEE DU CANADA, Métadonnées et vie privée: un aperçu technique et juridique, CAN IP 54-59-2014-IN, Gatineau (Québec), available at: https://www.priv.gc.ca/media/1793/md_201410_f.pdf, 2014.

[CON 17] CONSULTATIVE COMMITTEE FOR SPACE DATA SYSTEMS, Modèle de référence pour un Système ouvert d'archivage d'information (OAIS), Recommandation de pratiques pour les systèmes de données spatiales, Pratique recommandée CCSDS 650.0-M-2 (F), Livre Magenta, Version française, 2017.

[COO 92] COOK T., "The concept of the archival fonds: Theory, description, and provenance in the post-custodial era", in T. EASTWOOD (ed.), Le fonds d'archives: de la théorie à la pratique, Bureau canadien des archives, Ottawa, pp. 31–85, 1992.

[COT 04] COTTE D., "Le concept de 'document numérique', Communication et langages, Dossier : Du 'document numérique' au 'textiel', no.140, 2nd quarter, pp. 31–41, 2004.

[COT 15] COTTIN M., NESME M.-F., Système de gestion des documents d'activité (SGDA) d'après la norme ISO 30301, Session 2.4 (1st part) and Gouvernance, exigences de l'ISO 30301, Session 6.4 (2nd part), "Gérer les documents numériques: maîtriser les risques", MOOC, Conservatoire National des Arts et Métier, Paris, 2015.

[COT 16] COTTIN M., "La mise en œuvre de la nouvelle norme ISO 15489-2016", I2D – Information, données et documents, vol. 53, p. 60, 2016/4.

[COU 16] COUDRET S., DELTOUR J.-P., FERNIQUE A. et al., "Regards croisés sur l'archiviste numérique : entre rupture et continuité", La Gazette des archives, no. 244, pp. 233–244, 2016.

[COU 15] COUTURE C., LAJEUNESSE M., L'archivistique en 2015, considérations sur son état actuel et son avenir, in SERVAIS, P., Archivistes de 2030: réflexions prospectives, Academia/L'Harmattan, Louvain-la-Neuve, Publications des archives de l'Université catholique de Louvain, pp. 111–125, 2015.

[COU 14] COUTURE C., LAJEUNESSE M., L'archivistique à l'ère du numérique: Les éléments fondamentaux de la discipline, Presses de l'université du Québec, Quebec, 2014.

[COU 93] COUTURE C., LAJEUNESSE M., Législations et politiques archivistiques dans le monde, Documentor, Quebec, 1993.

[COU 97] COUTURE C., "L'évaluation des archives: État de la question", Archives, vol. 28, no. 1, pp. 3–31, 1996–1997.

[COU 99] COUTURE C. ET AUTRES, Les fonctions de l'archivistique contemporaine, Presses de l'Université du Québec, Sainte Foy, 1999.

[COU 82] COUTURE C., ROUSSEAU J.-Y., Les archives au XXᵉ siècle : une réponse aux besoins de l'administration et de la recherche, Université de Montréal, Service des archives et Secrétariat général, Montreal, 1982.

[DAV 14] DAVENPORT T.H., Stratégie Big Data, Pearson France, Tours, 2014.

[DEC 15] DECKMYN S., Document control, Session 3.4, "Gérer les documents numériques: maîtriser les risques", Conservatoire National des Arts et Métier, Paris, 2015.

[DEL 15a] DELMAS B., "De la diplomatique contemporaine à la diplomatique numérique. Retour sur l'expérience française", in GAGNON-ARGUIN L., LAJEUNESSE M. (eds), *Panorama de l'archivistique contemporaine: évolution de la discipline et de la profession : mélanges offerts à Carol Couture*, Presses de l'Université du Québec, Quebec, pp. 261–287, 2015.

[DEL 15b] DELMAS B., *Les données au péril des archives*, in SERVAIS, P., *Archivistes de 2030: réflexions prospectives*, Academia/L'Harmattan, Louvain-la-Neuve, Publications des archives de l'Université catholique de Louvain, pp. 129–144, 2015.

[DEL 12a] DELPIERRE N., HIRAUX F., MIRGUET F. (eds), *Les chantiers du numérique: dématérialisation des archives et métiers de l'archiviste*, Actes des 11ᵉ journées des Archives, Académia/L'Harmattan, Louvain-la-Neuve, 2012.

[DEL 12b] DELMAS, B., *L'archiviste, le numérique et l'avenir*, in DELPIERRE, N., HIRAUX F. and MIRGUET F. (eds), *Les chantiers du numérique : dématérialisation des archives et métiers de l'archiviste*, Actes des 11ᵉ journées des Archives, Académia/L'Harmattan, Louvain-la-Neuve, pp. 185–203, 2012.

[DEM 12] DEMOULIN M., *Quelques aspects juridiques de l'archivage électronique*, in DELPIERRE, N., HIRAUX F. and MIRGUET F. (eds), Les chantiers du numérique: dématérialisation des archives et métiers de l'archiviste, Actes des 11e journées des Archives, Académia/L'Harmattan, Louvain-la-Neuve, pp. 21–38, 2012.

[DEM 15] DEMOULIN M., VERNUSSET A., "La réversibilité des données et l'archivage électronique ou comment éviter la dépendance technologique", *Les Cahiers du numérique*, vol. 11, no. 2, pp. 115–145, 2015.

[DES 10] DESRICHARD Y., "Archivage et stockage pérennes : enjeux et réalisations", *Bulletin des bibliothèques de France (BBF)*, available at: http://bbf.enssib.fr/consulter/bbf-2010-03-0095-006, no. 3, pp. 95–97, 2010.

[DES 09] DESSOLIN-BAUMANN S. AND WIEGANDT C. (eds), "Dossier Records management, gérer les documents et l'information", *Documentalistes-Sciences de l'information*, vol. 46, no. 2, pp. 29–65, 2009.

[DIR 09a] DIRECTION DES ARCHIVES DE FRANCE, L'archivage électronique, Stage international des archives, available at: https://francearchives.fr/file/61df0ca72ea04bb87ebc59a3583 324ee7dfcb4db/static_2997.pdf, 2009.

[DIR 09b] DIRECTION DES ARCHIVES DE FRANCE, Exigences-types pour la maîtrise de l'archivage électronique, Spécifications MoReq2. Mise à jour et extension, Manuel et guide pratique, French translation by Marie-Anne Chabin, available at: http://www. archivesdefrance.culture.gouv.fr/static/2094, 2008.

[DIS 12] DIRECTION INTERMINISTERIELLE DES SYSTEMES D'INFORMATION ET DE COMMUNICATION, Archivage électronique: Un nouveau domaine d'expertise au service de la gouvernance des systèmes d'information, Paris, 2012.

[DRO 00] DROUHET G., KESLASSY G., MORINEAU E., *Records management : mode d'emploi*, Collection Sciences de l'information, Études et techniques, ADBS, Paris, 2000.

[DUC 77] DUCHEIN M., "Le respect des fonds en archivistique : principes théoriques et problèmes pratiques", *La Gazette des archives*, no. 97, pp. 71–96, 1977.

[DUN 15] DUNANT GONZENBACH A., FLÜCKIGER P., *L'archiviste à la croisée des chemins? La profession d'archiviste face à ces défis: se rendre indispensable?* in SERVAIS, P., *Archivistes de 2030: réflexions prospectives*, Academia/L'Harmattan, Louvain-la-Neuve, Publications des archives de l'Université catholique de Louvain, pp. 179–186, 2015.

[DUR 03] DURANTI L., "Pour une diplomatique des documents électroniques", *Bibliothèque de l'école des chartes*, vol. 161, 2, pp. 603–623, 2003.

[DUR 04] DURANTI L., CHABIN M.-A., "La conservation à long terme des documents dynamiques et interactifs : InterPARES 2", *Document numérique*, vol. 8, no. 2, pp. 73–86, 2004.

[DUR 12] DURANTI L., *Authentification des archives numériques: l'archiviste en tant qu'expert judiciaire*, in DELPIERRE, N., HIRAUX F. and MIRGUET F. (eds), *Les chantiers du numérique: dématérialisation des archives et métiers de l'archiviste*, *Actes des 11e journées des Archives*, Académia/L'Harmattan, Louvain-la-Neuve, pp. 115–213, 2012.

[FLE 12] FLEISCH F., "Les principes de gestion des documents d'activité économiques", *La Gazette des archives*, no. 228, pp. 175–192, 2012.

[FRE 13] FREY, V., TRELEANI M. (eds), *Vers un nouvel archiviste numérique*, Les médias en actes, L'Harmattan, Ina Éditions, Paris, 2013.

[GAG 15a] GAGNON-ARGUIN L., LAJEUNESSE M., *Panorama de l'archivistique contemporaine : évolution de la discipline et de la profession: mélanges offerts à Carol Couture*, Presses de l'Université du Québec, Quebec, 2015.

[GAG 15b] GAGNON-ARGUIN L., MAS, S., MAUREL D., *Les genres de documents dans les organisations: analyse théorique et pratique*, Presses de l'Université du Québec, Sainte-Foy (Quebec), 2015.

[GAG 11] GAGNON-ARGUIN L., MAS, S, *Typologie des dossiers des organisations: analyse intégrée dans un contexte analogique et numérique*, Presses de l'Université du Québec, Sainte-Foy (Quebec), 2011.

[GOU 16] GOUBIN E., "Les archivistes face au défi de la dématérialisation", *La Gazette des archives*, no. 242, pp. 149–159, 2016.

[GRI 09] GRIMARD J., *L'archiviste : constructeur, gardien et communicateur : mélanges en hommage à Jacques Grimard, 1947–2007*, Presses de l'Université du Québec, Quebec, 2009.

[GRO 05] GROUPE METIERS AAD-ADBS, "Comprendre et pratiquer le record management, analyse de la norme ISO 15489 au regard des pratiques archivistiques françaises", *Documentalistes-Sciences de l'information*, vol. 42, no. 2, pp. 106–116, 2005.

[GRO 11] GROUPE INTERASSOCIATION AAF-ADBS "RECORDS MANAGEMENT", *Le plan de classement des documents dans un environnement électronique: concept et repères*, Paris, 2011.

[GUY 15a] GUYON C., LONGIN C., ZELLER J.-D., "Open data et archivage électronique, quelles convergences?", *La Gazette des archives*, vol. 240, no. 4, pp. 385–396, 2015.

[GUY 15b] GUYON C., NAUD D., "Plus qu'hier et moins que demain? Exploration sommaire de l'usage sur Internet de quelques termes autour de l'archivage électronique", *La Gazette des archives*, no. 240, 2015-4, pp. 105–106, 2015.

[GUY 15c] GUYON C., "La pratique archivistique publique en France, entre adaptation et négociation : Expériences et réflexions d'une archiviste", *Les Cahiers du numérique*, vol. 11, no. 2, pp. 77–113, 2015.

[HAG 15] HAGMANN, J., "Gouvernance de l'information, Véritable innovation dans la gestion de l'information?", *Les Cahiers du numérique*, vol. 11, no. 2, pp. 15–36, 2015.

[HAS 13] HASHIMOTO FUENTES L., VERDO R., WATEL F., "La tradition de records management aux Archives diplomatiques et son adaptation à l'environnement électronique", in *Actes du colloque international de la Courneuve*, pp. 25–36, February 5 and 6, 2013.

[HIR 14] HIRAUX F., MIRGUET F. (eds), *De la préservation à la conservation. Stratégies pratiques d'archivage, Actes des 13es Journées des Archives*, Academia, Louvain-la-Neuve, 2014.

[HOL 15] HOLGADO S., VERNUSSET A., "'Petite Poucette' en trans....", *La Gazette des archives*, Association des archivistes français, Paris, no. 240, pp. 107–118, 2015.

[HOU 10] HOURCADE J.-C., LALOE F. AND SPITZ E., Longévité de l'information numérique : les données que nous voulons garder vont-elles s'effacer?, Report by the working group pérennité des supports numériques (PSN, France) common to the Académie des sciences et the Académie des technologies, EDP sciences, Les Ulis, 2010.

[HUC 08] HUC C., "La pérennisation des informations sous forme numérique: risques, enjeux et éléments de solution", *Médecine/Sciences*, available at: http://www.ipubli. inserm.fr/bitstream/handle/10608/6483/MS_2008_6-7_653.pdf, vol. 24 (6–7), 2008.

[HUC 10] HUC C., *Préserver son patrimoine numérique. Classer et archiver ses e-mails, photos, vidéos et documents administratifs*, Éditions Eyrolles, 2010.

[HUC 04] HUC C., "Un modèle pour l'organisation d'un centre d'archives numériques", *Document numérique*, vol. 8, pp. 87–100, 2004/2.

[HUL 13] HULSTAERT A., *Gestion des documents d'activité: enjeux documentaires et fonctionnels*, Onderzoeck-Recherche, available at: <http://blogresearch.smalsrech.be/? p=5983&goback=%2Egde_4344984_mmembe_277038578#%21>, September 2013.

[HUO 15] HUOT C., LEGENDRE J.-F., Données massives – Big Data: Impact et attentes pour la normalisation, AFNOR normalisation, Comité stratégique information et communication numérique, White book, June 2015.

[HUS 15] HUSSON L., "Système de gestion d'archives, gouvernance de l'information : une relation renforcée au fil du temps", *La Gazette des archives*, no. 240, pp. 167–168, 2015.

[ICA 05] CONSEIL INTERNATIONAL DES ARCHIVES, Les archives électroniques, manuel à l'usage des archivistes, ICA Études 16, Paris, 2005.

[IHA 10] IHADJADENE M., ZACKLAD M., ZREIK K., *Document numérique entre permanence et mutations: actes du 13ᵉ Colloque international sur le document électronique*, CIDE.13, December 16–17, 2010, INHA, Europia, Paris, 2010.

[ISO 16] ISO 15489 Information et documentation : Records management : Partie 1 : Principes directeurs, Partie 2: Guide pratique, ISO, Geneva, Révision 2016.

[JUN 15] JUNGHANS P., "Le big data pour construire une information d'anticipation", I2D-Information, données et documents, ADBS, vol. 53, pp. 12–14, 2015/4.

[KEC 14] KECSKEMETI C., LAJOS K., *Les écrits s'envolent: la problématique de la conservation des archives papier et numériques*, Éditions Favre, 2014.

[KER 15] KERN G., HOLGADO S., COTTIN M., "50 nuances de cycle de vie : Quelles évolutions possibles?", *Les Cahiers du numérique*, vol. 11, no. 2, pp. 37–76, 2015.

[KLE 18] KLEIN A., CARDIN M. (eds), *Consommer l'information. De la gestion à la médiation documentaire*, Presses de l'Université de Laval, CEFAN, 2018.

[LEB 09] LEBLOND C. (ed.), *Archivage et stockage pérennes : enjeux et réalisations*, Hermès-Lavoisier, Paris, 2009.

[LEM 15] LEMAY Y., *Préparer aujourd'hui les voix de l'avenir*, in SERVAIS, P., *Archivistes de 2030: réflexions prospectives*, Academia/L'Harmattan, Louvain-la-Neuve, Publications des archives de l'Université catholique de Louvain, pp. 285–304, 2015.

[LEM 09] LEMAY Y., "Archives ouvertes et archivistique", in LEBLOND C. (ed.), *Archivage et stockage pérennes : enjeux et réalisations*, Hermès-Lavoisier, pp. 93–117, Paris, 2009.

[LEP 11] LENEPVEU P., *Archivage électronique et records management: État de l'art et présentation de sept solutions*, ADBS Éditions, Tosca Consultants, Paris, 2011.

[LUP 00] LUPOVICI C., "Les stratégies de gestion et de conservation préventive des documents électroniques", *Bulletin des bibliothèques de France*, available at: https://core. ac.uk/download/pdf/12449783.pdf, vol. 45, no. 4, pp. 43–54, 2000.

[MAD 15a] MADAY C., Métadonnée, schémas de métadonnées, cours MOOC, "Gérer les documents numériques: maîtriser les risques", Conservatoire National des Arts et Métier, Paris, 2015.

[MAD 15b] MADAY C., "L'apport de la Gestion des documents d'activité (*Records Management*) à l'Ouverture des Données : Réflexions basée sur les pratiques", *Les Cahiers du numérique*, vol. 11, no. 2, pp. 149–166, 2015.

[MAK 10] MAKHLOUF SHABOU B., Étude sur la définition et la mesure des qualités des archives définitives issues d'une évaluation, Information sciences thesis, Faculté des Études supérieures, Université de Montréal-EBSI, 2010.

[MAK 14] MAKHLOUF SHABOU B., LEVEILLE V., "Le projet Records in the Cloud", *43rd AAQ congress proceedings*, Association des archivistes du Québec, available at: https://hesso.tind.io//record/586/files/Texte%20int%C3%A9gral.pdf, 2014.

[MAN 15] MANUELIAN É., "Il faut que tout change pour que rien ne change ", *La Gazette des archives*, no. 240, pp. 295–303, 2015.

[MAR 10a] MARGULIS A., "Identification des facteurs de succès d'implantation des SI en gestion documentaire moderne : une étude empirique", *Archives*, vol. 41, no. 2, pp. 45–112, 2009–2010.

[MAR 10h] MARLEAU Y., MAS S., SACKLAD M., "Exploitation des facettes et des ontologies sémiotiques pour la gestion documentaire", in BROUDOUX E. AND CHARTRON G. (eds). *Traitement et pratiques documentaires : vers un changement de paradigme?*, ADBS Éditions, pp. 91–110, Paris, 2008.

[MAS 15] MAS S., "Nouvelles problématiques de la classification des documents des organismes. À la conquête des espaces personnels d'information numérique", in GAGNON-ARGUIN L., LAJEUNESSE M. (eds), *Panorama de l'archivistique contemporaine: évolution de la discipline et de la profession : mélanges offerts à Carol Couture*, Presses de l'Université du Québec, Quebec, pp. 177–194, 2015.

[MAS 11] MAS S., *Classification des documents numériques dans les organismes : impact des pratiques classificatoires personnelles sur le repérage*, Presses de l'Université du Québec, Quebec, 2011.

[MAS 12] MAS, S., MAUREL D., ALBERTS I., *Actualité du records management : une expérience d'approche par la classification à facettes*, in DELPIERRE, N., HIRAUX F. AND MIRGUET F. (eds), *Les chantiers du numérique : dématérialisation des archives et métiers de l'archiviste, Actes des 11e journées des Archives*, Académia/L'Harmattan, Louvain-la-Neuve, pp. 75–106, 2012.

[MAS 14] MAS S., "La notion de facettes et son application dans un contexte de recherche dans les fonds d'archives: analyse des questions de recherche et de l'expérience vécue par des usagers novices", *Archives*, Association des archivistes du Québec, vol. 45/1, 2014.

[MAU 10] MAUREL D., "Repenser l'intégration des processus documentaires aux systèmes d'information organisationnels soutenant les processus d'affaires", *Colloque Spécialisé en Sciences de l'information (COSSI)*, Université de Moncton, Shippagan campus, 2010.

[MAU 09] MAUREL D., BERGERON P., "Quel rôle pour les archivistes dans la gestion de la mémoire organisationnelle?", *Archives*, vol. 40, no. 2, pp. 27–44, 2008–2009.

[MES 15] MEISSONNIER A., ROQUES R., "L'archiviste, les normes et le droit", *La Gazette des archives*, no. 240, pp. 135–151, 2015.

[MIN 13] MINISTERE DE LA DEFENSE, MINISTERE DE LA CULTURE, Programme VITAM. L'archivage des messageries électroniques / Preuve de concept, Paris, 2013.

[MON 16] MONINO J.-L., SEDKAOUI S., *Big Data, Open Data and Data Development*, ISTE Ltd, London, and Wiley, New York, 2016.

[NAH 15] NAHUET R., "Fonds d'archives et respect des fonds. Des vieux documents aux nouvelles formes documentaires", in GAGNON-ARGUIN L., LAJEUNESSE M. (eds), *Panorama de l'archivistique contemporaine: évolution de la discipline et de la profession: mélanges offerts à Carol Couture*, Presses de l'Université du Québec, Quebec, pp. 159–175, 2015.

[NES 15a] NESME M.-F., Exigences de l'ISO 9001 et de la gestion des documents d'activité, Session 4.5 "Gérer les documents numériques: maîtriser les risques", Conservatoire National des Arts et Métier, Paris, 2015.

[NES 15b] NESME M.-F., Chebbi A., Analyse des risques pour la gestion des documents d'activité, Session 3.1, "Gérer les documents numériques: maîtriser les risques", Conservatoire National des Arts et Métier, Paris, 2015.

[OTT 15] OTT F. (ed.), "Problématiques de la gouvernance de l'information à l'ère des documents numériques", *Les Cahiers du numérique*, vol. 11, no. 2, 2015.

[OTT 13] OTT F, "Les défis de la gestion documentaire face à la dématérialisation des documents", in Papy F. (ed.), *Recherches actuelles en Sciences de l'Information*, Hermès-Lavoisier, London, pp. 69–94, 2013.

[OTT 11] OTT F., "Gestion d'un dossier partagé à la Bibliothèque de l'Université de Moncton, Campus de Shippagan, Canada", *Commission nationale de normalisation 11 de l'AFNOR*, pp. 28–30, 2011.

[OTT 10] OTT F., "Comment initier les étudiants en gestion documentaire aux réalités professionnelles : études de cas à l'Université de Moncton, campus de Shippagan", *Actes du 2ᵉ Colloque Spécialisé en Sciences de l'Information: Information et organisation, nouvelles stratégies, structures et fonctions*, June 16–17, 2010, pp. 129–136, available at: http://www.umoncton.ca/Umcs/files/umcs/wf/wf/pdf/ACTES_COSSI_2010.pdf, 2010.

[RAJ 11] RAJOTTE D., "La réflexion archivistique à l'ère du document numérique: un bilan historique", *Archives*, vol. 42, no. 2, pp. 69–105, 2010–2011.

[RIB 14] RIBEIRO F., "The Use of Classification in Archives as a Means of Organization, Representation and Retrieval of Information", *Knowledge Organization*, vol. 41, no. 4, pp. 319–326, 2014.

[RIE 10] RIETSCH J.-M., MORAND-KHALIFA N., PASCON J.-L. *et al.*, *Mise en œuvre de la dématérialisation: cas pratique pour l'archivage électronique*, Dunod, Paris, 2010.

[RIE 06] RIETCH J.-M., CAPRIOLI E., CHABIN M.-A., L'archivage électronique à l'usage du dirigeant, FESISA/CIGREF, Paris, 2006.

[ROB 11] ROBERGE M., *Le schéma de classification hiérarchique des documents administratifs: conception, développement, déploiement et maintenance*, Éditions Michel Roberge, Quebec, 2011.

[ROU 94] ROUSSEAU J.-Y., COUTURE C., *Les fondements de la discipline archivistique*, Presses de l'université du Québec, Quebec, 1994.

[ROU 12] ROUSSEL S., "Le champ normatif de l'archivage électronique", *La Gazette des archives*, no. 228, pp. 60–78, 2012.

[SAM 15] SAMPIC M., Investigation électronique l'"e-discovery" américain, Session 2.5 "Gérer les documents numériques: maîtriser les risques", Conservatoire National des Arts et Métier, Paris, 2015.

[SEN 91] SENÉCAL S., "Une réflexion sur le concept de fonds d'archives : comment tenir compte du principe de provenance dans un contexte organisationnel dynamique", *Archives*, vol. 22, no. 1, Winter, pp. 41–52, 1991.

[SER 15a] SERVAIS P., MIRGUET F. (eds), *L'archive dans quinze ans. Vers de nouveaux fondements*, Actes des *14ᵉ Journées des Archives*, Academia, Louvain-la-Neuve, 2015.

[SER 15b] SERVAIS P., *Archivistes de 2030: réflexions prospectives*, Academia/L'Harmattan, Publications des archives de l'Université catholique de Louvain, Louvain-la-Neuve, 2015.

[SER 16] SERDALAB, La Gouvernance de l'information numérique dans les organisations, 5th Annual Digital Information Governance Report, April 2016.

[SER 17] SERDALAB, Protection des données: toute la vérité sur le RGPD, Comprendre les enjeux et conduire la mise en conformité, Paris, 2017.

[SOY 09] SOYEZ S., Directives pour la gestion et l'archivage numériques des courriels, Archives générales du Royaume et archives de l'État dans les provinces, manual 59, Brussels, 2009.

[SOY 12] SOYEZ, S., "Numérisation et substitution des documents: un chapitre singulier de l'archivage électronique", in DELPIERRE, N., HIRAUX F., MIRGUET F. (eds), *Les chantiers du numérique: dématérialisation des archives et métiers de l'archiviste, Actes des 11ᵉ journées des Archives*, Louvain-la-Neuve, Académia/L'Harmattan, pp. 107–114, 2012.

[VER 15] VERNUSSET A., Réversibilité des données et archivage, "I2D – Information, données & documents", *ADBS*, vol. 52, pp. 17–18, 2015/3.

[YON 15] YON C., "Du document papier à la donnée électronique, des solutions hybrides pour une gestion des archives unifiée", *La Gazette des archives*, no. 240, pp. 259–265, 2015.

Index

Printed in the United States
by Baker & Taylor Publisher Services